Editor's Note

Jonathan Wilson, Editor

C000212755

I got ill during the first week of Cup of Nations. In Mongomo I couldn't stop sneezing. By Malabo I was running a temperature and shaking. Midway through the first Group D double header I snuck off, intending to watch Cameroon v Mali from a bed in my hotel room.

I vomited, fell asleep, dreamed that Dwight Yorke had scored the winner for Sunderland against Manchester United — a terrible goalkeeping error — and woke up just in time to see Ambroise Oyongo scoring an 84th-minute equaliser for Cameroon. For two days I felt dreadful, sweating profusely but unable to stand the chill of air-con. I think it was just a touch of flu, but I lost weight and it wasn't until a fortnight later that my energy returned.

I considered returning home. The football wasn't great and the heat and humidity weren't helping my recovery. The food was deeply average, the hotel less than luxurious. I started to feel my age and more. What was I doing stuck here off the west coast of central Africa, a place the early Spanish colonialists had referred to as the Island of Death? I contemplated retirement from tournaments: do Chile and France, the easy ones, and quit at 40. That seemed

that. I could even go home for Chelsea v Manchester City.

And then the tournament woke up. Lots were drawn. Six goals were shared in the second half of the Congo derby. A highly controversial penalty led to Tunisia kicking a referee off the pitch. The second semi-final was held up by crowd trouble. The final reached an extraordinary denouement, Côte d'Ivoire's long deferred glory delivered at last by a goalkeeper whose haplessness seemed so often before to have stood between them and success. Chelsea v Manchester City turned out to be a damp squib.

This seemed a fundamental lesson. It's likely that, with the caveat that too many top teams seem over-reliant on individuals at the expense of real tactical sophistication, the football played in the Champions League over the past decade or so is the greatest football that has ever been played. There has never previously been such a concentration of talent among the top sides.

And yet that in itself destroys stories. Be rich enough for long enough and the Champions League will eventually turn up; success in Europe is no longer the quest it once was. And that's why, even though the actual football is significantly poorer than at club level, international football is still where the best narratives

2017, I'll be back in Ghana (or Gabon, Egypt or Algeria).

March 2015

Contents

The Blizzard, Issue Sixteen

CLASSIC FOOTBALL SHIRTS.CO.UK

THE MOST EXTENSIVE RANGE OF ORIGINAL SHIRTS ONLINE
HUGE CLEARANCE SECTION FULL OF 1000's OF BARGAIN ITEMS

GETAFE
£11.99

FC YOUNG BOYS
£19.99

LYON TECHFIT
£34.99

MARSEILLE TECHFIT
£22.99

VALENCIA
£19.99

STOKE CROUCH
£29.99

NAPOLI CAVANI
£49.99

NAPOLI HAMSIK
£44.99

SHORTS, SOCKS, BAGS, JACKETS ETC

FOOTBALL IS NOT A GAME. IT IS A LIFESTYLE.

CANNONIERE.EU

8

Groundwork

"We all cannot get back on our feet
if football does not recover here."

The New Owner

Sachin Tendulkar discusses his interest in football and why he's invested in an ISL team

By Dileep Premachandaran

As the legend took to the field, the no-name wandered around the owners' box. Sachin Tendulkar, the highest run-scorer in the history of international cricket, walked along the perimeter of the Jawaharlal Nehru Stadium in Kochi, soaking in the applause from the crowd, many of whom might once have cheered two of his five-wicket hauls. Alongside him was John Abraham, a Bollywood actor and model who had invested in the North East United Football Club.

Tendulkar, one of the owners of the Kerala Blasters, was dressed in the team's yellow shirt and jeans. He did a pre-match interview for television even as annoying dance music blared across the 75,000-capacity venue. A couple of times, you could see him leaning in to try to hear better and you couldn't help but think that 'Walk of Life', that epic sporting anthem sung by Dire Straits – one of his favourite bands – would have provided a far more appropriate soundtrack.

When his name was announced, Tendulkar was facing the pavilion that bore his name, behind the home goal. The collective roar brought back memories of his halcyon years, when those outside an Indian venue could tell if the boss was batting simply from the decibel levels. As he was then driven around the ground in a golf buggy, the non-playing members of the Blasters' squad slowly took their places on couches inside the owners' enclosure.

On the field, even the ball boys were mobbing Tendulkar. Off it, the unfortunates who hadn't even been named on the bench had an air of irritation about them. Dressed in training gear and Puma trainers, they fidgeted with their phones while trying to seem at ease on the black and white leather couches.

The yellow vuvuzelas were everywhere and the sound was deafening as the playing XIs emerged from a football-shaped tunnel with fireworks going off. It may not have been El Monumental and the Super Clasico, but it was hard to be cynical when 43,299 had come through the turnstiles for a match between two sides struggling for a play-off spot.

Minutes later, with the game about to begin, Tendulkar made his way to the owners box. Unlike the other couches, the one he sat on was bright red. In the stand immediately below, fans positioned themselves to take selfies with him in the background. He waved to the fans a few times, but once the game kicked off to the accompaniment of a relentless *chenda* [a percussion instrument used in temple festivals] beat, his concentration was absolute. While others took pictures or fiddled with their phones, Tendulkar's eyes flitted this way and that, following the ball from one end of the field to the other.

That buying a football club wasn't a vanity project for him had been amply clear when we had spoken earlier that afternoon. He had arrived from Mumbai only at around 2pm, but as soon as he was in the hotel he had gone to meet the players and chatted to them about the campaign and the key matches coming up. Synonymous with the national cricket side and then the face of the Mumbai Indians in the Indian Premier League for six seasons, what had prompted him to invest in a football team? "I believe we are creating something special here," he said. "I believe this is the foundation of that."

But why Kochi, 850 miles south of home? "I've always known that football is unbelievably big here," said Tendulkar. "There were a lot of players from this part of India who played for the national team, and now, there are not many. Hardly any, I would say. The whole idea was to see whether we could revive that football culture and the response has been spectacular.

"I was just going through some numbers with my support staff. They were saying, from the fan following or the support point of view [i.e. average attendances], we are the fourth-biggest league in the world [after the Bundesliga, the English Premier League and La Liga]! That shows what impact it has had. The support that we've received is really amazing. When that interest is generated, we're going to have more and more guys playing

football as well. And from there, we're going to find something special. All this got me excited and I thought this was one sport I should support.

"As a cricketer, wherever I went and played in India, I got support from all directions. For me, it's not like: 'I'm buying this team, so I'm against other teams.' I just want this tournament to be a success, I want people to enjoy playing and watching football."

Tendulkar said he had always played football as a child, in the playground at Sahitya Sahawas, the writers' cooperative where he grew up. Cricket was a constant, but according to the season, the kids would play hockey, football and hand tennis. He was never much of a football-watcher, though kickabouts before practice ensured that he never lost touch with the game. "All you need to do is carry one ball in your kitbag – the trainer or physio would have one – and we would get the football out and play on the cricket field," said Tendulkar. "Even till the last year of my career, I would play a little bit of football in the morning. Somehow, football has never had a direct relationship with me, but indirectly it's always been there."

In those early years of kicking a ball about, there was one hero, another small-statured man capable of awe-inspiring feats. "I obviously liked Maradona, because his flair and style were something I enjoyed," he said. "I also liked the way Brazil played, their style of play. Now, Ronaldo and Messi and all these guys are there."

Tendulkar, who has caught up with Roger Federer several times at Wimbledon –

"What a remarkable career @sachin_rt. Wish you the very best moving forward #ThankYouSachin," he tweeted when Tendulkar retired in November 2013 – has yet to meet any of the modern-day football titans, though he still chuckles about the one time he ran into the 'other Ronaldo', World Cup winner with Brazil in 2002, in Barcelona. Unlike Federer, Ronaldo wasn't too clued into cricket. "We were at a Formula 1 race," said Tendulkar. "But we didn't discuss cricket at all."

On the tour of England in 2002, Tendulkar and several other members of the Indian team watched Manchester United at Old Trafford. His eyes shone as he described how Sir Bobby Charlton had welcomed them. He has been back since, but admits that the intricacies of the game often pass him by. "I would be able to read what was happening on a cricket field, or what happens on the tennis court, to a certain extent. I would make out what's happening and be able sort of to preempt what would happen next.

"But I can't say that I know football to that extent. I'm getting to understand more and more now, slowly. But I understand just from a fan's point of view. But not a hardcore football fan or even serious player – they think at a different level."

As the game progressed without the Blasters getting the goal they craved, the frustration levels mounted. Ian Hume, whose itinerant career had already taken in Tranmere Rovers, Leicester City, Barnsley, Preston North End, Doncaster Rovers and Fleetwood Town, was their main prompter, but his strop after receiving a yellow just before half-time summed up the home team's night. Tendulkar permitted himself a half-smile.

There were few local delicacies on the owners box menu, which boasted pasta, paella and dim sum. The Blasters were playing in Brazil-1982 colours, but there was little Samba flair to their disjointed play. Michael Chopra, once of Newcastle, Sunderland and Cardiff, came on as a 63rd minute sub and looked as though he'd been enjoying the Kerala cuisine. His first act was an atrocious tackle on James Keene, a product of the Portsmouth Academy. Keene retaliated and saw red. The crowd roared, sensing that the man advantage would tilt the tie in their favour.

David James, their goalkeeper-coach whose career highlight with Liverpool – a Coca Cola Cup win against Bolton Wanderers in 1995 – had come nearly two decades earlier, paced the touchline anxiously. Chopra headed over when left all alone in the box. Next to me, I heard a sustained burst of swearing in Malayalam. A few minutes later, I asked the swearer his name. Sushanth Mathew had played a couple of games earlier in the season but, at 33, he wasn't even seen as a young prospect. His place – on a couch a million miles away from the action – sort of summed up the state of Keralan football in the past decade.

It was one of the issues that Tendulkar spoke about most passionately. India's best player, Sunil Chhetri, wasn't part of the Indian Super League, having been prevented from playing by his I-League club. Chhetri had an unhappy spell with the Kansas City Wizards in Major League

Soccer, a sad repeat of the experience that Baichung Bhutia had with Bury in the late 1990s. Without its Cha Bum Kun or Hidetoshi Nakata, India will always struggle to grab the headlines.

IM Vijayan was perhaps the best all-round talent the country has produced in my lifetime. So poor that he used to collect used soda bottles at the Municipal Stadium in Trichur – a couple of hours drive from Kochi – Vijayan epitomised Keralan football when it was at its strongest. There was talk of playing contracts from Malaysia and elsewhere when he was in his prime, but he was so painfully shy that the leap never materialised. Even if he had gone, you fancy it would have ended as it did for a homesick Barry Ferguson at Blackburn.

Kerala, while not being able to boast of a Jim Baxter or Kenny Dalglish, has mirrored Scottish football's decline, and Tendulkar has enlisted Vijayan's help to try to put things right. "He comes for the matches and we've watched a couple of games together," said Tendulkar. "He is one name we would want to be involved on a long-term basis with local schools. I think he would speak a different language with young footballers, a common person going there and motivating them. Just his sheer presence would be a motivating factor.

"We have also met the chief minister and asked for his support, which he has extended. Also, the opposition party, the police, the sports minister. From every direction, people want to support and it will only help if everyone is thinking of how to raise standards and enthusiasm for football."

Tendulkar can recognise a footballing hotbed when he sees one, having spent the summer of 1992 playing for Yorkshire as the county's first overseas professional. Despite the proximity to Elland Road – Leeds won their last title that May – and Hillsborough, he never got to a game. "I didn't go, not even once," he said with a slightly perplexed expression on his face.

On the field, as the clock wound down, North East United substituted Joan Capdevila, whose 60 caps for Spain encompassed glory at Euro 2008 and the 2010 World Cup. The Blasters continued to huff and puff, with Chopra fluffing another chance. Next to me, Mathew was on his feet in frustration. At the final whistle, he thumped the couch and walked away.

A week later, more than 60,000 were in attendance when the Blasters, who had sneaked into the play-offs in fourth place, took on Chennaiyin FC, the table toppers, in the first leg of the semi-final. Hume, whose career changed forever at the age of 25 when a Chris Morgan elbow left him with a fractured skull, was magnificent that night, with windmill-tilting runs and deft passes to teammates.

In the 86th minute, with the Blasters 2-0 up, Mathew was sent on. As a Chennaiyin attack broke down near the Blasters area, the ball was funnelled to Hume. From what some would call the quarterback position, halfway between his area and the centre-circle, Hume stroked a pass to the right wing. Mathew sprinted forward to collect it. He then cut inside, evaded a couple of defenders and lashed a shot towards the far corner.

Mathew was born in Ambalavayal, in the hilly and picturesque Wayanad district of Kerala. He came through the ranks at FC Kochin, where Vijayan once played, but his best years were spent in the colours of the now-defunct Mahindra United. During his time on the couch against North East United, he had spent the half-time break trying to keep his toddler from running amok. When the game resumed, he called his wife and handed the child over. You could almost sense his relief.

His goal in the semi-final was the sort you'd be happy to score on a PlayStation. For a 33 year old at the fag end of his career to do it in the biggest game that he'd ever played — that was something beyond the realms of fantasy. Mathew yanked off his shirt and set off on a celebratory run. He was later booked for his troubles, but no one cared. No other goal exemplified what the fledging league could do for Indian football.

The Blasters lost the final, to Atletico de Kolkata — a team part-owned by the La Liga champions — after the latest of late goals. Consolation came in the shape of the Golden Ball, for player of the tournament, for Hume and the awareness that a football-crazy region had taken the team to their hearts. Tendulkar, instrumental in the IPL's growth, was convinced that the ISL too could sustain similar interest. "I don't see why not," he said. "If it's entertaining, why would you not want to be part of the action? I feel it's only going to get bigger from here."

Structurally, however, the ISL has only made the Indian football scene even more confusing. It ran for just over two months from October to December 2014. In January 2015, the I-League, the competition featuring India's most storied clubs — Kolkata's East Bengal and Mohun Bagan — kicked off. Their season will end on May 17. In addition to this, there are still local leagues in places like Kolkata and Goa, and cup competitions like the Federation Cup and the Durand Cup, which goes back more than a century. For Indian football to progress, there will need to be an ISL/I-League merger that also ensures players and teams don't waste time on big-fish-small-pond tournaments.

Tendulkar reckoned that football missed out on the gravy train in the post-economic liberalisation 1990s simply because it wasn't marketed as well as cricket. He was merely being modest. Vijayan and Bhutia aside, there were no players even capable of competing on the Asian stage; let alone at the highest level. That problem remains.

Hope comes in the shape of young men who are eschewing the IPL's considerable appeal to kick a bigger ball around. On the day of the ISL final, I spent some time with Nishant Bhatt, a 16 year old who is one of the stars of Bengaluru FC's youth side. Ashley Westwood, a product of the Manchester United Academy who went on to play for the likes of Crewe Alexandria, Sheffield Wednesday and Wrexham, coaches the team, which won the I-League at the first attempt in 2013-14.

Bhatt's parents run a coaching scheme called Stadium Soccer in Bangalore and have invested considerable time and resources on his progress. He has yet to catch Westwood's eye, but knows that strong performances with the youth team will mean opportunities to train with the big boys. And although he was on the other side of the divide, he couldn't help but be enthusiastic about the possible impact of the ISL. "I haven't seen all the matches," he told me. "I had training quite a few evenings. But it's been great to see people talking about football on TV and elsewhere."

Bhatt plays as a striker, and you can only imagine what it would mean for a kid that age to play alongside the likes of Alessandro del Piero or David Trezeguet, who featured for Delhi Dynamos and Pune FC in the ISL's first season. Such players, like Nicolas Anelka – who turned out for the Peter Reid-managed Mumbai FC – may be well past their best, but Tendulkar insisted that they hadn't been signed up just to raise the glamour quotient.

"The whole idea is to reach world-class standards, and help Indian football players get that exposure of rubbing shoulders with international stars," he told me. "What I thought cricket did with the IPL was that it allowed players, especially the younger lot, to spend time together with foreign players. You can only learn from such experienced names, and that is what the ISL is doing for Indian football. I think, in time to come, the standard of ISL play will get better. In the process, so will Indian football.

If that happens, one of cricket's all-time greats will allow himself a quiet pat on the back. The winds of change may have arrived too late for some like Mathew, wonder goal or not. But for kids like Bhatt with stars in their eyes, the future seems limitless. After half a century of treading water, Indian football may finally be on the move. Ⓑ

Death of the Giant Killers

Hereford United are one of the most celebrated minnows of English football, so how could they collapse into bankruptcy?

By Louise Phillips

On a dark Friday afternoon in a small courtroom the week before Christmas 2014, Hereford United Football Club (1939) Limited was dissolved. The owner Andy Lonsdale had failed to arrive with proof that he had £1million to pay the club's creditors. "I'm instructed that the transfer has been made," Lonsdale's lawyer told the progressively incredulous judge, "Mr Lonsdale is stuck in traffic." He conceded that he had personally seen no evidence of the transfer taking place. The liquidation order was uttered with such little fanfare that some of the supporters and reporters in Courtroom 7 were initially unsure it had actually happened.

The hearing followed a five-month boycott which had seen the club attracting gates of barely 400. The previous evening Lonsdale had reneged on his promise to address a meeting of the Hereford United Supporters' Trust. Instead, HUST members and the local MP had discussed plans for a supporter-run phoenix club they hoped to rebuild.

Outside the High Court, fans expressed sadness and relief when they spoke to reporters. As far as they were concerned, their club had been dead since the summer. Hereford United had been torn apart by the arrival of its controversial owner, which had set fan against fan

and exposed the lack of ownership safeguards in the English game.

United's supporters followed their club for decades, at home and away on windy terraces from Carlisle to Canvey Island, keystones against the rapacious free-market plunder of the upper leagues. Fans spent the better part of the 2013-2014 season fundraising as their club teetered on the brink of bankruptcy, shaving their heads, auctioning memorabilia and organising charity walks.

Five years ago the club was in League One. But cash was already tight and after being relegated they were taken over in 2010, with David Keyte, a local accountant who is said to have played for their reserves, installed as chairman. "I shall be continuing the prudence that Graham Turner has set for this club," he said.

His four years in charge were marked by economic difficulties and a decline in form. Hereford United were relegated from League Two at the end of the 2011-12 season. The first winding-up order was served over unpaid VAT and PAYE bills in October 2012. Those bills were paid with the money generated from an FA Cup first round win and £20,000 raised by fans.

Hereford United's board responded to the constant threat of administration with ill-conceived schemes and increasingly brazen requests: the Pitch Maintenance Fund, a Hereford United Debenture Scheme launched by Michael Portillo. In December the club's board asked supporters to chip in: "We need to raise £35,000 over the next 14 days."

Steve Niblett was the club photographer for 11 years. "Predominantly it's been unpaid, that never really came into it," he said. "It was just the love of doing it." He could recognise about 1000 supporters by face and over 100 by name. "After Christmas [2013] some of my friends who worked there weren't being paid... They were just getting sporadic little bits of money. I know the youth players in April had only been paid £7 since Christmas. I mean it was really bad, it really was. It was financial mismanagement. I don't think David Keyte is a nasty bloke, I really don't. I think he's just very incompetent."

HMRC served Hereford with two more winding-up orders between March 2013 and January 2014. The club continued to collect thousands of pounds from fans at matches. In February, the youth team assistant manager, the goalkeeping coach and two first-team masseurs were made redundant. The manager Martin Foyle left in March after two years. His winding-up order against the club over unpaid wages was issued in May.

Hereford's fans kept going to games, shaving their heads, organising charity walks and passing the bucket. Niblett said that the money raised never made

its way into people's wages. "I sold a lot of my memorabilia, shirts and things like that... quite often they paid by PayPal, so I'd just transfer it to my bank account and go round to people's houses and give them the money."

On the last day of the season he took a bucket to the Aldershot game and raised £600 for the players who had just secured Hereford's Conference Premier status. Exemplars of dedication and professionalism, they were frequently repaid with empty promises.

In April the Hereford United Supporter's Trust made an offer to buy the club for £1 and pledged £220,000 to help clear the debt. Just over a month later the club announced that a London businessman named Tommy Agombar had purchased Hereford United for £2. Agombar said he'd met with the HUST chairman Chris Williams shortly after taking over. "I said, 'Chris, listen, let's take the club forward, me and you. You're the Supporters Trust, lovely, we need the supporters, I'll come in with my money. I'll put in 300, you put in 300, we've got 600 bags there.' He went, 'Well, I can't do that, Tom.' I said, 'But you've told me you've got all this money,' and he went, 'No, I've got pledges.' I went, 'So what you've really got is IOUs.' They're worth nothing, you can't buy a cup of tea with them."

"None of that is true," said Chris Williams. "We got pledges of sufficient numbers to bid, but the owner felt the regime that has taken over the club had better opportunities and more finances that we did, and he chose to sell it to Mr Agombar for £2." Seven days after Agombar bought the club. Hereford United were expelled from the Football Conference.

"We were talking to Mr Agombar and trying to support his activities to bring the club together," recalls Williams. "But he made a number of promises and those included paying the bond that the Conference League required for us to stay in the league, and he failed to do that so we were kicked out of the Conference, which meant we then had to apply to the Southern League to get into a football competition which is two leagues lower than we'd managed to stay in."

Supporters were in an uproar. They unearthed old stories about the new owner they posted on an unofficial fans forum called Bulls Banter. In 1987, Agombar had been sentenced to 10 years for stealing lorries of mink skins, designer clothes and £100,000 worth of cigarettes. "It's not the vicar coming along to buy the football club, is it?" said Keyte when he confirmed the story. "He was 27 years of age, with a group of other lads who came up with an idea that they didn't get away with."

The club had signed a 30-year lease for the Edgar Street stadium with Herefordshire Council in February. Fans worried Agombar was solely interested in the development opportunities at the Merton Meadow and Blackfriars ends. On June 12 it emerged that he had asked the council to transfer the leases allowing development to a company under his ownership. Jesse Norman, the MP for Hereford and South Herefordshire, asked the Council to defer making any decisions about the Edgar Street leases for a month.

Speaking to Steve Sabel and Kev McCall, fans who confronted him outside a meeting with Herefordshire Council officials, Agombar denied he was only interested in the leases. A video of their encounter, "HUFC Fans meet Tommy Agombar", was posted on YouTube. Agombar was accompanied by a sombre adviser named Andy Lonsdale, then one of two presidents at Bedfont & Feltham FC.

"I went to Feltham 15 years ago, [when] the club was close to closing," Lonsdale told me. "I ended up investing a whole lot of money, paying off all the bills and turning it into a club that's in credit at the bank. The council then decided to take the roof off the ground, we got demoted for [having] astroturf and ended up ground sharing for a few years. And two years ago we merged with another local club. It's now called Bedfont & Feltham."

Lonsdale's CV on the Company Check website was posted on Bulls Banter. He has held 21 appointments at 17 dissolved companies. His longest current appointment was 14 years at Seagrave Haulage Limited. Lonsdale spent 2006 to 2012 registered as a disqualified director by Companies House and in 2008 he was convicted of dumping 600 lorry-loads of contaminated waste on green-belt land.

Of particular concern to the fans was Lonsdale's role at Feltham FC. In 2007 the club was granted permission to build a new stadium on the site of its former ground. Five times the permitted volume of soil and building rubble was dumped at the arena over the course of five years, during which time no stadium was built. The disposal work was carried out by a since-liquidated company called All Transport Limited, run by

Lonsdale. "At the outset there was a lack of clarity as to who the Council was dealing with," stated the Report of the Feltham Arenas Scrutiny Task & Finish Group. "The proposal and agreements were with Feltham Football Club (FFC). Yet the importing of soil was to be undertaken by a company owned by Mr Andy Lonsdale."

In July Lonsdale confirmed he'd left Bedfont & Feltham to advise Hereford. On August 4 he was announced as the new chairman. Fans marched in a mock funeral procession from Edgar Street to Herefordshire Council with a 7,300-signature petition rejecting the proposal to transfer development of the land leases to Agombar. The London Bulls supporters group called for a boycott of the club on July 3 and HUST followed a week later.

"The leases say that football has to be played at Edgar Street forever," Lonsdale said. "There's development at both ends. The fans have known that since day one. The fans have actually put on Bulls News copies of the leases for everyone to read, yet they still think that we want to develop the whole of Edgar Street, which we don't... No development's going to happen there for at least two years, so we've got to develop the football."

"That's what the leases say," said Williams, "and that's what the covenant on the ground said, but we know that if you pay enough money you can eliminate those conditions."

Agombar said development talks had been in progress for five years prior to his purchase of HUFC, with plans for residential units for the Meadow End

and retail units and possibly a hotel at the Blackfriars End: "When I took over the club... [David Keyte] said, 'Look, I want something out of the club.' I said, 'You've took £1.3m out of it, David, so what more do you want?' 'Well when the development is done, I want £300,000 out of the development.'" (David Keyte has declined to respond to this allegation).

Lonsdale and Agombar were unprepared for the online backlash: the evidence of past misdemeanours fans tracked down and the forums where they organised and shared information. "In this country everything is transparent and can be seen on Google," said Lonsdale. "If anyone's abroad, you can't see that, can you? So they get away with it. If someone from Canada came over here, they can't look at their past, can they? If you're a British citizen, it's there to be seen. The internet is a good thing and a bad thing. It's very easy to find things out on it."

"If they really wanted to connect with the fans from day one, they should have been open and honest," said Steve Niblett. "That's all it would have taken."

"Let me tell you what HUST and the supporters are trying to do," Lonsdale said. "Everything we say they try to discredit. That's why we don't put out a lot of PR on the social media. We don't talk until we know for definite it's a fact."

John Harold Edwards and Elke Thuerlings were announced as directors on June 26. Thuerlings had previously held directorships at two companies engaged in environmental and consulting activities. Edwards was the company secretary or director at 12 companies involved with waste management, the sale of machinery and industrial equipment. July 1 brought the appointment of Philip Peter Gambrill, the company secretary of Savannah Construction Limited, a firm involved in the construction of residential and non-residential buildings.

By July, Hereford's physiotherapist, kitman, groundsman, club secretary, media secretary and webmaster had left the club, as well as staff involved with accounts and sponsorship. "It was almost physical intimidation, almost," recalled Steve Niblett. "I think they were making all these promises that they'd be paid by the end of the week and none of them got paid. So questions were asked and they did nothing, nothing to keep the staff at all. It was almost like constructive dismissal."

"You can listen to all kinds of people and what they've got to say, they're not for the club," Agombar said when asked about Niblett's statement. "How can I bully anybody? Listen, the simple thing they do is: 'I'm not coming in to work in the morning, but this is the bill you owe, quite simple.'"

Agombar's appointment as director was terminated on June 18 when he failed the owners' and directors' test, but he remained United's majority shareholder. He attended the first game of the season when Hereford lost to St Neots in the EvoStick Southern League. Three days later, "A Message from the Directors" was posted on Hereford United's website. Signed "Elke & John", they urged "anyone who is allowed to vote for the (upcoming) Company Voluntary Arrangement to do so" and confirmed that Agombar had failed the FA's owners' and directors' test. John Edwards was photographed standing on the pitch buying Agombar a season ticket. Agombar attended all of the home and away matches, where he enjoyed a warm rapport with the Hereford United fans who opposed the boycott.

"I've become a supporter. That's what I've done, I watch all these games. 'Cause I'm backing me mate and he's not going to fail."

His shares in Hereford United were sold to a purchaser of distressed debts called Alpha Choice Finance Limited. Alpha's owner, Alan Gerald McCarthy, had been the director of a dissolved company called Infiniti Consortium Limited. Infiniti's registered address was the same Herne Bay, Kent address as the dormant Philip Gambrill & Company Pension Scheme Limited, which was headed by Peter Philip Gambrill, who was appointed to Hereford United's board in July.

"But that doesn't mean anything, does it?" countered Lonsdale. "Philip introduced [McCarthy] to Tommy, I think... Basically, Alan buys distressed debt. Tommy needed to get rid of his loans and his shares, and Alan was the only one who was willing to buy them at the time."

The MP Jesse Norman had written to the FA with his concerns about Agombar's suitability and later pressed them to make public the results of the owners' and directors' test. Norman cited inadequate disclosure about the status of the owners' and directors' test, whether the insolvency has been properly handled and whether individuals should be allowed to drop in and out of the Companies House director's register as contributing factors to the current situation, as well the pernicious aspects of the football creditors rule.

"What the football creditors are saying in effect is if a club is worried about getting relegated, it can load up on debt in order to buy and sell players and the other clubs will trade with it on the basis that they know they'll get paid out first."

Creditors gathered in Edgar Street's Starlite Room to hear the nominee Marc Landsman present Hereford United's CVA proposal. Elke Thuerlings, John Edwards and Andy Lonsdale sat with Landsman at the top table. Philip Gambrill, subject to an individual voluntary arrangement, did not attend. At the shareholder's meeting the CVA failed when 61.7% of members voted in favour of the voluntary arrangement and 38.3% of members voted against it. Landsman said he expected the club to be wound up by the High Court in September.

But it wasn't. The main claimant was paid and Hereford United's winding-up order was adjourned in the High Court for 42 days, then they were granted another extension, then an adjournment of 15 working days – the club's eighth.

In June, Jesse Norman had contacted the Southern League and the Football Association to warn them Agombar was unlikely to pass the FA's owners' and directors' test. He had phoned Agombar "very soon after he'd invested in the club to find out what his intentions were, and

to find out what kind of person he was, and I got cut off – so I didn't regard that as a very encouraging sign."

"He told you that?" said Agombar, who told me Norman had hung up on him after phoning to ask when the staff were going to be paid.

"And I basically said, 'Jesse Norman, shouldn't you be sorting out the major problems that you have in your town, rather than phoning a businessman up, about when is he going to pay his wages?' There's businesses all around Hereford who have not paid their staff or perhaps not paid their bills, does he phone them up every day?"

In September, Norman secured a debate on the floor of the House of Commons focusing on the future of non-league football. "Football clubs are not purely private organisations," he said. "They are not merely the private playthings of their owners – they are public as well. What gives the clubs their life and energy, even in the Premiership, is the passion and love of their fans."

Norman described his attempts to warn the FA that Agombar was unlikely to meet the requirements of the owners' and directors' test and their refusal to make the results of the test public. He called the events at Hereford United "a catastrophe for the club, for the city, for the county and for Bulls fans everywhere".

Agombar called Norman "a politician who wants to jump on the bandwagon and bring a club down. Why don't he say to people, 'Please, give them a chance, please let them see what they can do within a year.'"

"The FA have been toothless," said Steve Niblett. "How can you do a fit and proper test after you've bought yourself into the club? It's ridiculous, absolutely ridiculous."

"In late August, early September," the HUST chairman Chris Williams recalled in November, "I spoke to Tommy Agombar and said to him, 'Look, we've got to work together, we've got to get this thing to go. We want to try to sort this out, we need to get together to talk about it. If you send me a letter from a solicitor guaranteeing that football will continue to be played at Edgar Street, for the foreseeable future, I'd ask the Supporters Trust to call off the boycott and ask the fans to go back and support the team.'

And he said, 'Yes, I'll do that.' This was on a Friday night, and he said, 'Yes, you'll have that in your email inbox by Monday.' And that was the end of August, early September, and I still haven't received that letter."

"Yeah, I did say, 'Yeah, I'll get the letter, I'll get a letter for you,'" Agombar conceded, "But then as I put the phone down, [I thought,] 'What's the point?' My lawyer said to me, 'He knows in the leases that football's got to be played at Edgar Street.' What did he expect me to do? Build on the middle of the pitch?"

Ellistown and Ibstock knocked Hereford out of the FA Cup in September. HUST organised a protest at the televised October 8 match between Kidderminster Harriers and Welling United, chanting, "We want Tommy out!" throughout the match. Fans were divided between those who attend matches and the much

larger number who wanted the club to be liquidated so they could build a supporter-run club like Chester FC.

"They're not doing us any good at all," said Eddie Pobiega, who attended matches for 46 years and didn't support the boycott. "At the end of the day we want the club to survive. So you've got to pull together, haven't you? So the gates we're having or not having are not helpful and we could do with some of those thousand odd people coming back to us."

"[It wasn't] about supporting Hereford United," said Chris Williams. "It [was] about protecting Edgar Street so that Herefordshire can have the potential to play league football for the future. As soon as that stadium goes, that opportunity is lost forever." In September Herefordshire Council added its name to the list of creditors for £65,000 in rent arrears, business rates and legal fees. On October 24, the Council announced it had attempted to take possession of Edgar Street and issued proceedings against the club for forfeiture of the leases and repossession of the ground. "In response to this action, we can confirm that HUFC has paid outstanding sums due to the council."

"I'm not going to give in," Lonsdale told me in October, "We're here to win the war. It's a war of wills between us and the fans. Not all the fans, some of the fans. The fans are actually brilliant, a lot of them, but we're not going to give in."

I asked Steve Niblett if he thought it was possible the impasse might have been the result of ham-fisted public relations and a series of misunderstandings. "No, not at all. Not at all," he replied. "We're not thick, we know what's going on. This guy's trying to pull a fast one."

Fourteenth in the table, Hereford United struggled along. 43 players were involved in the season, with only 13 accumulating 10 or more appearances. The club returned to the High Court on December 1 and told the Registrar a £1.5million investment from Newell Properties Developments Ltd. had fallen through due to "aggressive social media". On December 10, Alpha Choice Finance issued the statement that it was ending its involvement with Hereford United after "many weeks of harassment and misinformation". The same day Andy Lonsdale – who had passed the FA's owners and directors test in October – announced that he was the new owner.

Staff and players still weren't being paid. The left-back Daniel O'Reilly, who left the club in October, told the *Hereford Times* he was owed a month's wages. He said players were paid in cash with handwritten payslips and Agombar remained involved with the club: "Tommy once deducted us £20 for not training even though we weren't getting paid."

On December 15, a Monday morning, the club was granted a four-day extension after Lonsdale's lawyer argued that the 15-working-day adjournment had included two weekends. The supporters who filed into the courtroom on Friday afternoon were half-expecting another extension.

The liquidation order took about five minutes. Hereford United's results were expunged from the Southern League, with any future matters to be dealt with by the office of the Official Receiver. The creditors, among them Steve Niblett, Wye Valley Brewery, ID Sports and Leisure, Mowtech Landscape Contractors and Quickskip Hereford Ltd, would remain unpaid. The players were left without a club.

"We've been lied to from day one as far as we're concerned, we had a lot of promises and obviously nothing's come to fruition," Hereford's manager Jon Taylor said on BBC Hereford & Worcester Sport, "In hindsight, I should have believed what the supporters were saying."

HUST issued a statement that a plan was already in place to secure the use of Edgar Street: "Hereford United is the supporters that have had the club at their hearts, in many cases for generations of their families, and the spirit of the club will live on through each and every one of us." In early January HUST announced an open meeting and a member vote on the acceptance of a partnership proposal from the Jon Hale Benefactors group. Hale had been among a group of local businessmen who'd approached Herefordshire Council with plans for a phoenix club, Hereford FC, back in August.

The Hereford FC proposal states that HUST will be able to own up to 50% of the club by buying shares, with all profits funnelled back into the club. The club will offer the stadium's development rights to the Council, with no profits assigned to the benefactors. The FA has indicated that in order for a phoenix club to be accepted next season matters must be resolved by March 1. Ⓑ

Building the Dream

As the political wrangling continues over Qatar's World Cup, what's the reality on the ground?

By James Corbett

At the edge of an empty man-made lagoon near to the shore of the Arabian Gulf, I count skyscrapers looming from the dust. The road, lined on one side with partition hoardings and on the other with palm trees, ends 50 metres ahead. Saplings are planted down the middle. In the blinding light I can see eight towers under construction, three already built as well as a nine-storey building that seems to be occupied. There is a sense of order and eerie quiet. It is Friday, the day of rest and prayer, so no construction is taking place. It is just me and a taxi driver, blinking into the sunshine at Qatar's blank canvas.

This is Lusail, a city which is still being built. In seven years time it will host the World Cup final.

"Expect Amazing" was the slogan of Qatar 2022 when it bid to host the greatest show on earth, but four years down the line I hadn't expected this. Having toured Brazil and South Africa on the eve of their tournaments and seen the global scrutiny because stands or walkways or roads hadn't been completed on time, I was aware of the unique pressure hosting status brought to a nation. But in Lusail I found something else. This wasn't about missing bits of infrastructure, this was about an absent city.

Qatar 2022 is a concept that always required a great leap of the imagination. The heat, the lack of football pedigree, and the size of the country are all factors that for most observers should have precluded it from even being a contender to host the World Cup.

I'd followed Qatar's story almost from the very start. It seemed, at first, patently absurd. The idea of the World Cup in a desert nation that had never come close to even qualifying for the tournament seemed like one of those ruses dreamed up by a western PR agency playing to the vanity of an egotistical sheikh. It all seemed such a hopeless and naive undertaking. In May 2009 I'd sat in a conference hall at Wembley Stadium as the president of the Asian Football Confederation, Mohamed Bin Hammam, a Qatari, had not even mentioned his own country's bid. If Bin Hammam wasn't going to talk it up, who would?

As a succession of established and emerging football nations launched their bids through 2009, Qatar's seemed the odd one out. Even Indonesia, with its chaotic and corrupt football leaders, could at least boast one of the most football-mad populations in Asia.

But on visiting Qatar for the first time in November that year, what the bid committee presented did at least offer some coherence: a compact World Cup, cooling technology overcoming the heat factor at least on the pitch and in fan-zones, potent messaging as a World Cup for the "entire Middle East", not just Qatar's 2 million, predominantly migrant, population, and lots and lots of money to overcome the country's infrastructural shortcomings. It did still require a leap of faith to believe it could ever be pulled off, but there was some practicability underlying the bid.

Yet through 2010, something quite palpable changed. Qatar ran an excellent campaign, something that tends to be overlooked now. Its stadium plans were eye-catching, its international and domestic legacy pledges bold and it provided a viable solution to the on-field problems posed by heat. More significantly, the country's government began putting together trade deals with several nations that had representation on the Fifa Executive Committee. Bin Hammam also clicked into gear, forging alliances that would prove crucial on the day of the vote.

"The one thing that has significantly changed over the past year was perceptions," the bid chairman, Sheikh Mohammed, told me in October 2010. "People are now taking us much more seriously, taking our message much more seriously." He acknowledged that in the first days of the bidding process this was very different. "It was very much, 'Who are these people? Where are they coming from? Why are they doing this? What does it mean to them?'"

Yet exactly how or why Qatar won on 2 December 2010 remains shrouded in

mystery. The scent of corruption lingers strongly and it seems improbable that the Fifa Executive Committee were capable of making an honest decision. Significant allegations have since been made about many of its members and Bin Hammam has been banned from football for life after being implicated in a cash-bribery scandal ahead of the 2011 Fifa Presidential election. Despite some excellent investigative journalism and a controversial Fifa-commissioned investigation by the New York attorney Michael Garcia, we are not much closer to the truth.

Quite apart from the compromised process that crowned it victor, Qatar, too, has been engulfed in opprobrium. Indeed its success has sometimes threatened to become the greatest PR disaster of all time. From being accused of being too hot and too small to host the World Cup, discussion of its host status has, since 2010, encompassed a vast and sometimes bewildering array of concerns, including corruption, accusations that the country is a haven for modern-day slavery, that the football calendar can't cope with a tournament moved to avoid the summer heat, that Qatar funds terrorism, that it has simultaneously become too powerful within world football for its own good and yet cares nothing for the game. At times the narrative has simply spiralled out of control: one website making the absurd calculation that 48,000 guest workers would lose their lives building the country's World Cup stadiums.

Four years on from its bid victory I spent a week in Qatar. Was it the slave state of global renown? What was the mood like for an organising committee that for some had assumed pariah-status? Was there any sense of football mania? Would the country overcome the "logistical challenges" Fifa's own inspection team had pointed at ahead of the vote and be ready? Above all, would Qatar actually host the World Cup?

The initial signs that Friday morning in Lusail did not seem positive. Superficially the area had changed little since I'd last been there in 2010. With 12 years leeway it had seemed ambitious but nevertheless plausible that Qatar, with their huge petro-dollar wealth, could make an entire city rise from the sand. By late 2014, it had started to seem optimistic.

"People tend to forget that a city is like a tree," Lusail's developers had proclaimed hopefully in 2010, when Fifa's inspectors were in town and we journalists who had followed the bid circus to Qatar had questioned the lack of development. "Without a proper foundation underground, nothing above will flourish."

Four years on, the fruit from these roots seemed particularly sparse. Was the same true for the rest of the country?

I wanted to see a football match in Qatar, but not in the way that I'd seen games there before. There was such a variety of experience in those encounters that at once reflected Qatar's wealth and its multiculturalism. The most memorable experience had been at a World Cup qualifier between Qatar and Indonesia, when the local expatriate community had easily outnumbered their hosts and provided colour and noise while their compatriots were easily beaten. These matches had been watched from the press box. This time, however, I wanted to go as a fan, planning to take public transport and sitting with Qatari spectators.

One of the perceptions is that the 2022 World Cup is being hosted in a country without a true appetite for the game and will leave a legacy of white elephant stadiums. It is, according to Brian Glanville, a "wretched little anonymity of a football country". The national team had been hotly tipped ahead of the Gulf Cup and this was one of their final warm-up matches. As the weekend commenced, would the crowds be lining up to see off The Maroon?

"Where do I buy a ticket?" I asked a Nigerian security guard after I arrived 30 minutes late, Doha's sclerotic public transport system having proved beyond me. The guard simply laughed and waved me towards the VIP entrance. I told him I didn't want to go there and he laughed again and, shaking his head, pointed the other way to an empty ticketing cubicle. An attendant, sitting outside eating his supper from a polystyrene tray, ignored me and another security guard beckoned me inside. No one, it seemed, was paying their way in.

There were around 2,000 spectators in a stadium built for six times as many, including around 60 North Korean supporters watching impassively on the opposite side of the pitch, and 200 in a stand assigned for families. I sat with the bulk of the spectators, a mixture of Palestinians, Egyptians, Bangladeshis, Sudanese, Indians and East Africans, interspersed with some Gulf Arabs

– mostly teenage boys – who were distinguishable by their brand new iPhones.

The game was untidy and leaden-paced. Qatar, who had six players seemingly of West African origin in their starting XI (the QFA insisted that all were born in the country to guest worker parents), were much bigger and more powerful than their opponents. The mismatch seemed to reflect a meeting of two political extremes: one absolute regime that starved and stole from its population, the other that indulged its citizens in every conceivable way. There appeared to be relief at half-time and the ground emptied, as spectators filtered outside to pray or claim free food packages, comprising a chicken sandwich, juice and water. A Qatari boy complained "the chicken tastes of stones".

After the interval, the Koreans imploded. Qatar streamed forward and scored twice in three minutes, adding a third on 55 minutes. The crowd were roused and rose and clapped to the rhythm of the game, encouraged at times by what can only be described as an official cheerleader, who marched along the front of the stand imploring people to make more noise. Was it stage-managed? There was an element of that. The majority of supporters were guest workers bussed in to see the game, although, when asked, no-one admitted taking money to be part of the crowd.[1] Most seemed to enjoy themselves. For some it all became a bit too emotional and security guards had to intervene gently as two Qatari teenagers started throwing punches at each other. The game ended 3-1.

When Qatar was awarded the 2022 World Cup the country sat 112th in Fifa's World rankings and had never come close to qualifying for a World Cup. No host country in the history of the World Cup has ever had such poor pedigree. When South Africa, about which concerns were also voiced as to its suitability as a football nation, was awarded the 2010 finals it was 39th in Fifa's rankings.

What will the World Cup mean for Qatari football? "We've really been able to use World Cup 2022 as a platform to spread football culture," says Germay Amanuel, a projects manager for the QFA. "From hosting World Cup 2022 we've been able to expand football, we've been able to expand the number of registered players, we've been able to expand the number of diverse and different expat nationalities who are participating in football here, we've been able to expand women's football."

While the standard of the Qatar Stars League is improving and less reliant on high profile players, such as Pep Guardiola and Gabriel Batistuta, looking for a final payday than previously, the league continues to struggle for local fans. Supporter affections usually lie with La Liga or the Premier League, which are available cheaply via satellite TV. There exists a deep-rooted TV culture that leaves stadiums empty. Week in, week out most games are played before barely a handful of spectators.

---

[1] *This is a big problem in Qatar: a January 2014 survey by Qatar's Ministry of Development Planning and Statistics suggested that paid fans may be turning large numbers of Qataris off live sport.*

"If you are playing in Europe there is more pressure than here because you play to win," the former Norway international defender, Pa Modou Kah, told me in 2011 when he was playing for Al Khor. "Here you play to win as well, but in a different environment. There are no spectators. Everyone watches the game at home. In the long run, that has to change."

Germay Amanuel says that the issue is not using the World Cup to 'create' a fan culture. "Lots of people aren't aware of the history of football in this country. We used to have full stadiums, we still have full stadiums, but along the way we probably lost a bit of momentum," he says. He points to the "really serious derbies between Al Arabi and Al Rayyan" which he likens to a smaller scale version of some of Europe's *clasicos* as evidence of Qatar's passion for the game. A turning point was the late 1990s when "all sorts of forms of alternative entertainment came in and the explosion of technology", including wall-to-wall broadcast of overseas leagues. As a way of regaining momentum behind the domestic game, he has led the QFA's development of an amateur league involving 16 teams made up from across Qatar's guest worker communities that utilises the country's professional sporting infrastructure and effectively exists as a the third tier of the Qatari football pyramid. The aim is to give immigrant populations a stake and sense of ownership in the domestic game and build the sport holistically. "Hosting the World Cup is a real blessing because it gives us the platform to really reignite that football culture again," he says.

When pitching to be World Cup hosts, Brazil and Russia argued that the progress of their domestic football was predicated on the need for world-class facilities and only the World Cup could secure that necessary investment. Qatar, on the other hand, already had sporting facilities – including the Aspire Zone and a score of high quality but perennially underused stadiums – that exceeded its needs.

But really, Qatar 2022 was about something else. "Essentially the vision of Qatar 2022 as a bid is not just about a vision for the World Cup, it's a vision for a nation," its bid chairman, Sheikh Mohammed, explained to me in Johannesburg in December 2009. "And the master plan for Qatar is essentially the master plan for the World Cup as well." What he meant was this: World Cup sporting facilities and stadiums would form the keystones of Qatar's urban development plan; the World Cup, as he saw it, would no longer be just about football or stadiums and transport upgrades, but about changing the entire complexion of a country. "One of the milestones is bringing those things together and making sure the whole world can see that the World Cup is no longer just about the development of football as a sport in a nation or any given region, it's about the development of a whole country."

Six months later in Zurich, at the handover of the bid books, he said, "For us to provide a bid that is essentially providing an outcome for 12 years from now, it talks about the confidence that we have in hosting such a tournament. It will require huge investment – but nothing that can't be done." In short, it was, and remains, a bet on the future – both in terms of football and the entire country.

Nearly eight years out from the finals – a point at which most previous tournaments had still to be awarded – it was too hard to judge whether Qatar would be ready or not. Work was under way on some of the stadiums and there was no doubt in my mind that the country had the money and political will to build them on time. There was a new airport and a nearly completed metro. But the suggestion of Supreme Committee officials to conceive of their tournament "along the lines of an Olympics" was a big jump when the World Cup had never been staged like that before or in such a small host city.

Football, of course, was and is important to the Qataris, even if it didn't always seem obvious in the stadiums. Inter-Gulf competition remains fierce. The twice-weekly football discussion show, *Al Majlis* on the Al Kass network, which assesses Qatari and Gulf football in detail, suggests an obsessive interest in local football. Is this enough? Probably not. Certainly Qatar is not Brazil and it's not Germany. The World Cup used to be a reward for what a country had achieved in football. Now it is an agent for what a country wants to achieve on and off the pitch.

As World Cup hosts and finalists, there will be much focus on the progress –or lack of – of the Qatar national team. There is an awareness, too, that many people will want to see Qatar fail on the field. The Qataris remained optimistic. In 2011, al-Thawadi told me, "We will see Qatari players in La Liga and Premier League by 2022 and young budding players from Europe will be wanting to come here."

There was little sense of progress towards that dream at the Lekhwiya Stadium, but his other belief, that by 2022 the country will be able to "show everyone that we have players who are talented and can compete with the rest of the world" and qualify for a World Cup on its own merits, may not be unrealistic. Three weeks after the North Korea match, Qatar beat their neighbour Saudi Arabia to lift the Gulf Cup. As well as a significant act of giant killing and regional one-upmanship it elevated Qatar to fifth in Asia's rankings and 93rd in the world, above recent World Cup qualifiers such as Australia and New Zealand. The Maroons may not be in contention for the 2022 crown, but with such progress they may not bring disgrace, either.

If nobody cared much about Qatar v North Korea on the pitch, off it the relations between the two countries were swiftly brought into sharp focus. The day after the game the *Guardian* published shocking revelations about guest workers in the country, focusing on the 2,800 North Koreans based in Qatar. It explained the sixty or so bedraggled Korean fans we had seen at the previous evening's game.

Impeded by economic sanctions and trade bans, North Korea's leader Kim Jong-un had hit upon the ruse of exporting labour to bring in hard currency to North Korea. Qatar was one of the destinations, although it transpired Russia and even Poland and the Czech Republic had received North Korean workers. The *Guardian* alleged that up to 90 per cent of the salaries of these workers, sent on three-year rotations, were expropriated by the North Korean government. "They work constantly," the manager of a tower project, which employs about 50 North Koreans, told the newspaper. "I have even built a room for them so they can rest without having to go back to their labour camp."

There was no suggestion that any of these workers were employed on World Cup stadium building sites, but the link was immediately made in other reports and on social media. "It seemed like we had reached a point where the organisers of the 2022 World Cup couldn't possibly get more cartoonishly evil," began a report by the US website, *Deadspin*.

Over the past two years, Qatar 2022 has become the touch paper for the vast and largely unreported issue of *kafala*, the system of sponsored labour prevalent in a number of Gulf states. In Arabic *kafala* literally means 'guardianship'. The translation is telling, for the system removes many freedoms an independent adult would enjoy, binding foreign workers to a single 'sponsor' who must, under the law, also be their employer, and places all sorts of restrictions on the guest worker, as if indeed they were a child. It allows the sponsor to monitor their stay and exit from the country; they cannot change job without permission; once a guest worker leaves Qatar they cannot return to Qatar under a new sponsor for two years. "Sponsors," Amnesty International says, "can have a significant influence over the lives of migrant workers."

The system is supposed to balance the rights of the worker and employer. In practice, Amnesty says, "it creates an excessively unequal power relationship, in which workers have limited and ineffective avenues open to them if they are being exploited. If workers arrive in Qatar to find that they have been deceived about the terms and conditions of their work during the recruitment process, or are subjected to abusive working or living conditions by their employer, the question of whether or not they can change jobs depends on their employer – the very person responsible for their abuse." If a worker has cause to complain about wages, accommodation and so on, a sponsor can simply withdraw their sponsorship and force them to leave.

Qatar, of course, is not alone in using *kafala*. What World Cup host status has done is highlight a broader problem that a western audience might otherwise have known nothing about.

In September 2013, the *Guardian* published a devastating exposé of the conditions migrant construction labourers endure in Qatar. It was a catalogue of human misery, documenting evidence of forced labour on a World Cup infrastructure project, non-payment of wages, confiscation of passports. Most shockingly, an accompanying film showed the bodies of some of the 44 Nepalese workers to die on Qatari building sites that summer being returned home for their funerals in Kathmandu.

"I think it would shock anybody," Hassan al-Thawadi told me in his office, 15 months after publication. "I think it shocked everybody. At least some of the videos that were shown, of course they shocked me." Was he aware that people lived that way in his country? "In terms of what I saw on the *Guardian*? No, not to that extent, no."

It was indeed a piece of journalism that shocked. It also ramped up pressure on the Qataris another notch. From being a matter that lay on the periphery of the debate about their World Cup – a debate that was still dominated by the heat, the size of Qatar and probity of its voters – human rights became a core issue. Nobody wanted to see football's greatest show built in stadiums that for some families were memorials to sons and fathers who had died building them.

Qatar's labour problems fall into three categories. Firstly, there were evident safety problems on building sites, which, exacerbated by the blistering heat, were causing high numbers of worker fatalities, some from preventable accidents, others by the stress of working long hours in the heat. Secondly, low wages and poor living conditions, combined with unscrupulous employers and recruitment agents who were late in paying wages and demanding huge fees for themselves, left many guest workers indebted and poverty-ridden. Thirdly, and at the root of most of its labour problems, lies the *kafala* sponsorship system, binding employee to the employer. This system creates a work environment in which there is little chance of progression to better paid work. Guest workers are left reliant on the goodwill of those that brought them to the country for their survival. *Kafala* also mitigates against social mobility. If a worker was any good at their job, why would an employer ever let them leave? This further undermined by Qatar's trap of low wages, high living costs and administrative obduracy and chaos.[2]

"It's not a World Cup being built on the blood of innocents," said al-Thawadi at the time of the guest worker issue exploding into the public consciousness. "That is unacceptable to anybody. We will be eradicating these issues." Blatter met the country's emir and declared Qatar was "on the right track" in dealing with workers' rights. The law firm DLA Piper were commissioned by Qatar's government to draw up an independent report recommending changes to the country's labour laws. It engaged with a wide range of stakeholders, including Human Rights Watch and Amnesty International, and pulled no punches in its widely leaked 139-page report, recommending the effective abolition of *kafala* and the introduction of comprehensive worker rights.

When Qatar's Ministry of Labour held a press conference in May 2014 shortly after the submission of the DLA report, it was expected that sweeping changes would be announced. What followed

---

[2] *Nor were these conditions solely the domain of uneducated migrant labourers from the developing world. Even footballers, such as the French-Algerian midfielder Zahir Belounis, could become victims of Qatar's Kafkaesque labour laws. He became stranded in the country for two years after a contractual dispute with his sponsor club, who refused to allow him to leave. Even when he became the global face of the struggle against kafala, causing François Hollande and others to intervene, not to mention huge embarrassment for his hosts, nobody, it seemed, could break the impasse.*

was an excruciating cherry-picking of some of its recommendations – with most, including the *kafala* question, overlooked – that infuriated reformists within Qatar and human rights groups alike. Repeated and continual criticisms that change was nowhere near fast enough certainly held true.

Nicholas McGeehan, Human Rights Watch's Gulf researcher, recalls his "disbelief" at this fudge. "The DLA Piper report wasn't perfect but it was a lengthy, serious and impressive document that contained recommendations which, had they been adopted and enforced, would have moved this issue forward significantly," he says. "The Qatari authorities seemed to get a case of last-minute nerves and canned the report, and instead announced a series of steps which included better housing, wage payment protection, but very minimal changes to the law."

This apparent failure gave ammunition to the extreme sides of the debate. For the elements within Qatar, insistent that there is nothing wrong with the country's treatment of guest workers, the thin veneer of reform was proof that everything was okay and that Qatar was indeed a progressive nation. For the cast of individuals, ranging from the head of the International Trade Union Confederation (ITUC), Sharan Burrow, to the Fifa Executive Committee member Theo Zwanziger, who denounced the country as the crucible of modern slavery, it was more evidence that nothing would ever change.

The ITUC in particular has pulled no punches about what Fifa should do with the World Cup: its campaign website

is rerunthevote.org. More so even than the *Guardian*, it has cast into the global consciousness the idea that Qatar is a pariah state and has inextricably linked football and the World Cup with *kafala* and worker deaths. Thousands of column inches have quoted Burrow, an Australian schoolteacher and trade unionist, who has been an implacable critic of Qatar 2022 and whose polemicising has brought the wretchedness of *kafala* to a wider audience. "Qatar," claims Burrow, "is a country without a conscience."

But where does the truth lie about Qatar? Is it the slave state that some maintain it to be, or is it just like many developing countries, in which a wealthy elite presides with impunity over an impoverished and disenfranchised working class? Are the native Qataris, who make up just 15% of the country's 2.1 million population, a tyrannous and ruthlessly exploitative people, or is it actually more complicated than that? What are Qatar 2022 doing about it? And what about the men who are actually building all these stadiums?

Friday afternoon in early November and a walk around Doha's main souk and its neighbouring bus station offers a glimpse into the world of the country's guest workers. It is their day off and thousands of men mill around, shopping, chatting, hanging out. Many sit aimlessly, disconsolate, bored. On Al Ahmed Street, a block from Souk Waqif, where families and tourists frequent its restaurants, Filipino men loll indolently. Some watch a gigantic TV lodged in the back of a van, bearing the logo of Al Murshid Unit (strap line: "Where morals and culture flourish"), broadcasting a religious discussion show in Arabic. The men look on, tired and uncomprehending.

Everyone has a story about being ripped off, for it is a fact of life for guest workers in Qatar. The scorn is usually reserved for the middlemen who brought them there, employers who acted like tin gods as the law permitted and the system that failed most people when things went wrong. There was the Bosnian builder not paid for six months. When he took his case to court, it took four years for the outcome to be decided: he got his work permit back, but not any of the money that was owed to him. There was the Ethiopian who worked at the Pearl Development, a vast luxury retail and residential project on an artificial island, wasn't paid after a month and walked out to work illegally elsewhere. The Nepalis, whose conditions were subject of the *Guardian's* devastating investigation, were spoken of by other guest workers as a pitied underclass, whose recruiters had a reputation for corruption and brutality that went without parallel.

Most seemed to view the Qataris merely as distant overlords whose aloofness and negligence had allowed their misery to prosper. The "what do you think of Qatar?" invariably elicited a grunt that spoke more loudly than words. "The Qataris are so arrogant," a Kenyan named Khalid hissed in disgust. "They think that money can buy them anything." Direct accusations were rare, but the one I heard from an Ethiopian shocked me. "The big problem with the Qataris is not on the building sites, it goes unseen," he told me. "They hire maids from my country and others. The Qatari men fuck them, then won't have them in their houses and tear up their sponsors' permit. They are left with nothing."

"Women who report sexual abuse also risk being charged with 'illicit relations' – sexual relations outside of marriage – a 'crime' normally punished with a year in jail and deportation," noted Amnesty in a 2014 report. Those who end up pregnant can face a worse fate: forced removal of their child, who ends up in a Qatari orphanage, and deportation for the mother.

Away from downtown Doha, which, beyond the gleaming skyscrapers of West Bay and the opulence of its magnificent Museum of Islamic Art is dirty, polluted and impoverished, the buildings thin out. Behind the car dealerships and nascent shopping malls of Salwa, the environment starts to resemble a moonscape. Not yet desert, it is a bleak scene of building sites, broken rock, dust, rubbish and heavy machinery. In Saniya, one section of highway is lined by a mile-long procession of dust-stained JCBs, cranes, steam rollers, dumper trucks, bulldozers, excavators, buses: tens of thousands of tonnes of machinery that is transforming the face of Qatar.

Behind this cavalcade live many of the men who are making the building happen. Their homes are concrete barracks with open terraces and small kitchens, where they live several to a room. Externally, they resemble the low-rise blocks not dissimilar to some 1970s social housing projects you see across Britain. Up close, the reality is far bleaker.

This is Qatar's dirty secret. A few kilometres from where the some of the wealthiest people on the planet reside in luxury, those servicing their economy live in filth and degradation. To describe these as "slave camps" is manifestly incorrect – residents are free to come and go as they please – and conditions are perhaps no worse than homes I've seen in the slums of Brazil or South Africa. But juxtaposed with such proximity to Doha's wealth – the malls, the five star hotels, the palatial family homes – the effect of such poverty is startling.

I entered the courtyard of one such block. Rubbish and broken masonry was piled everywhere. A boy sat on an old office chair, thumbing a cheap smartphone. A group of men stood around a carrom board – an Indian variation of billiards – engrossed in the game.

Around the side of the building was more rubbish and the stink of sweat, cooking oil and shit. A Bengali teenager came up to me and asked in English what I wanted. I told him I wanted to look around.

Wordlessly he led me around the block, while his neighbours looked on, bemused. In one open doorway, flies buzzed around the air aggressively.

"Is that the bathroom?" I asked, trying to hide my disgust. Broken porcelain and tiles smashed from the wall lay around, and the place was smeared with the splatter of excrement.

"You want to use the toilet?" he asked, misreading my question.

"No, I just want to look. Can I see a bedroom?"

"You want a room?" he asked.

"No, I just want to look."

We moved on, the boy hesitant now. I stood in the open doorway of a fetid room. Tired men lay in the near darkness, their pathetic belongings around them, while an ancient air-conditioning unit wheezed. This was the bedroom that five of them shared and which housed everything they owned here. It was perhaps 12m^2.

On the passageway outside, a man with a beard and broken teeth started barking in a language I didn't recognise. The boy's bemusement gave way to anxiety.

"Who are you?" he asked. "What do you want?"

"I'm just looking."

"Are you a labour inspector?"

"No, a reporter."

He looked at me in disgust, turned his back and disappeared into a room, slamming the door shut behind him.[3]

A few miles away from the Saniya barracks was a compound housing Qatar's two churches, the Catholic Church of Our Lady of the Rosary and an

[3] *My experiences in Doha's slums were relatively fleeting, limited by language barriers and concern that those that assisted me would meet trouble. As I was alone my own security was of concern too. Infinitely more comprehensive surveys of worker abuses and case studies exist in Amnesty International's 2013 report "The Dark Side of Migration: Spotlight on Qatar's Construction Workers" and Human Rights Watch's 2012 report "Building a Better World Cup."*

adjacent Coptic Church. On Fridays, the compound comes alive with every guest worker community under the desert sun.

From 6am until 7.30pm no fewer than 17 masses are held in the Catholic Church – in English, Konkani, Tagalog, Sinhala, Arabic, Malayalam, Urdu, Tamil and Syriac. There are three separate masses for children and a baptismal service. While there were some Europeans, the place was mainly full of those from Qatar's guest-worker working class and mercantile communities: Filipinos, Sri Lankans, Egyptians, Ethiopians, Kenyans, Nigerians, Lebanese and Colombians.

Outside, Indian parishioners oversaw a labour exchange. People came with CVs and application forms and their details were logged onto a computer.

"We have many parishioners who cannot find staff and parishioners who are looking for new jobs," explained Joseph, an Indian who was overseeing the project. "We have people needing masons, builders, drivers, cooks, engineers, painters, domestic staff, accountants, secretaries. You name it. We have 200 applicants at the moment but more than 400 jobs on our books."

I asked him about those who had fallen foul of their employers or were in hardship.

He shook his head sadly. "We really can't help them. They must leave the country and return."

Wherever I went in Doha there seemed to be an underlying sense of alienation, disappointment, of being there purely for business, in order to remit riyals to make a better future elsewhere. But here,

as the November breeze blew in across the desert, was a sense of community, belonging and optimism.

Nor was every guest worker experience I heard hopeless. There has been an influx of East Africans over the past few years who – perhaps because they speak better English than other communities – seemed better equipped to navigate expat life and all its absurdities. Most whom I spoke to viewed Qatar as a means to an end, few were happy there and most had been screwed over in one way or another. They grumbled about the low wages and relatively high living costs. But most went home each year and came back of their own accord.

John, an Ethiopian driver, had first come over in 2011 to work on the construction sites.

"It was very hard and very hot, we sometimes worked 14 hours a day," he told me. "In summer it became so hot that sometimes they switched our shifts to the night." Besides the heat, he said he had no problem with site conditions, but the accommodation was grim – "six to a room" – and the food provided by his company was mundane – "chicken and rice every single day". After six months he saw out his contract and found work at a couple of different hotels in West Bay before returning home. When he returned it was as a painter, and after a spell back in Ethiopia he came back again in 2014 working as a driver, albeit on the wrong kind of permit. He was aware – although not especially anxious – that if he was caught he risked being incarcerated at Doha's notorious detention centre and then kicked out.

His main complaints were about the visa system that necessitated him paying around 3000R (£550) for a visa each year, most of which went to a middleman, and the high cost of living.

He explained the economics of life in Qatar. It cost him 1000R (£185) per month to rent a one-bedroom flat in Al Rayyan, which he shared with two friends, but while it was small it was clean. He paid 100R per day to rent his cab and 75R for his fuel. Taxi fares averaged 15-20R in the city, so he would have to make at least 10 journeys per day to break even. But there was money to be made, he said, to which the pair of iPhones that sat on his dashboard attested.

His ambition was to study in Los Angeles, where he had family. He worked every hour he could to realise that, but the margins were small and so the dream remained distant. It frustrated him that there was no access to education in Qatar, no access to anything except work as a means to an end.

I asked him what he did in his free time.

"I go to church and watch football."

I asked him if he'd seen any in Qatar, which lays on its Stars League for free or for a very nominal amount, but he seemed perplexed by this notion. A lack of engagement from his hosts rendered live football an alien concept. Football for him meant watching La Liga or the Premier League on the country's heavily subsidised satellite channels.

Two days later I was given the Supreme Committee's take on the guest workers who will make Qatar's World Cup dream a reality.

Farah al-Muftah is one of the faces of the new Qatar. Young, US-educated and eschewing the traditional headscarf, she is, according to one of her colleagues, "very driven, unwavering in her focus in spite of the obstacles". A legal counsel at the Supreme Committee, she also heads the Qatar 2022's Worker's Welfare Committee (WWC).

When we meet at the Supreme Committee's West Bay offices, she tells me about the Workers Welfare Charter, which was released in March 2013, and provides "contractually binding" standards to all of Qatar 2022's contractors, subcontractors and service suppliers, which she says are comprehensive "covering all areas from recruitment to repatriation". These principles are as wide ranging as health and safety, employment standards, ensuring wages are paid on time, grievance processes and access to information. Accommodation facilities, she says, are inspected at tender stage and compliance is a pre-requisite. If tender is granted a contractor is made subject to continuous "ad hoc inspections".

While human rights groups have given cautious welcomes to Qatar 2022's WWC, the ITUC issued a condemnation when it published its full guidelines in February 2014. "Qatar's new World Cup worker welfare standards do not deliver fundamental rights for workers and merely reinforce the discredited *kafala* system of employer control over workers," it said in a lengthy rebuke, which claimed that the charter was "a sham for workers" and alleged that they "reinforced a system of forced labour with *kafala*."

I put it to Al-Muftah that while Qatar 2022 worker conditions may be being improved, the root of the criticism facing Qatar was the *kafala* system. Reforms to *kafala* were going through the legislative process, she said, by "at the latest is the end of this year [2014] or early next year."[At the time of writing, in mid-January 2015, this has not come to pass]. She added. "As far as the comment about everything being tied to the *kafala* system I'd tend to disagree with that in the sense that conditions are important and issues other than the *kafala* are addressed."

I asked why anyone would take at face value the country's commitment to reform when it was dealing with regimes like North Korea to bolster its work force. "I'm not going to get into politics," she replied. "What I can see in that specific story is that the report should have been taken to the Ministry of Labour for them to take the action they're mandated to take."

The problem with assertions like this is that Qatar's Ministry of Labour has so far proved singularly unable to deal adequately with the multitude of labour problems it has, or even to recognise that criticism may have some basis. The *Guardian's* 2013 reports were variously described by an undersecretary of the Ministry of Labour as "a conspiracy driven entirely by political motivations" and "an effort to undermine Qatar and an attempt to spoil its hosting of the 2022 World Cup". These conspirators, he said, needed "indirect excuses" to achieve the end of Qatar's host status "among them

the releasing of false reports not linked to the facts around the situation of the workforce in Qatar."

"It has been proven time and time again that state enforcement mechanisms are the problem not the solution," says Nicholas McGeehan. "Qatar 2022 know these mechanisms don't work which is precisely why they propose a special layer of protection for the workers on their projects. It's understandable that Qatar 22 would say this, but we know and Qatar 22 know that workers who are not on the high-profile projects will not be adequately protected from serious abuses."

The other problem Qatar 2022 faces is that while it may have praiseworthy initiatives to ensure stadium workers are well treated, there were no such guarantees for those building supporting infrastructure. The World Cup does not exist in isolation – for instance, the BBC has estimated that 0.1% of construction in the country is World Cup related – and many of the roads, hotels and other structures will go up regardless. But who is looking out for these workers? If a stadium is built without any casualties that is good news, but less so if the road leading up to it is littered with worker's corpses. I put this to Al-Muftah and she replied, "At a minimum, any contractor doing business has to comply with the labour law. To its credit, the labour law is very good. It's just a case of enforcing and implementing." When I pointed to the Ministry of Labour's less than glowing reputation, she said that they were increasing its number of inspectors and their training levels. Whether such faith is rewarded remains to be seen.

"A two-tier system is not an acceptable legacy, especially when the second tier of workers continue to be subjected to a system that makes them highly vulnerable to forced labour," says McGeehan. "Cooks, domestic workers, road sweepers, gardeners and all the other workers who make their living in Qatar are as deserving of their basic rights as the select construction workers who will enjoy this enhanced protection. If these welfare codes are a stepping stone to wider reforms then that's fine, but they must not be implemented as an attempt to circumvent long-term reform."

Earlier in the day, a Belgian project manager overseeing renovations to the national stadium had told me that there were clearly workers in Qatar working in unacceptable conditions, but that responsible contractors such as his own adhered to safety standards that exceeded those laid down locally, indeed were comparable with the European Union. As we were shown around his well-organised building site that was in evidence.

But what sanctions would Qatar 2022 be able to take against unscrupulous contractors? "The last resort is termination of contract," said Al-Muftah. "You don't want to terminate a contract and leave a worker in that situation. I'd sooner work with a contractor and make sure that we're actually uplifting the standards." She says that there is an element of enlightened self-interest for contractors to maintain good work conditions and gave me the example of two work camps that adhered to Qatar 2022's standards and one that didn't. "Productivity increased, there was less sick leave, less absenteeism and in general the workforce was more happy and productive."

One of the main challenges Qatar 2022 faces in relation to its charter is ensuring that workers had not had to pay onerous recruitment fees in their country of origin. "The recruitment fee discussion is very difficult because it involves multiple players," she said. "So you have to cooperate and collaborate with the sending countries to ensure that there's alignment in policies and making sure that [workers] are not getting charged recruitment fees at the state of origin and when they come here you find out that they've been charged. It's a very complex situation because you're talking about different jurisdictions and making sure that they're aligning."[4]

I asked her about some of the news coverage of Qatar's labour problems, specifically the images of coffins being sent back to Nepal. "I think on just a basic human level it's shocking when you see something like that," she said. "But the most important thing is you are actually doing things to address it and I know that the Workers' Welfare Committee and the government are doing things that address that."She added, "What has been reported is the bad. What I'd like is for us to showcase the good."

A few hours later, she got her chance.

It was dinner time at the workers' compound near the Al-Wakrah Stadium, 25 kilometres south of downtown Doha, when we arrived. As ever in Qatar, it was not quite what

I expected. The hour-long journey, through ceaseless rush-hour traffic, had taken us from the gleaming West Bay area past the car dealerships and hidden slums of Doha's fringes and briefly into desert, which will surely be swallowed up by the city's sprawling mass before long. The road then traced the edge of endless new-build developments, the high walls enclosing clusters of town houses, apparently Doha's suburbia. And then, quite unexpectedly, we pulled into one of them.

This was Compound 41. Inside the vaulted gates was the sort of soulless suburban development sold to British pensioners made good in Spain: a semi-pedestrianised street, perhaps 50 three-storey townhouses, parking lots, trees. It was a scene of order and developer-brochure idyll, but for a line of Asian men clutching tin trays and dinner tickets snaking from one of the buildings.

"Is this your workers' paradise?" I sniped to the press officer.

This compound was home to 468 workers, employed by HBK Contracting, a vast Qatari-owned building and engineering conglomerate. According to a noticeboard in the administration block, 108 were working on the Al Wakra Stadium site, comprising 89 labourers, 6 junior staff and 13 administrators; the rest were employed on other projects in Qatar's building boom. The houses had been subdivided into dormitories. Each room contained three curtained off areas which contained single beds. There were two lockers, a set of shelves and a pin board. The rooms were clean, bright and air-conditioned. There was a municipal area with a TV and DVD player, bathrooms and laundry areas; although the site manager explained that laundry was done for them, free of charge. "Some of them like to wash their smalls themselves," he said.

Another building housed a computer suite with internet access and a small library, although it seemed difficult to imagine many residents picking up a copy of *The Edge* – "Qatar's Business

---

[4] *This explanation initially seemed somewhat vague. When I followed up two months later via email, Al-Muftah repeated that recruitment restrictions were subject to "complex legal questions related to international law and the laws of sending countries", but sent me a very detailed explanation of Qatar 2022's best practice, which suggest that the mechanisms, at least, are in place.*

When asked about the Worker's Welfare Committee in general, Humans Rights Watch replied, "HRW has consistently been impressed and encouraged by Qatar 22's openness and the willingness to engage on these issues. In the regional context, sitting down and meeting with HRW and Amnesty is significant and creditable. We're also encouraged by the steps they plan to take to protect workers on their projects, as we are impressed by the Qatar Foundation's efforts. The challenge for them is to make their welfare codes work and if they can demonstrate that they do then that will be a positive. But what Q22 are trying to do is to guarantee workers' rights in a sector where there has been very limited reform and which is beset by abuse and exploitation. They would have a much higher chance of succeeding if their efforts were being complemented by meaningful legislative reform."

Magazine" – or flicking through Qatar 2022 Welfare Standards (in English) after a hard day's work. There was a mosque, and adjoining it a block with a 12-metre swimming pool and well-equipped gym. It was like visiting a very large youth hostel rather than the Qatari answer to *Auf Wiedersehen, Pet*. It was certainly a world away from the slum I poked around in Saniya.

Of course, nobody who works 12-hour six-day weeks for a few hundred dollars per month is living in a workers' paradise, no matter how tolerable their living conditions. The menu board in the mess hall spoke of the long days these men had to endure: breakfast served from 4.30am, lunch at 12pm and dinner at 7pm.

"The workers are all happy here, yes," declared the enthusiastic site manager, a plump, moustachioed south Indian man in his fifties, dressed in a black suit. He proudly showed me the menu, which had regional variations and changed daily; the men were being served fried fish and dal as we watched over them. He invited me to inspect the kitchen's complaints book. There was page upon page of "no food complaints", although the previous week someone had evidently taken exception to the bread and scribbled, "Roti no good. I want khubz."

There was, of course, an element of stage management in our tour. When we sat down with four workers, there were three journalists and a translator talking to four workers, but also watching over us a press officer, the omnipresent site manager and four other Qatar 2022 staff. Yet the workers didn't seem too perturbed.

"The facilities we used to get earlier were not so good, but now I am very happy living in this accommodation," said Rajesh Kumar, a 39-year-old builder from the Indian state of Uttar Pradesh. When pressed about how many to a room he had previously been living, he went immediately off message, telling us how he had shared a room in a Portakabin with nine others as recently as a year ago while working on the construction of the Qatar Foundation's building. The Qatar Foundation is supposed to be overseeing various reforms to the way that the country's guest workers are recruited and treated.

"This is a big improvement from the past five years," he added of his current home. An old man wearing a Delhi Public School T-Shirt chimed in, saying that it was much better than where he lived in India.

I asked him how site conditions varied between Qatar and India and he replied, "The facilities we get in Qatar are very high. Here we find that safety people are always behind us, and we are always getting cold water and lemon juice in the hot summer. Here the climate is not always extreme heat; it is a pleasant heat now."

What, I asked, was it like working in Qatar's summer heat? The men conferred with the translator, who answered rather blandly, "It is very difficult for the men working during the day."

Another journalist asked about the standard of the bread. The workers talked among themselves in Hindi before the site manager interposed: "The chapati issue is closed!"

We asked if they were allowed to keep their passports. The removal of passports from workers was something that human rights groups have been severely critical of; it was also against Qatar 2022's own rules. The men became more animated on this question than anything else, as if we'd asked a profoundly ridiculous question. "No," the translator explained, "they do not keep their passports. To keep their passport is a responsibility. They see it as the responsibility of the company to keep them safe."

When the question came to money, the men were coy about what they earned – although we were told it ranged from 800-1300 riyal per month (£150-£240). It seemed a pitiful amount for so much work, but when we asked what they spent it on they were more expansive. Rajesh told us that 70% of his salary went home to support his wife and three-year-old son. Besides daily household expenses and savings for his son's education, he had just built his own three-bedroom house in his village.

Was it the best house in his village? "It's much better than the other houses," he boasted. How much longer would he stay in Qatar? "Ten years."

In a consulting room, bearing the sign "WE ARE HERE FOR YOU" on one wall, Dr Buddaraju, the camp's friendly doctor, listed the workers' health problems: scabies, diabetes, allergic reactions to working in heat and sand, sweat rashes, as well as all the attendant scrapes and pains of manual labour. Some were pre-existing conditions that came with the workers from their countries of origin. "They are better here. They make some money and at the same time their health is taken care of," he claimed.

Dr Buddaraju was responsible for 2000 workers contracted to work on various building sites. Like many of his patients he was from the Indian subcontinent. He compared life in Qatar favourably to that back home, although for the blue-collar workers it seemed to me to be the exchange of one kind of poverty for another.

What was the most common source of death? "In Qatar? Road traffic accidents." But on building sites?"We don't see that here," he replied with a momentarily confused look. We asked him about heart attacks brought on through heat stress or overwork, but he claimed not to have encountered any such cases and tapped the wooden desk for good luck. One worker was diagnosed with a brain tumour and treated. "As a matter of fact it's not the physical illness which they suffer from, it's probably the mental illness," he said. "They are away from their homes, they have their anxiety neuro-system. For those who are serious we refer to a psychiatrist, but they are very few. But many of the workers from India are from the same areas, the same streets even. They share their problems."

"Why have they come here?" the doctor concluded as we stood up to leave. "To earn money. The quality of living here is definitely better than what it was in India or Sri Lanka. But it's about balance. You lose something, you gain something."

Our time in Compound 41 was drawing to a close, but the site manager was keen to show us the gym and swimming pool. The workers were filtering off to their dormitories – indeed one had started to fall asleep during the interview – after a long day, and so the place was nearly deserted but for a few security guards, one of whom another reporter fell into conversation with.

As we were waiting to leave, there was a sudden exclamation as my colleague marched a slightly bewildered man mountain of a Kenyan security guard to the entourage of other reporters, welfare staff and site management and confronted the press officer."He sleeps six to a room and yet all these other workers live like this!" he said.

It was an excruciating moment, not just for the press officer and well-meaning welfare officers but also, I suspect, the guard himself, who had just had his lower status so rudely confirmed. As the situation diffused, the guard, it transpired, was employed through the site's security subcontractors and lived elsewhere, and wasn't a direct or even indirect hire of Qatar 2022 and so not subject to their rules. That was the horrible reality of the Kenyan's existence in Qatar.

We left awkwardly, one of the welfare officers protesting, "We can't enforce our standards on people not contracted to us."

In so doing, she cut to the heart of Qatar 2022's labour problem.

Back at the Supreme Committee's West Bay headquarters I wanted to get a sense of what it was like to face a daily onslaught of vitriol, how it felt to face the backlash against what had arguably become the most hated sporting event since the 1936 Berlin Olympics. What is it like working in the eye of the storm? What do they make of the almost daily torrents of anger?

With Hassan al-Thawadi, Nasser al-Khater, the Supreme Committee's affable communications and marketing director, is Qatar 2022's public face. I have known him five years and like many journalists spoken to him at the time of some of his project's gravest moments. Even at times of utter crisis, he has always expressed a sense of confidence, but now, in his office in Doha, with a replica of the World Cup beside him, that seems dimmed by a sense of weariness.

He speaks of "fighting" a five-year long "media war", of "worrying" about the rhetoric and negativity that surrounds Qatar 2022, of critics who go on criticising regardless of measures that are taken to address their concerns, that "there is always going to be that cynicism and that criticism", of future battlegrounds ("I think possibly the environment is something that is going to come up. Possibly LGBT," he adds). In a world of polished platitudes and sound-bites, his frustration is palpable. "I have to admit I expected there to be issues. However I didn't expect the frequency or ferociousness," he says.

At times, this frustration seems understandable. Many words have been written about Qatar, plenty of which make eloquent and detailed cases against the country's host status and elucidate concerns about its many shortcomings, some of which the Qataris have still fully to address. Many others, however, are merely click bait, while some have racial undertones. Even major publications, such as the *New York Times* with its army of fact-checkers, have published serious inaccuracies about Qatar 2022. At times, a readiness to rely on assumptions and rumours as the basis for stories has backfired horribly for publications. With a few notable exceptions very little actual reporting has been done by the world's press on and within Qatar.

I ask Al-Khater if the media has failed Qatar. "If there is a failure, I think their failure is to their audiences and their readers, not to us," he says. "Yes, we're disheartened and discouraged...As a whole there are a lot of people who don't care what the reality is. They know the line that matters, they know the line that sells newspapers, they know the line that people want to read, they know the line that gets a lot of clicks on their website and they're going to keep biting it."

We talk about the plethora of worker rights stories to have emerged over the past 18 months and he expresses his concern at many of the issues to be raised as well, explaining some of the ways the Supreme Committee have worked with NGOs to address them. "We engage with Human Rights Watch and Amnesty International because we feel they're sincere and genuine," he says. "We demonstrate that we're willing to work and listen and exchange ideas and opinions when there is a real genuine effort and intention behind it." When I mention the ITUC, however, his eyes narrow. Its general secretary Sharan Burrow has become Qatar 2022's *bête noire*, an outspoken critic who lambasts its every move with instantaneous derision. "To be honest with you I've lost interest in reading and following what they're doing," he says dismissively.

"From the very beginning I've felt their intentions were disingenuous."

I ask him what the most difficult time was since December 2010. "I think there are many low points," he says. "I think there was one point when human rights and political issues and the [Michael Garcia] investigation came together and it just seemed to...for lack of better words...the perfect storm. I think that's behind us.... The worst is behind us."Having shared similar conversations with his opposite numbers in Brazil and South Africa on the eve of their World Cups, I can't help but feel that he's being optimistic.

If Al-Khater allowed his frustration to surface occasionally, Hassan al-Thawadi was still the consummate politician. I'd also known him since the start, interviewing him five or six times. The messaging drilled into him during bidding — we're a young nation, this is a World Cup for the whole of the Middle East, a compact finals, we'll have stadium cooling technology, and so on — remained inherent in his responses. Any nuances to the official line remained framed in the occasional pauses he gave before answering.

Has Qatar 2022, in light of the continual bad press, inadvertently become a PR disaster, I ask. Straight away he responds in his rapid-fire American accent, "This is why our World Cup is so important for us. It's about the Middle East, we're an Arab nation in the end. What the World Cup offers is the ability to pause for a second and celebrate together on that common platform, which is football, which is the World Cup, which is the greatest sporting event in the World. This is a positive opportunity. We need to utilise it for the positive sense! It is a journey we have to go through. There is an incredulous belief about a Middle Eastern nation hosting the World Cup and I think that all this does is increase our commitment to showcasing this as a Middle Eastern World Cup. And it will change perspectives." I put it to him that many other football stakeholders from the region feel disengaged from Qatar 2022 and he lists various initiatives the Supreme Committee is involved in at this level, pointing out that Qatar are still a long way out. A lot, however, will need to be done to generate the genuine sense of shared ownership across Africa for the 2010 finals.

When I ask about the perspective the world currently has about his World Cup, he again begins listing off the multitude of things that Qatar has done to try to show that it will be a good and capable host. "There was a lot of effort that was put in there, it wasn't something that was written on the back of an envelope," he says. Finally he addresses the question: "For me it's a bit disappointing because nobody is willing, because people aren't raising the questions...the lack of belief and the surprise at the fact that Qatar won it – *how could Qatar win it?* – and some writers have very colourful descriptions of it. But you've seen the work that we've done, a lot of people have seen the work that we've done, a lot of people have seen us building relationships and pumping hands with whoever it was, talking to people, doing the work, making presentations, wherever we're at trying to be meticulous. A lot of those people who were there during that journey, I don't hear them as outright critics."

Momentarily his tone changes: "I hear other people, who were never involved in that journey, who never got exposed to us, who never saw us, who never visited Qatar, who never saw our final presentation, who never talked to us, who never bothered even opening doors with us raising their concerns and doubts. For me it is disappointing."

The Middle East is a region awash with conspiracy theories and for years Qatar 2022 officials have muttered darkly of facing plots from jealous neighbours, desperate to remove their 2022 crown. Of particular consternation has been a succession of stories demonising the country as a supporter of terrorism, notably Isis and Hamas, and even linking football officials and the World Cup to terror. Qatar's complex and sometimes meddlesome foreign policy as well as its 'open door' diplomatic approach, which gives access to groups such as the Taliban, has unquestionably brought the state into contact with groups most would consider deeply unsavoury. Wealthy individuals in Qatar and the government have made donations of finance and weaponry to rebel groups in places like Libya and Syria, some with hard-line Islamist leanings, exacerbating already bloody and complex civil wars and reaping a terrible human toll. The US Treasury Department have described Qatar (along with Kuwait) as "permissive jurisdictions for terrorist financing". But the Qatari government vehemently deny sponsoring terrorism.

In September 2014, the *New York Times* reported "an unlikely alignment of interests, including Saudi Arabia, the United Arab Emirates, Egypt and Israel" seeking to depict Qatar as "a

godfather to terrorists everywhere".
Israel opposes Qatar's support of
Palestinians in general, but particularly
Hamas. Egypt, Saudi Arabia and UAE
are angered by its support for the
Muslim Brotherhood, the latter two
countries breaking diplomatic ties
for a period with Qatar over this
issue. The report referenced the US
lobbying company Camstoll, manned
by ex-US Treasury staff and retained
by the UAE, and was followed up by
investigative website *The Intercept*. It
was subsequently alleged in a lengthy
feature by Glenn Greenwald that UAE
had paid Camstoll more than $7m to
spend "enormous of amounts of time
cajoling friendly reporters to plant
anti-Qatar stories. Their strategy was
clear: target neocon/pro-Israel writers
...all eager to promote the *Qatar-funds-
terrorists* line being pushed by Israel."
The efficiency of this murky campaign,
concluded Greenwald, "demonstrates
how American public perceptions and
media reports are manipulated with
little difficulty."

I referenced this tenebrous PR proxy-
war to Hassan and he let out an audible
sigh. There was a pause. I thought
momentarily he was going to vent his
spleen, but instead he smiled and said,
"Any sort of disagreement or issues that
arise are always disappointing for us, the
Middle Eastern world, an Arab nation
and so on. But in the end our focus
goes back to the sporting event. As a
matter of fact our focus is reinforced
when it comes towards the World Cup
in the Middle East. This is why we want a
World Cup in the Middle East. The World
Cup we look to as a common platform;
towards bringing people together. It's as
simple as that. This is our opportunity.

This something we need to utilise even
more so, to the extent that if there are
any differences, this World Cup goes
towards resolving them."

I put it to him that the modern history
of the Middle East is defined by self-
defeat and infighting. Is this a threat to
Qatar 2022? "No. No. The reality is that
there is significant support towards the
World Cup in Qatar," he claims. "At the
grassroots level you know there is that
support. You talk to people and you see
that support. There is that excitement
about the World Cup in there. In the
end as Middle Eastern nation and in the
Arab world we are passionate towards
football. The World Cup is the ultimate
prize, so there is that excitement there.
For us we're working towards making
that World Cup has a very positive
impact...'And then he was away again,
selling the virtues of Qatar 2022.

Have there ever been moments of
doubt? A pause. "There have been
moments of stress." Such as? Another
pause, before Hassan the politician
answers: "Moments of stress. But in the
end, you look at the positives out of
this..." and he's away again, describing
his hopes of changing Qatar and
perceptions of the Middle East. I ask
again, about being under global scrutiny
and having people close to him like
his brother Ali, who is also his deputy,
named in newspaper stories. Al-Thawadi
seems to bristle for a moment at the
mention of a family member before
composing himself.

"You know yourself," he smiles. "If you
can look in the mirror and be proud of
what you've done and confident of what
you've done, you just move ahead."

In the realms of international super-villainy, Mohamed Bin Hammam cuts an unlikely figure.

We're sitting in front of the fountain at his Doha palace. Six lanes of traffic thunder by not 50 metres from his vast two-building home, a short drive from Aspire. Darkness has fallen and Bin Hammam, now aged 65 and slightly shrunken beneath his dishdasha, grinning, is holding court.

Even Fifa anoraks could scarcely invent this scene. To his right sits Manilal Fernando, the corpulent Sri Lankan lawyer and former Fifa Exco member, for years Bin Hammam's closest ally in Asian football and now banned for life from football for reasons Fifa have never cared to reveal. There are a handful of African federation heads, a former Premier League footballer, a television executive. Bin Hammam's youngest son, a child of 10 or 11, plays around the guests, at one moment approaching his father and kissing him tenderly on the nose. To Bin Hammam's left, drinking tea, is me.

It is two years since Bin Hammam withdrew from all football-related roles and was immediately banned by Fifa from football for life for "conflicts of interest". Depending on your perspective, this is shorthand either for taking on Sepp Blatter as Fifa president in May 2011 or for his part in a huge bribery scandal that unfolded in the Caribbean while he was on the election trail, leading to his withdrawal and ultimate disgrace. His name was further tarnished when a cache purportedly containing millions of emails was leaked to the *Sunday Times* by a "concerned Fifa official" in June 2014. The so-called

"Fifa files" showed Bin Hammam's nexus of largesse in the three years running up to the abandoned election and included scores of cash payments of up to $200,000 paid to African football officials, lavish hospitality and direct payments totalling $1.6m to his nefarious former Fifa colleague Jack Warner.

Miraculously, this vast cache of documents asked no hard questions of Blatter, nor did they cast any light on Bin Hammam's time as Sepp Blatter's lieutenant in the late 1990s. Bin Hammam had been a decisive supporter of Blatter when he sought to succeed João Havelange as Fifa president in 1998. Campaign funds and a private jet courtesy of Qatar were put at Blatter's disposal and he ultimately carried the day in the Paris Congress vote over the Uefa president Lennart Johansson. When the Swiss secured re-election in Seoul in controversial circumstances in 2002, Bin Hammam was again by his side. Even as late as June 2010, ahead of the South Africa World Cup, Blatter publicly referred to Bin Hammam as "my brother Mohamed".

To those who closely follow football politics, the Fifa Files said more about the world Bin Hammam inhabited than the man himself. He was a player — and they showed that by 2011 he was probably a more powerful player than Blatter — in what was, and remains, a corrupt and opaque system. They also demonstrated that he was by turns a brilliant and ruthless politician.

There was, of course, another interpretation, advanced by the *Sunday Times*: that Bin Hammam's scheming was intimately linked to Qatar's successful bid for the World Cup. Its headline said it all: "Plot to buy World Cup".

Along with the Qatar government and the bid team itself, Bin Hammam was the third component behind its stunning victory. Each strand was interdependent but ultimate success was entirely reliant upon all facets. Bin Hammam, as AFC president and a powerful Fifa Exco member of 14 years standing, was the link with the 21 other voters and the most important component of Qatar 2022's victory. Put simply, he brought a minnow football nation to the top table of the game's global government. He did the lobbying behind the scenes, cut the deals and cleverly built a platform – via a deal with Spain-Portugal, who were bidding for the 2018 finals – that formed the basis of its victory. Ultimately, however, the reasons thirteen other Fifa Exco members voted for Qatar remain, with a few exceptions, largely or entirely unexplained.

The *Sunday Times* tried to expand on his role by explaining that the four African votes Qatar received were linked to Bin Hammam's munificence. Bin Hammam had flown many African federation heads to Doha and Kuala Lumpur on junkets, handing out $400,000 in cash. A subsequent series of bank transfer payments were also made to many of these men and women. It was a damning indictment of the Fifa system in which nepotism and corruption are allowed to flourish and ultimately of Bin Hammam too, who partook in it. The problem with this theory, however, was that no one who directly benefited from Bin Hammam's generosity actually had a vote for World Cup 2022. Instead, it appeared, he was currying favour for the Fifa presidential election six months after the 2022 vote.

Qatar 2022 invariably distanced themselves from Bin Hammam, as they always have done since his fall. Their continued assertion is that he had no official role with the bid team. But as ever with Qatar, the reality was more complex. When I interviewed the bid's chairman, Sheikh Mohammed, in an executive box at Stamford Bridge two months before the vote he told me that Bin Hammam was the bid's "mentor". "He's always been advising us and always been by our side," he said. "He's definitely our biggest asset in the bid."

And here, four years on from that day in London, as we talk in his garden about Gulf politics, his boyhood club, Liverpool, the changing face of Doha, the engineering business that made him wealthy and to which he has returned to lead, our families, but never really the strange and dysfunctional football family that has exorcised him ("That is all in the past, we move on.") Bin Hammam still seems to me a far bigger asset for Qatar than he ever has been a liability. He is relaxed, genial, incredibly knowledgeable; certainly not the monster of popular perception.

I'd previously seen him in late 2011 as the fall-out from his demise continued to reverberate. He was more expansive then about the forces that sealed his fall and he still plotted to clear his name, despite the apparent wealth of evidence against him. Whistleblowers from four Caribbean football federations had said they were offered $40,000 in envelopes after attending Bin Hammam's campaign pitch in Trinidad and Tobago, allegations which were accompanied by damning photographic evidence. Bin Hammam had no doubt as to who was behind this sting. He had been banned from football but maintained his innocence and had seemed in a state of shock. Then it was less than a year after Qatar 2022's victory and he had appeared sure at one stage of following that by taking football politics'top prize for himself. Instead he found himself humiliated, disgraced and ostracised.

In July 2012, Bin Hammam won his appeal before the Court of Arbitration in Sport, which cited lack of evidence but added that his behaviour was "not of the highest ethical standard" and that "it is more likely than not" that he was the source of the money brought into Trinidad and Tobago and distributed by the former Fifa vice-president Jack Warner. Nevertheless, it overturned his life ban.

There was, however, to be no return to football for Bin Hammam.

On 11 December 2012, Blatter was back in Qatar for the opening of the Doha Goals conference. He visited Qatar 2022's Supreme Committee and then held talks with the Emir, Sheikh Hamad. What went on in that meeting? Was a deal done to save Qatar 2022 in exchange for Bin Hammam's silence? Were the secrets of Qatar 2022, Bin Hammam and Blatter closed for good that afternoon?

We will probably never know. Maybe it was just a courtesy visit. Perhaps the Emir – like many world leaders – knew the value of stroking Blatter's ego by granting an audience. But two days later the Fifa ethics committee announced that it had closed its investigation into Bin Hammam. There would be no more questions asked. No one from Fifa would probe his role in Qatar 2022's victory

or indeed Sepp Blatter's ascent to the Fifa presidency. On Saturday December 15 Bin Hammam sent letters to Fifa and the AFC, resigning his positions on the Fifa Exco and as AFC president, saying, "I do not want to spend any more of my life fighting trumped up allegations and to focus instead on my family and businesses." 48 hours later there was another development: Fifa banned Bin Hammam for life again.

Fifa controversies tend to drag on for years before reaching their inevitable, unsatisfactory conclusions. The ISL bribery case lasted 13 years by contrast, but in this one the door swung shut with unprecedented speed following a remarkable series of coincidences.

As we sat down to a lavish buffet in one of Bin Hammam's reception rooms and Manilal Fernando took centre stage, telling us about Sri Lanka's transformation since the end of its civil war and his pride in his son who was to study medicine in Manchester, it became clear that Bin Hammam was not going to be giving away any secrets that night. To an outsider, it was a strange, convivial occasion.

Later, as one of Bin Hammam's sons drove me back to my hotel through the Doha evening, past the Aspire Zone and Khalifa Stadium, which in 2022 will host the World Cup opening game, the words his father once uttered to me came back: "No one has done more difficult things for Blatter than me." Whatever could he have meant? Was it suppression of this knowledge that simultaneously finished Bin Hammam and will save Qatar 2022? Will we ever know? Ⓑ

After the Earthquake

How football is playing its part rebuilding the shattered communities around Fukushima

By Felix Lill and Javier Sauras

Masaki Moriyama is unsure whether he's allowed to smile. During the game that has just finished, the 12 year old conceded two goals that he normally would have saved. One shot from far away slid through his hands, another one from the wing sailed into the box and Masaki got down too late. The goalkeeper looked insecure, which the other team noticed. Happily, his teammates still managed to score twice to secure a draw, although their opponents were much weaker than them.

Masaki and the other Nihonmatsu FC players are now sitting on a heap of sport bags, covered in blue training jackets, analysing their imperfect performance. They need to win the next game, the final one of the group stage, otherwise they won't make it through to the second round. Disappointment and anxiety are in the air. "Come on boys", shouts their coach as he claps his hands in encouragement. "We can still make it. The next game will be ours!" In some of the children's eyes a glimpse of optimism is visible, others seem proud of having scored goals, regardless of what their coach is telling them. But Masaki, sitting slightly apart from the group, cannot get rid of his somewhat sad look. He knows he has been the weak link and that things might look better now if it hadn't been for his errors.

As the coach finishes his short motivational speech, most of the boys run to their parents or to watch the other teams playing. On this rare day, an early Sunday afternoon in spring 2013, Fukushima City seems alive again. It is the first tournament in the open air in two years. The once proud sporting facilities, hosting two football pitches, a baseball field and tracks for athletics, have not been in use since spring 2011. But today, all of this is forgotten. Contaminated soil is still here, bundled in brick forms, covered up and packed together within easy reach, lying around less than a minute's walk away on the same sports terrain. But at least, the kids are playing again. All looks like good fun. Mostly.

As his mates have got up from the heap of bags, Masaki Moriyama, a boy with short dark hair and a chubby face, prefers to stay seated. "This is not my real team," he whispers. Masaki spent his first footballing years in his hometown, Namie, located less than an hour from these spacious sports facilities in Fukushima City. Masaki never wanted to play for Nihonmatsu FC, a local team he once battled against together with his friends from home.

But like many others, Masaki has not been on home soil for a while. He's not allowed to because nobody knows the exact dangers that still linger there. "Our club still exists, but only on paper," says Masaki's father, who is approaching his son to cheer him up. "Nobody is using the ground in Namie anymore. They might actually shut everything down eventually." Masaki is listening to his father's words and looks even sadder now.

"Dad, I want to play with my old friends again."

"I know, my son. One day, you will." But none of them seem to believe it.

In March 2011, Masaki, his younger brother and his parents were given one day to pack their most important belongings and leave everything else behind. The government had found that radiation levels in Namie were so high that it would have been irresponsible, if not negligent, to allow people to continue living there. Once the Moriyama family heard about the evacuation order, some of the things Masaki just had to take along were his gloves and the jersey of Eiji Kawashima, the number-one goalkeeper of Japan's national team.

But as the family of four settled in a temporary housing in Fukushima City, it soon became apparent to Masaki that most things that were important to him inevitably belonged to his hometown and didn't fit into his suitcase. Many of his friends have been settled in other parts of Japan, his school has been closed ever since, and his room, with a J-League blanket on his bed and football posters on the walls, has remained abandoned. Masaki has no idea what it looks like today, and perhaps he never will.

The events of 11 March 2011, have transformed the lives of the 100 children who are playing their favourite game on this sunny Sunday in Fukushima City. In some way, they changed the life of every person in Japan. Four years on, everybody can recall what they were doing and where they were when, in the early afternoon, the ground shook with a magnitude no living Japanese had ever experienced. At the epicentre off the east coast, the quake measured a striking value of 9.0, which was unprecedented even in Japan. Shortly after, the news reported a 20 metre-high tsunami wave approaching the coast.

TV pictures showed people, cars and whole buildings being washed away. The waves also knocked out the nuclear power plant in Fukushima prefecture, leading to meltdowns in three out of six reactors. The plant is located right on the coast, around 250km north of Tokyo, the biggest metropolis on the planet. Analysis would show that it was largely a matter of luck that no clouds carrying nuclear steam approached Tokyo – the wind just happened to blow the other way, saving the livelihoods of up to 35 million people. Instead of heading south, the winds took the nuclear poison to the north and east, which meant that not only did around 2,000 people die from the earthquake and tsunami, but at least 300,000 had to leave their homes.

Masaki Moriyama's fate is one out of thousands. The refugees took shelter in all parts of the country and around half of them are yet to return to their homes. In the most highly radiated places, such as Namie, a resettlement date is still unknown despite ongoing decontamination works. Most temporary homes that the government has provided lack space for privacy and sometimes walls are said to be too thin to keep people warm in winter. But since so many people not only lost their homes but also their jobs after the catastrophe, there is often nowhere else to go.

This reality has made a youth football tournament, which once would happen every other weekend, a special occasion in Fukushima City. The prefecture's capital has grown in response to the evacuation orders. It's located 60km inland from the east coast and has somewhat controversially been deemed safe enough to live in. But outdoor activities for children have long been largely prevented because of radiation worries. Gyms have been overcrowded and many children stopped playing sport.

Football is certainly not the Japanese public's primary worry these days. However, the so-called "triple disaster", the trinity of earthquake, tsunami and nuclear cataclysm, may have crippled the development of the country's most popular sport among the young. In the worst case, Japan has lost a generation of talent. "Many of my old friends have stopped playing because their parents wouldn't let them," says Moriyama as he takes the hand of his protective dad. "I am never going to stop. But maybe I'm just lucky that my parents still allow me to play."

Countless young Japanese have not been so lucky. The appearance of the abandoned towns in Fukushima prefecture, such as the village of Iitate, explains why. Iitate is located 40km from the reactors and was once home to 6,000 people. In April 2011, six weeks after the beginning of the nuclear disaster, high radiation levels were suddenly identified in the air. People had to escape in a matter of hours. Ever since, Iitate has been labelled a 'ghost town' and the description is not far-fetched.

On the doorsteps of the once inhabited houses, wild grass is growing. A few streets are blocked with red-and-white tape and barriers to indicate those areas where radiation is so high that it is dangerous to enter even for just a short time. Here and there, fixed Geiger counters give the current radiation level, which oscillates according to the direction of the wind Even for a place as small as this, the level of silence in Iitate is remarkable. All one can hear are birds and dogs that have taken over the place.

Iitate's junior high school was once the place where the village's dreams, hopes and youthful illusions were vibrant. Today, there is not much but sadness. Leaves and bird droppings float on the contaminated water in the swimming pool, the sports ground in front of the school's main building is covered with the traces of vultures. On the doorstep to the dressing-room lie two pairs of boots; next to them is a football with almost no air pressure left.

Norio Kanno cannot get these pictures out of his head. He is the mayor of Iitate and for four years has been administering his abandoned hometown from an office in the outskirts of Fukushima City. "We were a village full of hope and potential. We also had a good football team," he says in improvised headquarters packed with cardboard boxes. "It makes me sad that this happened to us. I am doing all I can to get as many people to move back to Iitate very soon. But radiation levels are still very high."

Kanno does not expect that Iitate will ever be the same again. Young people are less likely to return to the village than the elderly, and talented young footballers have lost four years of systematic training. The situation is similar in other parts of the Tohoku region. Fukushima was once the national hub for football education: Japan's national football association's elite training centre, the J-Village, is located in the area. But since 2011, the centre has had to be used as a sort of crisis management control tower.

Football has been booming in Japan for years and the country's progress has been notable. In the early 1990s, the sport was still minor compared to baseball or sumo, but today these two disciplines envy the following and sponsorship money football is attracting. Japan established the J.League, the country's first professional football division, in 1993. During the league's early years, aged stars like the Brazilian Zico, the German World Cup-winner Pierre Littbarski, the Englishman Gary Lineker and the Spanish striker Julio Salinas went there to cash in before retirement and draw Japanese crowds into the stadiums. In 1998, Japan's national team qualified for a World Cup for the first time.

Since then, Japan have qualified for every World Cup and have become Asia's leading national team. Instead of importing expensive international stars who have already had their day, today's J.League teams are known for their exports of young talent. At the 2012 Olympics in London, the women's national team won silver, while the men just missed out on bronze. Elsewhere in Asia, countries have been copying Japan's youth development.

Will the 2011 catastrophe one day be known as a long-term drawback to the country's much-praised footballing system? Hardly anyone denies this possibility. Toyoharu Takata, vice-president of the J-Village, has even put it the other way round: "We all cannot get back on our feet if football does not recover here."

But the impact of the triple disaster has been so varied that positive football developments have emerged too. 80km north of Fukushima City, Sayaka Suzuki is distributing flyers at an entrance to the Yurtec Stadium. They depict the line-up of the heroes of Sendai. Half an hour before kick-off, the chants of the home team's supporters are clearly audible from far away. Vegalta Sendai, the only J.League club from the Tohoku area, are playing against Sagan Tosu, a team from the south-west.

Their boisterousness is common in Japan's otherwise quiet football scene that often associates loud and vigorous support with hooliganism. In Sendai, however, the chanting has become a crucial part of the team. "This really only started after the tsunami," Suzuki, a short and skinny woman with a high voice, says as loudly as she possibly can. Suzuki is a proud Vegalta supporter, as most people from Sendai are. The city did not suffer nuclear radiation, but parts of it, including the Yurtec Stadium, were severely damaged by the earthquake and tsunami.

The J.League's itinerary follows the calendar year, so the disaster hit only days before the 2011 season was scheduled to start. At the time, Vegalta Sendai were a new member of Japan's top-tier and the lack of experience as well as the limited budget meant that avoiding relegation would be considered a success. "Nobody expected the team to make it, but there was hope," Suzuki recalls. The earthquake and tsunami shrunk this hope to a glimmer. Because of fears of nuclear radiation, one foreign player asked for his contract to be dissolved immediately. For the same reason, Vegalta's management could not attract any new players. Who would still go there?

"We were struggling so badly, we had no idea how to move forward," remembers Morishige Matsuba. He is responsible for the club's strategic planning. At the point of the disaster, Matsuba had only just come to Sendai to join the club and he admits that he was also wondering whether to cancel the appointment. He might have done so, he says, if the cause hadn't suddenly become much bigger than football: "So many Vegalta supporters had died, others had lost their homes, or at least everybody knew someone to whom something terrible had happened. Then, the stadium was damaged too. If everyone jumps off the ship now, I thought to myself, Vegalta and football in the whole Tohoku region might collapse."

Many people had similar thoughts. When Vegalta played their first home game of the 2011 season, with some weeks delay, the Yurtec Stadium was packed with people dressed in yellow and blue, the club's colours. Suzuki, who was also at the opening match, says the atmosphere on that day was "surreal". "Some were laughing out of joy to see their friends

alive, others were crying in mourning. Suddenly, Vegalta had become so much more than a football club." To some, it became a new home. Shortly before the final whistle, a huge banner moved through the stadium and topped all emotions of the day. It made a promise to everyone, the players as much as the supporters: "Thank you to our friends. We will not lose a game until we have our city back."

What sounded like the hubris typical in any football stadium would be turned into reality, bit by bit, week after week. The underdogs Vegalta did not lose their first match, or the second, or the third. Meanwhile, the stadium was rebuilt for €2.3 million and the supporters imported one classical football chant after another. "We're Not Gonna Take It" by Twisted Sister became an evergreen in the Yurtec Stadium, as much as "Take me Home," borrowed from John Denver's "Country Roads". The supporters joined in and screamed them at home and away games. There was hardly a minute during a Vegalta game when the fans were not making a huge noise.

"This was new to the J.League," Suzuki says proudly. Vegalta supporters interpreted football in a way previously unseen in Japan. And it must have helped the players to stand up against their often stronger opponents. Vegalta remained unbeaten for 11 games and, over the whole season, they only lost two games in the Yurtec Stadium. When the season came to an end in December 2011, Vegalta were fourth, a remarkable achievement for relegation candidates. A year later, Vegalta Sendai came second, qualifying for the Asian Champions League.

Although Vegalta Sendai are now back to mediocrity, the club's story has become recognised nationwide as a phoenix rising from the ashes. It is also Tohoku's role-model for resilience and fighting spirit. Even Europeans have been inspired. The British filmmakers Douglas Hurcombe and Geoff Trodd travelled to Sendai to produce a documentary about the club. "Vegalta really has this punk mentality you also find at some European clubs," Hurcombe says. "The area is dominated by farming and fishing and was a slow developer culturally in the history of Japan. So there had always been a bit of an inferiority complex among the people, which had manifested itself as a brash, bold defiance among the fans – especially when they played the 'big city' clubs like Tokyo." But when Vegalta in 2008 signed Makoto Teguramori as head coach, things started to change. Teguramori is not only a Tohoku local, but had also acquired coaching skills under Arsène Wenger during his time at Japan's Nagoya as well as Arsenal – valuable experiences that few coaches in Japan have.

"Technically, the team played in a very similar style to the Arsenal sides of Wenger's early career," says Hurcombe. "The only thing they lacked was self-belief." In 2011, though, the team and the whole club transformed the freedom of being the underdog and the pain of destruction into an incredible resilience. *Football, Take Me Home*, Hurcombe and Trodd's documentary – which is yet to be released – focuses on the club's ultras and how their support of the team has also cheered up the whole city. "We felt that it was a great metaphor for everyone who had to start again, build again, and learn to live again after the tragedy," Hurcombe said.

But in a sense, a movie about the recovery of Sendai can only tell part of the whole story. The biggest city in Tohoku was able to mobilise the necessary resources for reconstruction relatively easily. Elsewhere near Japan's notoriously underprivileged east coast, there are few signs of progress even four years after the catastrophe. Where whole villages were washed away, a full recovery to pre-disaster levels is impossible. This is true for football as much as for all other facets of life. One of Norio Kanno's colleagues once tried to count all the football clubs that now exist on paper but have no training sessions, no coaches, no players... In the small office, two officials said they estimated the number to be in the hundreds.

In the areas where the disaster's destruction cannot be seen or felt but only be measured with cutting-edge technology, the dominant emotion is not pain for the losses suffered. It is anxiety that every raindrop, every breeze and every breath can have life-changing, life-shortening consequences. Back in Fukushima City at the youth tournament where, on the surface, everyone is having a great time, Juan Saldívar walks away from the populated football pitches to talk straight.

The Mexican is the man who organised this youth tournament and someone who has his very own connection to the Tohoku area. Nine years ago, Saldívar was transferred to a semi-professional football club here, believing his new team would be playing professionally the following season. When the project had failed and after Saldívar had spent a few years trying to win promotion, he decided to end his career in response to the disaster and dedicate himself to youth coaching. His work proved more necessary than he would ever have dared to believe. Because the number of football teams had declined so radically, partly due to a sudden lack of available facilities, it had become difficult even to organise games and tournaments. Saldívar started to rent an indoor pitch and invited schoolchildren to come and play again. And he spent months talking to city officials and parents to put together this outdoor tournament.

"The biggest obstacle is probably the parents," Saldívar says at low volume as he checks whether anyone is listening. A strong wind is blowing around his ears. "And I can understand them. Who would want their child to be unsafe?" Saldívar raises his left hand to catch some of the wind. "We don't know if this is contaminated. Things can change in a matter of days or even hours." But on the other hand, Saldívar wants Fukushima's children to enjoy life. "Sport has the ability to relieve stress and football happens to be the most popular. It's very important not to lose that culture here. You can really see it today: the kids are smiling when they are allowed to play."

That Sunday afternoon in spring 2013 was an attempt to reboot. Juan Saldívar had been hoping even more teams would come to play, with more players on each team. But not every parent wanted to trust him that the sky, the wind and the air would remain free of excessive radiation. Many of those parents who did arrive with their children were carrying Geiger counters. Before each match, they would hastily walk over the pitch to take measures of the air at grass level. "If the radiation is too high, we're going home, you understand,"

Yukari Miura, the mother of seven-year-old Amane says, worried that her daughter might get grass in her mouth. "But she loves playing football, so what can I do?"

Amane and her mother live in Fukushima City, 60km away from the crippled nuclear power plant. Some of their family in Tokyo have been telling them to leave the area. "My aunt says it's unsafe to live here. But we don't want to move away. Amane also just started playing football here recently."

Most people in the areas that have shown elevated radiation levels have asked themselves whether to move away or not. Saldívar is one of them. In late 2014, his Fukushima venture had to come to an end. In an email, he explains that his family wanted to leave Fukushima because of fears of radiation. At first, only Saldívar's two children and his Japanese wife migrated away. "I had to stay there a bit longer," Saldívar writes, "to support Fukushima's youth football. We have been playing tournaments against teams from other prefectures of the country and you can notice that the children from Fukushima lack physical strength and speed. I believe it's because we cannot play and practise enough."

Saldívar might never return to Fukushima City. His seven-year-old daughter is now playing football though. If she's a big talent as Saldívar hopes, she might one day join Japan's women's national team, world champions in 2011. Now that the little girl no longer lives in Fukushima, her father thinks, he chances for sporting success look a bit better. Ⓑ

56

Interview

"...because of the player's friendship with homosexuals, his fights with his girlfriend or his connections with the Workers' Party."

Reinaldo

The former Brazil striker explains how he expressed his opposition to the dictatorship

By James Young

Not all revolutionaries get the fame, or the notoriety, they deserve. Before Sócrates and the *democracia corintiana*, and after Tommie Smith and John Carlos in Mexico City, a different Brazilian rebel with a cause was raising his fist in both protest and celebration. José Reinaldo de Lima, better known as Reinaldo, Atlético Mineiro's all-time leading scorer with 255 goals and the *Seleção's* centre-forward during the ill-fated 1978 World Cup campaign, has not been granted a place in the hall of fame of Brazilian greats alongside the likes of Garrincha, Pelé, Tostão and so many others. That is a shame – for Reinaldo's is a life lived to the fullest, both on and off the pitch.

A few weeks after Fifa-approved Brazil unfurled itself in front of the planet – filled with gleaming new stadiums, corporate sponsorship and levels of public safety and infrastructural efficiency jarringly unfamiliar to those who live here – it was revealing to sit down with Reinaldo and remember a very different nation – the Brazil of the 1970s, when a country largely isolated from the rest of the world lay under the yoke of a 21-year military dictatorship.

"The pay was good for footballers back then," Reinaldo recalls. "Not spectacular, but good, compared with what most

people got. But the economy was very different. The currency was worth nothing and there was hyperinflation. You can't compare it with today. It was a closed economy. There were no imports. The only things people could buy, even footballers, were records or books. It was another reality. Brazil was a very shut-off, rural country in those days."

As is so often the case in societies that lack the freedom and entertainment options that so many of us take for granted today, it was football that filled the gap.

"Football, going to the stadium, was the leisure activity of the masses back then," remembers Reinaldo. "Crowds of 80,000 or more were common. And all the great stars played here. I played against Pelé and Rivellino when I was still just a kid."

Reinaldo's rise to fame is another story that feels very much of its time. Born in 1957 in the small town of Ponte Nova, 170km from Belo Horizonte, his success appears a simple, almost predestined process.

"I picked up a reputation for being a good player when I was very young, playing at school and in street games. I was only eight years old when I played for the local junior team. I was up against much older boys and as there were no boots for really young kids in those days, the club made a special pair for me. A few years after that, in 1971, the Atlético youth team came to play in Ponte Nova. The coach of our team knew the *Galo* [1] manager, Barabatana, and recommended me to him. Then Atlético took me to Belo Horizonte, to their headquarters in Lourdes. There were lots of boys there and we slept under the stands. After a week my mum came to see how I was getting on, because there were no phones in those days."

When one thinks of the pantheon of Brazilian stars, beginning with arguably the country's first footballing idol Arthur Friedenreich and running through to Neymar, it is tempting to think that there must be a certain complacency in the country when it comes to the emergence of young *craques* – who, in the past at least, seemed to be as plentiful as *botecos* in Rio de Janeiro. Even in such a rich footballing environment, however, some manage to stand out from the crowd. Reinaldo was one of them.

"I was pretty lucky," he remembers. "I was there for a trial, but one day we played in a training game against the first team, who were the Brazilian champions at the time. The manager was Telê Santana [coach of Brazil at the 1982 and 1986 World Cups]. I came on at the end of the game. No one knew me, but I scored, and dribbled and passed the ball pretty well. I did enough in 20 minutes to catch their eye. So they gave me a contract. I was the top scorer for the juniors that year, with 38 goals. Suddenly I was famous. They called me the 'baby *craque*'."

Much glory was to follow. Reinaldo became a professional when he was just 16 ("only Pelé started younger than me – I was the youngest in the league," he says) and, despite a string of debilitating knee injuries that would restrict his powers in later years, soon established himself as one of the brightest stars in a league dripping with talent, finishing as the Campeonato Brasileiro's top scorer in 1977 with a remarkable 28 goals in 18 games. Unfortunately, Atlético's eternal role as Brazilian football's bridesmaids (after winning the first official national championship in 1971, the club went 42 years before lifting its next major trophy, last year's Copa Libertadores) meant major silverware was to elude him throughout his career, though Galo were league runners-up in 1977 (when the team went unbeaten, only missing out on the title thanks to an away-goals defeat against São Paulo) and 1980.

Regardless of goalscoring awards or titles, however, there is no doubting Reinaldo's remarkable talents, which can be verified by a quick YouTube search. Strong, fast and graceful, he possessed a remarkable flair and coolness in front of goal. "If it hadn't been for the injuries and the knee surgeries... Reinaldo is the player who would have come closest to rivalling Pelé," said no less a judge than Zico on Brazilian TV last year.

"Reinaldo was a genius," said Marcelo Oliveira, his former Atlético teammate and

[1] *Atlético's nickname, meaning rooster.*

current manager of Cruzeiro, Galo's Belo Horizonte rivals and the reigning Brazilian champions, in another TV interview. "I've seen him do everything, score every type of goal, whether he's sliding into the box, scoring with his head, flicking the ball over the defenders, dribbling round the keeper, or his speciality, feinting, then finishing with utter coolness. I agree [with Zico]... he first injured his knee in a game against Atlético Paranaense, and I don't know if the surgery was performed badly or not, but he ended up suffering from it for the rest of his life. He was such a special player." As the interview comes to an end, Oliveira's voice begins to crack and his eyes moisten as he remembers the glories – and disappointments – of his friend's career. "We played together, spent our free time together, for many years. He would come over to my house, I would go over to his house," Oliveira explains. YouTube will also reveal the brutality of some of the tackles attacking players were subjected to in those days, which undoubtedly contributed to the ruined state of Reinaldo's knees and the nagging sense that despite all that he achieved there would have been even more to come, had it not been for the injuries.

One of those disappointments came at the 1978 World Cup. Reinaldo began the tournament as Brazil's first-choice No. 9 and scored the *Seleção's* opening goal of the competition in a 1-1 draw against Sweden. But Brazil's bid to lift the *Mundial* on enemy soil would ultimately end in failure. Set against the backdrop of General Jorge Videla's military *junta* and the dirty war, a relatively stilted Brazil side (at least in comparison to the much feted boys of summer from 1970 and 1982) made its way unspectacularly to the second round and into a group with

the hosts, Poland and Peru. After Brazil and Argentina fought out a goalless draw, the qualifying spot for the final came down to goal difference. Argentina needed to score four against Peru to edge out the old enemy – they got six. The conspiracy theories that have swirled around Brazil ever since (Peruvian goalkeeper Ramon *'El Loco'* Quiroga was born in Argentina, a shipment of grain was said to have been sent to Lima in thanks, the *junta* reportedly agreed to imprison (or "disappear") a number of Peruvian political dissidents) have gained credence following the declaration last year by former Peruvian senator Genaro Ledesma that a deal was struck between Videla and the Peruvian government during the tournament. Reinaldo has no doubts. "Of course it was a fix," he says. "It was obvious Brazil were going to win. We went home unbeaten."

Even though Brazil's campaign ended in frustration, the tournament marked the most high-profile (at least in an international context) sighting of Reinaldo's traditional clenched fist goal salute. While the World Cup in Argentina would be ultimately overshadowed by the horrors of the political environment that surrounded it, back home Brazil was being smothered by a less gruesome but equally abhorrent military regime.

Inspired by *ufanismo* (basically the nationalistic trumpeting of Brazil's endless natural riches and dizzying potential, often at the expense of reality), the *Seleção's* glorious 1970 World Cup win was co-opted by the Brazilian government as a patriotic symbol of the country's progress. How did Brazil's people, and its footballers, deal with the fact that their sporting success was being used to promote a dictatorship? As Reinaldo points out, the times were very different and awareness, political or otherwise, was limited. "There was a certain sense of helplessness. Even as players, we didn't have much perspective in terms of our careers. It was just the Campeonato Mineiro and the Campeonato Brasileiro and playing for Brazil. There was no talk of going to Europe. The World Cup was our only chance to see how other countries played. When we saw Holland play in 1974, we were amazed. We didn't know anything about football outside Brazil.

"But on the other hand, our isolation gave us real determination. 'I'm going to beat England,' we used to say, or, 'I'm going to beat Germany.' It was our dream from when we were kids. It's different today, but then there was a real glamour, a grandiosity, in playing at somewhere like Wembley. The games had tremendous importance for us, and we really wanted to win. They matter today too, but they're absorbed by other things. There was a campaign for reaffirmation going on, a lot of talk about national pride and being proud to be Brazilian. Of course it was all a political strategy in the end."

In such a setting, his raised clenched fist was clearly an inflammatory, political manner of celebrating a goal. "It was a revolutionary, socialist gesture," he explained once on Brazilian TV. "I started doing it in 1976, in the middle of an era of repression, to try to accelerate the arrival of the democratic process." Today, he makes something of an unlikely revolutionary hero. Thick-set and bald, he looks much like the other overly garrulous elderly gentlemen who

spend their mornings sitting outside the Tres Corações café in the leafy Savassi neighbourhood of Belo Horizonte, arguing about Galo and Cruzeiro.

According to Reinaldo, while a resistance movement existed in Brazil in those days, society on the whole was not a hotbed of political debate. "Really the masses didn't know what was happening," he recalls. "And those that did, didn't protest. There were reprisals, or even disappearances. So people behaved themselves. And of course we weren't educated, so we didn't have strong opinions. We were told all the time that Brazil was a great country and that the economy was growing by 10%."

"I felt isolated," he says of his political stance. "There were no organisations for players, or workers of any type, in fact. There were no unions. Any type of association was banned, even things like building meetings in apartment blocks. It was a dictatorship, after all. None of the players I knew were politically engaged. The life of a footballer isn't really part of society. Plus in those days footballers were ignorant. Plenty of players couldn't read or write. It was common. It was difficult time for Brazil in general."

According to popular belief, Reinaldo's opposition to the dictatorship ultimately cost him a place at the 1982 World Cup. "Telê [Santana] should have taken me to the World Cup. But I had my political position and he was a reactionary," the player is on record as saying. Santana's son Renê has said that his father did not select Reinaldo due to injury and that he "had not kicked a ball in six months" – despite the fact that Reinaldo had in fact played regularly for Galo in the 1982

Campeonato Brasileiro, which ran until the spring of that year.

In January 1982 *Placar* magazine wrote that "in the second half of 1981, Telê began to snub Reinaldo, either because of the player's friendship with homosexuals, his fights with his girlfriend or his connections with the Workers' Party," while Santana himself said that "the only thing Reinaldo knows how to do is play football. But they like to make him think he is an intellectual who needs to help the Indians, Lula [Brazil's Workers' Party president from 2003 to 2011], and Frei Betto [a writer, religious and political figure who spent four years in prison during the dictatorship]."

The threat of rather more serious reprisals than being dropped from a football team was never far away. "In football you are a public figure. My protest came when things were already relaxing and opening up in Brazil, slowly. People had started taking their heads out of the sand. But the directors and presidents of the clubs were linked to the military. So of course we suffered retaliation. Not openly or obviously like it would have been in the past, there were no murders or disappearances, because by this stage things were changing [the most brutal years of the dictatorship, known as the *Anos de Chumbo* ("The Years of Lead") were between 1968 and 1974]. But I knew they had a file on me and I was being watched. The CBF [the Brazilian football federation, known as CBD at the time] was run by the military, from the president to the trainer." In 1974 the president of the CBD was Admiral Heleno Nunes, while the coach of the *Seleção* in 1978 was the former military man Captain Claudio Coutinho.

Reinaldo says he had little contact at the time with Sócrates, who was noted for his political activism. "It wasn't as planned as that," he says. "We were timid, very reserved, for a long time. Even the press. When I gave interviews it was for the alternative press, the left-wing press, the unions who were just starting to appear. It wasn't for the *Estado de Minas* or *O Tempo*, the big newspapers. Not to talk about politics, anyway."

I talked with Reinaldo twice – once over lunch at an echoing, almost empty Italian restaurant in Belo Horizonte and a few weeks later over a coffee at the *Tres Corações*. Unsurprisingly, it wasn't long before the conversation turned to the World Cup, the current troubled state of Brazilian football and of course the 'Massacre at the Mineirão' – Brazil's 7-1 semi-final humbling against Germany.

"The 7-1 can have a positive effect. It should serve as a spark for change in Brazilian football. From the current legislation down to the directors, both at the clubs and the CBF," says Reinaldo. "It's a joke. José Maria Marin? He's a torturer! [A reference to the CBF president's shady pro-military, right-wing political role during the dictatorship]. These old wolves. He's more of a crook than Ricardo Teixeira. Do you remember when he stole that medal? [Soon after his appointment, footage emerged of Marin pocketing the winner's medal of a young Corinthians player at a youth tournament] They're playing with the feelings of the Brazilian people. They're a stain on Brazilian football."

The often shambolic conditions of the Campeonato Brasileiro, plagued by low crowds, fan violence, an overcrowded, chaotic fixture calendar and clubs that seem perpetually on the verge of financial ruin, is an easy target for Reinaldo's wrath. "Did you watch the World Cup?" he asks me. "And you watch the Brazilian league too? Isn't it a like a street kick-about in comparison? Did you see Germany, even Bosnia, control the ball and pass it? Brazil players can't control the ball. Why can the European players do what Brazilians can't? We have to get organised in our tactics, the way we play the game. We aren't organised at all."

Warming to his theme, Reinaldo explains his theory on what has gone wrong with Brazilian football. "What killed Brazilian football was something everyone can see but no one talks about," he says. "Brazil doesn't have wide players. There's no one to open the game. Holland has them. Even Japan has them. Every team has players that can open up the game. That's what changed, ever since Telê Santana. There are hardly any teams in Brazil that play with wide players. That was the tactical change."

Reinaldo, who dabbled briefly in politics, and recently (unsuccessfully) managed the Minas Gerais lower division teams Villa Nova and Ipatinga, now runs a junior team near his home in Nova Lima, which he says gives him a unique perspective on the effects that the country's social progress has had on Brazilian football. "At the start of every year 300 kids turn up, all dressed in replica kits, with boots. And I think wow, these kids must know how to play. They're certainly dressed like footballers, anyway. Then they play and they can't do anything. They want to become Messi and Ronaldo in a day. Maybe three or four of them will be OK.

But a real star, a diamond, is very rare. Kids don't play football anymore. Where do you play, anyway?" He points out the window of the restaurant at a busy street filled with traffic. "You used to be able to play football out there. Not now. It's easier to play on the computer."

Chewing on his *bife à milanesa*, Reinaldo is lively, affable company. Yet he carries with him a sense, not of bitterness, but of mild regret, perhaps that in the end, stymied by injury and his refusal not quietly to accept the stunted state of his country, all that glorious, expansive talent did not result in more – more major trophies, more World Cup appearances, a greater, longer lasting awareness of his ability among football fans outside Brazil. Zico compared him to Pelé on the pitch – but it is hard to imagine Pelé today huddled over an espresso and a cigarette in the Praça da Savassi on a chilly Belo Horizonte morning.

Life did not run perfectly smoothly after he hung up his boots, either – in 1997 he was sentenced to four years in prison for involvement in drug dealing, when three men were arrested in possession of cocaine in a car registered in his name. The verdict was overturned on appeal and Reinaldo was cleared of any wrongdoing, but not before his involvement with the drug had come to light.

"In those days it was snowing cocaine in Brazil. We had easy access to it and little information about the dangers. It's a very seductive drug. It takes you prisoner. I wasn't an addict or anything like that and it was after I'd stopped playing. It was just for a couple of years, but I saw how it can destroy you. Now I just have one or two beers. I never even have a hangover."

The ghoulish spectres of his past, Reinaldo believes, were involved in his arrest. "I was never a drug dealer," he says, "but I was charged with being one. It had a lot to do with what went on in the dictatorship. It wasn't an accident."

There is also bitterness over the way he has been treated by the club for which he sacrificed so much. "In Brazil an ex-player is a disease. You devote your entire life to football, but after your career is over you have no place in the game. The president of Atlético [Alexandre Kalil] said he doesn't want ex-players, idols, hanging around the place. He wants the fans to sing his name instead, a guy who has never kicked a ball. Ex-players at Cruzeiro have a card to get into the stadium. I don't. I'm Atlético's all-time top scorer, and it's hard for me to get into the stadium to see a match. It's all about the ego of the directors these days. They exploit the clubs. What contribution do they make? I took kickings and beatings for Atlético, I was operated on countless times. At the club's centenary celebrations, none of the old players were invited. It makes me sad. I don't want money. I just want to be treated with respect."

Respect. It sounds like the very least a man like Reinaldo — one of the most gifted players ever to emerge from the famed Brazilian production line of talent, and who, in the strength and courage of his convictions, puts better known but more politically acquiescent legends, such as Ronaldo and Pelé, to shame — deserves.

Which would probably be a good place to end. But perhaps talk of being snubbed by blowhard football chairmen, or undervalued by the fickle, media-and-success driven world of international reputation, is not the right way to sign off. And YouTube clips never tell the full story of a player or a life. I decide to put in a call to another Belo Horizonte footballing legend, Tostão, one of the heroes of Brazil's 1970 World Cup win. Tostão's career ended far too soon when, in 1973, aged just 26, problems with his vision forced him to abandon the game. Reinaldo made his debut for Atlético that same year, though the two never played against each other. Now a columnist for the *Folha de São Paulo* newspaper and one of Brazil's most intelligent football thinkers, Tostão, while a warm and highly educated speaker, is not always enthusiastic about talking to journalists, particularly when called at home, unannounced, on a Friday morning. When the subject turns to Reinaldo, however, he cannot say enough.

"He didn't play for as long as he should have, because of the injuries. But he was a truly spectacular player," he enthuses. "If he'd played more he would have achieved everything that Romário and Ronaldo did. He even played a little like Romário in his younger days, the way he would carry the ball from deep, and his finishing, fooling the goalkeeper then chipping it over him. There is a slight sense of missed opportunities, because he could have achieved more. But Reinaldo was majestic."

64

Tournaments

"I know I am not big in stature
or talent but I remembered my
mother loves me."

The Improbable Rainmaker

How a derided reserve goalkeeper brought Côte d'Ivoire's long wait for a trophy to an end

By Jonathan Wilson

The helicopter that had hovered over the stadium all game passed low over the stands. Then it came back again, lower. And again, even lower so that when it crossed the tribune at the western end of the stadium, fans fled and a swarm of inflatable orange hands, clap-sticks, empty water bottles and scraps of paper were swept into the air. It came one more time, passing perhaps 30 feet above the top of the stand, by which time smoke grenades had been released.

Behind the goal, a line of Ghanaian fans huddled in fear, protected to an extent by local riot police, but still having to dodge the occasional missile. Red-shirted Equatoguinean players approached in despair, hands out, trying to calm their own fans. Ghana's players stood in the centre-circle, sporadically shaking their legs to keep loose. An announcement came over the loudspeaker, urging fans to remember the image of the country. The word *"vergüenza"* – shame – was repeated. It only inflamed the situation, prompting a further hail of water-bottles to be hurled at police.

Eventually the stand behind the goal and the main stand were cleared of home fans. The mood among some remained strangely cheery. As they were hastened along the aisle in front of the press-box, one inadvertently knocked off a colleague's laptop charger, apologised, rescued it from the churn of feet and handed it back. After a delay of 40 minutes, the game restarted. There were eight minutes plus injury-time remaining; they lasted perhaps three before the Gabonese referee Eric Otogo blew the final whistle.

Ghana won 3-0, and had played extremely well, particularly given the absence of Asamoah Gyan because of a pelvic injury sustained when he was kicked by the Guinea goalkeeper Naby Yattara. That, though, was not what will be remembered from the second semi-final. The first sign of trouble had come when Iban Edu, a player notable for being quick, irritating and immaculately groomed, had dispossessed Wakaso Mubarak midway inside the Ghana half, giving him a clear run on goal. The tackle seemed clean – and the linesman, who was no more than 15 yards away didn't flag – but Otogo deemed it a foul. Iban Edu, who plays in a constant bubble of fury, harangued Otogo and was rapidly joined by four or five teammates. A couple of bottles were lobbed towards the pitch.

Ghana were clearly the better side and, unlike Tunisia in the quarter-final, they took on Equatorial Guinea at football, rather than seeking to scrap and to spoil. Again and again Wakaso hit Christian Atsu with rapid long passes from deep in midfield and he soon exposed Rubén Belima's shortcomings at left-back. Four minutes before half-time, Atsu laid in Kwesi Appiah, who was tripped by the goalkeeper Felipe Ovono. Equatorial Guinea protested, but the decision was clear-cut. Jordan Ayew converted the penalty.

As Ghana celebrated by the bench, Equatorial Guinea kicked off quickly, charging through an empty half at Razak Braimah's goal. Otogo called them back and, as he was surrounded, more bottles were thrown, aimed mainly at the celebrating Ghanaian players. Equatorial Guinea's discipline deserted them and, as they threw men forwards for a corner, Ghana hit them on the break, Atsu leading the counter before laying in Wakaso to make it 2-0. This time the hail of bottles was heavier and when the half-time whistle blew soon afterwards, Ghana's players were unable to leave the field until riot police had formed a *testudo* with their shields. The start of the second half was delayed until a similar shelter had been created – despite pleas from Equatorial Guinea players for their fans to calm down – after which Avram Grant, notably unconcerned, led out his players.

A tense second half was played out at half pace until, with eight minutes remaining, Appiah crossed for Dede Ayew to add a third. Bottles rained down and then the missiles began to be directed at the 500 or so Ghanaian fans in the western corner of the north stand. It later became apparent that it wasn't just plastic water bottles being thrown, but glass beer bottles and stones, even half a plate and a piece of mirror. The Ghanaians, panicking, made first for the top corner of the stand,

where they were at least protected from anything hurled from the west stand and then fled down to the front of the tribune. It was widely reported that they'd forced the gate, but later inspection showed no damage: either the gate was already open or stadium security had released the magnetic lock. As the fans spilled through, police escorted them onto the running track, where they became targets for the west stand.

In the press box, there was a strange sense of dislocation and disbelief. Only twice did it feel that this could develop into something really serious: briefly when it seemed the Ghanaians may fight back and attack the west stand, and then when riot police, batons raised, cleared the main (south) stand. The Ghanaians, though, were admirably restrained and the evacuation actually passed off reasonably smoothly. The police, once they took action, ultimately responded well in quelling mounting tensions. Yet certain images remain. A ball boy, terrified in his uniform black shirt and orange shorts, hiding behind two medics. The back of an advertising hoarding streaked with blood. A photographer, a friend, hiding behind an inflatable Pepsi can as missiles peppered the track around him. An Equatoguinean couple sitting – defiant? dumb? drunk? – in their team's red shirts as an exasperated policeman prodded the man with the end of his baton. The Ghanaian fans, a fatalistic calm having settled over them, waiting outside the stadium for buses to ferry them away.

Was it a major incident? In terms of casualties, no, but in preventing the game from continuing, absolutely. For a long time, it seemed impossible that the game could carry on: what, after all, was the point with Ghana already 3-0 up? Then, slowly, realisation dawned. The television feed, beholden to the Confederation of African Football (CAF), had cut away from the violence almost as soon as it began (which is why most of the footage of the incidents, shot by a South African cameraman from the back of the press box, features the freelancer Nick Ames and me in the foreground).

And what sort of incident was it? Ostensibly, this was a home crowd reacting petulantly when its dreams of a final were taken from it, yet it was noticeable that the police became as much of a target as Ghana's players and fans. The outward appearance is of a placid population that has bought en masse into the propaganda of Teodor Obiang Nguema's regime, or is at least too weary or too frightened to fight. But opposition voices were quick to suggest that the relative anonymity of the football crowd – as so often before, in so many places – had permitted dissent to kindle. Obiang is 72 and his son, Teodorin, is making desperate attempts to persuade the world he isn't the free-spending playboy he has appeared. If the oil money is running out, what does that mean for the future of Equatorial Guinea?

There was other, more immediate, politicking at play. By insisting the game went on, by going through the charade of playing out those final minutes, CAF could create a simulacrum of normality. In the future, people looking at the results will see a game that Ghana won 3-0, not a match that was abandoned after 82 minutes with Ghana leading 3-0. Image is everything: that the tournament

was staged at all was testament to the demand that the show must go on.

When Morocco withdrew from hosting the Cup of Nations in November, it left CAF with a major problem. "Once you postpone this event, it will open the door for everybody to ask for a delay of any competition and we will no longer be credible and cannot organise anything," the CAF president Issa Hayatou said. "We will hurt our sponsors and partners. Everyone will say we are not ready and finally it is CAF that will pay the piper."

But as well as finance, there was an issue of credibility. "You know, we have a problem with French clubs which will not release our players if we move the Africa Cup of Nations," Hayatou went on.

There was also the issue of pride. The Cup of Nations was established in 1957 as a direct response to what CAF saw as Africa's under-representation at the World Cup. In that sense the tournament stands as an expression of African self-reliance, which is one reason CAF has resisted numerous calls to make the tournament once every four years in line with the Euros, the Copa América and the Asian Cup. Hayatou, over the past fortnight, has repeated again and again that CAF has never in 57 years postponed the Cup of Nations, for disease, war or political upheaval. For Hayatou and for CAF it was a point of principle that the tournament went ahead.

Quite why Morocco pulled out was something of a mystery. It has invested significant sums in football infrastructure, making a bid to host the World Cup and staging the Club World Championship. The Cup of Nations seemed a logical part of that strategy of self-promotion. Presumably the reasoning was that fear of Ebola would have such an impact on Morocco's tourist industry that it made more economic sense to accept CAF's sanctions – which eventually amounted to a ban for Morocco from this and the next two Cups of Nations, a $1million fine and €8million damages. The actual threat, though, was minimal, given that only one country afflicted by Ebola, Guinea, qualified, and that their travelling support and media could probably be numbered in double figures. Even more bafflingly, with Guinea banned from playing in Conakry because of the epidemic, they played 'home' games in Casablanca.

As CAF cast about for alternate venues, it turned out there was only one viable option – in Africa at least. Equatorial Guinea, having co-hosted the 2012 Cup of Nations with Gabon had the experience, two functioning stadiums and a further two under construction. It also had the wealth and the political will. Given it had a little under two months from being announced as hosts to the opening game, Equatorial Guinea did a remarkable job. Construction of the stadium in Mongomo was completed and a pitch laid, while improvements were made in Ebebiyin. Rudimentary press facilities were installed; sometimes the wifi even worked after half-time.

The biggest problem was hotels, less in Malabo than on the mainland. Tunisia arrived to find a three-hour power cut and no water. Burkina Faso moved because there weren't enough rooms. Claude Leroy, the Congo coach, spoke of the worst facilities in his eight

Cups of Nations. DR Congo stayed in a bizarre holiday camp near Bata airport that featured a lot of sinister men in sunglasses and no wifi until the second week. For journalists, finding accommodation on the mainland was hugely problematic.

I was one of five British journalists who'd booked flights from Malabo to Bata the day before the opening game. Three years ago I'd stayed in a hotel called the Sueño, run by a struggling French couple, but there seemed to be no trace of it online and I assumed it had gone out of business. The day we were due to fly there, we still had nothing and met in a café that morning to discuss our options. Somehow Brian Oliver, the former sports editor of the *Observer*, who was already in Bata, got wind of some rooms being let by a Mr Chang. We called him, negotiated a rate, and found ourselves staying in a Chinese restaurant. Chang himself came to meet us at the airport. He was young, friendly, extremely lean and muscular and had a bodyguard who carried an AK47. His fleet of cars, including at least one Porsche, suggested either that Chinese food is extremely profitable in Equatorial Guinea or he has some sort of sideline.

Before the opening games, the streets were packed, lines of white and blue taxis left gridlocked by the decision to shut the coast road to all but CAF officials and the teams. As we looped way east of the city before turning south towards the stadium, we passed the Sueño, still very open, and adorned with a photograph of the Congo team.

The stadium in Bata has an official capacity of 35,000 and in many ways is extremely well-appointed. Its major drawback is that everybody has to approach along one road and pass through a single gate. Three years ago, a crush there led to smoke bombs being fired by police to disperse a crowd, a scenario that was repeated ahead of the second group games this time round. Even when we arrived for the first games, five hours before kick-off, there were signs of problems to come as a few fans encroached beyond a barrier, police raised batons, and those fans ran back in a panic, into a line of other fans who were arriving behind them. By the time we left after the game, the gate hung buckled from a single hinge. Before the second game, against Burkina Faso, frustrated ticket-holders hurled rocks at police. Between the two games, it became so busy in the stadium hotel that they had to close off the bar; a producer for Al-Jazeera saw one irate local pull a gun in an attempt to gain admittance.

Equatorial Guinea took the lead against a sluggish Congo, Middlesbrough's Emilio Nsue taking advantage of a generous offside call to finish neatly. He was denied a second by an incorrect offside call and Congo battled back to level through Thiévy Bifouma. Leroy was furious, although it was unclear whether he was alleging skulduggery or ineptitude when he described how before the game the air-conditioning failed on the team bus, which then took 70 minutes to complete a 10-minute journey. Equatorial Guinea responded with an official complaint about the disallowing of Nsue's goal and alleging there was a "conspiracy" to "complicate" their progress to the second round. Gabon then beat a disappointing Burkina Faso with surprising ease.

Internal transport in Equatorial Guinea wasn't easy, but fortunately in the week before the tournament I'd been contacted by Chris and Melvyn, who worked for a British consultancy overseeing a construction project in Mongomo. They'd read a piece I'd written about the difficulties of finding accommodation and had very kindly offered the use of an apartment belonging to a colleague of theirs who was stuck in Britain with visa issues. Even more generously, they offered us the use of their office manager, Edu, as a driver. He picked us up in a Toyota Hilux at Chang's and, with four packed into the back, drove us through the jungle to Ebebiyin.

We arrived about four hours before kick-off in the first game there and popped into the town's one major hotel looking for something to eat. We were shown to the dining room, where the Cape Verde team were already tucking into a buffet of rice and various meats. When they left, the Minister for Sport, Francisco Pascual Obama Asue, arrived with his entourage. He happily agreed to an interview. He was very keen to assert that Equatorial Guinea had never volunteered to replace Morocco as hosts. "It was CAF who asked us and we said yes," he said. "They had no other solution. We were the last resort. CAF asked who could do it and if no one could, it would have gone to Qatar. It would not have been good for this tournament, a celebration of African football, to be cancelled or moved outside Africa. So for that reason the

President agreed. Africa has to consume what is African."

This is very much the image the president Obiang Nguema, who took power in a coup in 1979, is trying to portray: Equatorial Guinea is taking an increasingly important role within Africa, hosting the African Union summit in 2011, for instance, as well as the two Cups of Nations since then. There's clearly a reluctance, though, to appear too pushy. "We do not seek to be a protagonist," Obama said. "When we are asked, we are ready to help. There is a sense of satisfaction, of course, that the rest of Africa trusts us to do it."

There's also a sense of a future being prepared. Oil production has peaked – rough estimates suggest that the tier-one oil companies will start withdrawing in 2030 – and that the fall in the price of oil at the back end of 2014 has created major financial difficulties for the government, while causing those tier-one companies to consider backing out of costly deep-water drilling that remains only just financially viable. Clear information on how much hosting the tournament cost is difficult to find, but South Africa reportedly spent £25million to stage the 2013 edition, taking over from Libya at short notice (although not nearly so short as the notice Equatorial Guinea had). Obama could give no precise figure for the cost of the tournament beyond a vague figure of £10.5million each for the new stadiums in Ebebiyin and Mongomo.

Whether the government has overreached or not, the scale of the infrastructure projects – roads, water, electricity – is impressive and much

needed. That said, there is still much to be done: although the La Paz hospitals in Sipopo and Bata, funded by Israel, are excellent, they remain out of the reach of locals. The main hospital in Bata is so basic it doesn't even have an incinerator: needles are buried in the forest, while the story is told of a man who had his leg amputated and was given it to take home when he was discharged; he threw it from the taxi window, where local children played with it until it was eaten by dogs. With such obvious deficiencies, President Obiang's various vanity projects, his many palaces, his private helicopter that was once dispatched to Ebebiyin to pick up a cake, become even less justifiable.

Even hosting the tournament, for all the good it may do in terms of boosting Equatorial Guinea's profile and enhancing its prestige within Africa, has been questioned. Before the opening game in Bata, an opposition leader, Celestino Nvo Okenve, was arrested for handing out flyers and T-shirts urging people not to support the tournament by attending games and the human rights activist Santiago Martin, a member of the opposition, was detained for planning to lead a demonstration against the tournament.

The Equatoguinean exile Juan Tomás Ávila Laurel wrote a blog post that was reprinted in the *Guardian* in which he pointed out that "Many [Equatoguineans] barely have roofs over their heads, for the majority live in horribly overcrowded houses and sleep in whatever living-space is left over to them. We won't even mention drinking water, schools or centres for professional training." Laurel has a political axe to grind, but the basic truth of what he says is indisputable. Yet the argument is not as simple as he suggests. For one thing, if only those nations with adequate provision for healthcare and education were permitted to stage tournaments, the list of hosts would be impossibly short; and for another, there is surely some value in the happiness and pride that can be stimulated in a host nation by positive results.

The stadium in Ebebiyin is basic, with a horseshoe of stands and one end left open to the jungle, but it's more than good enough for group games, even if the pitch did cut up alarmingly – although hardly surprisingly, given it had been laid a matter of weeks earlier. Most significantly, it was full. Three years ago, other than for games involving the hosts in Bata, matches in Equatorial Guinea had been notable for their poor attendances – not that that is exactly unusual in Cups of Nations. This time, prices were set low, some going for as little as 500XFA (58p – or the price of any taxi journey within a city), while Obiang had personally paid for 10,000 tickets in each of the four venues to be distributed to fans. "We have to give solemnity to the Nations Cup. It is necessary to buy tickets to fill the stadiums," he said. "Let those who have the means help the poor." That's an intriguing take on his social policy, but it did suggest the extent to which, for him, this Cup of Nations is about spectacle.

The opening games in Ebebiyin may not have offered too much of that from a football perspective, although Yannick Bolassie's equaliser for DR Congo against Zambia was a goal of great beauty as he ran on to a cut-back from the right and creamed the ball into the top corner from just inside the box. Tunisia's 1-1 against Cape Verde was rather less

memorable. In fact, the whole group faded quickly from the recollection: Cape Verde were dogged and dull, a disappointment after the fluent team of two years ago, while Zambia lost their nerve having taken the lead against Tunisia, conceding two soft goals. In the end, a draw between Tunisia and DR Congo took both through.

Mongomo remains just as weird as it was when I passed through three years ago. The development has moved on apace and there is now a library and museum to go with the palace and the 8,000-capacity basilica, the second-largest Catholic place of worship in Africa. It still feels as incongruous as Portmeirion, an Italianate folly rising from the jungle. The new stadium was full for the opening games as Senegal overpowered a limp Ghana side and won 2-1 with a late goal from Moussa Sow. Afterwards Avram Grant cut an uncomfortable figure, shoulders hunched as a bat fluttered above his head in the press-conference room and he faced a barrage of criticism for his decision to switch to a back three shortly before the tournament.

Algeria, the pre-tournament favourites, fell behind to South Africa, whose goalscorer Tokelo Rantie missed a penalty soon afterwards. It was then that the goalkeeping situation that had always looked a potential weakness became a major issue – a phrase that while undoubtedly true sounds almost offensively banal given the context. After the murder of Senzo Meyiwa in October, the most experienced candidate to keep goal for South Africa was Darren

Keet, who had won just four caps. He played against Algeria and, although he made one stunning double save with the score at 1-0, he was responsible in varying degrees for all three goals South Africa conceded in the final 23 minutes. From Algeria's point of view, it was an emphatic conclusion to a game in which they'd been largely undistinguished.

It didn't immediately get better for them as they faced an improved Ghana, the return of Asamoah Gyan from what was described as "a mild dose" of malaria inspiring them. Gyan looked exhausted by the end of the game against Algeria but in injury-time, with the score at 0-0, he summoned the strength to run on to a long pass from Mubarak Wakaso and hit an awkward bouncing finish across Aymen Mathlouthi and in at the far post. With Senegal drawing with South Africa, who again threw away a lead, that meant all four sides could conceivably have made it through.

An early goal from Riyad Mahrez against Senegal put Algeria in control of the group and when Mandla Masanga scored with a brilliant volley against Ghana, South Africa were a goal from joining them. They were forced deeper and deeper, though, as they had been in their opening two games, and goals from John Boye and Dede Ayew gave Ghana a win that took them through with Algeria, who eventually won 2-0.

In Malabo, it was a story of West African giants crashing into each other with great force. Guinea were the romantic choice, having won their last two games to qualify despite being banned from

playing matches at home because of the Ebola crisis. They brought a surprising number of fans, one of whom stood in front of the press box dressed in a green, yellow and red jester's costume brandishing a banner that read, in French, "God is great! Come on Guinea, the team of Ebola!" They started well against a sluggish Côte d'Ivoire and took a first-half lead through Mohamed Yattara. When Gervinho was sent off just before the hour for lashing out amid some general pushing and shoving, a Guinean win began to seem possible. Hervé Renard brought on Seydou Doumbia, went to a 3-4-2 formation and, as Guinea tired, the substitute found the equaliser. The Guinean press was furious, one journalist directing a diatribe against the coach Michel Dussuyer, accusing him of being overly negative, and storming out. A physical Mali then forced a 1-1 draw against a Cameroon side that lacked the spark it had shown in qualifying.

Côte d'Ivoire were only moderately improved in their second game, Max Gradel hitting an 84th-minute equaliser after Bakary Sako had given Mali the lead with a superb finish. When Ibrahima Traoré, winning a second successive man of the match award — "one for mam, one for dad," as he put it — equalised for Guinea against Cameroon, all four sides in Group D were locked on two points, with two goals scored and two conceded.

Café Malabo has the best juice, the best wifi and some of the best food in town, so three of us decided to go there to watch the final games in Group A. Equatorial Guinea had drawn 0-0 with Burkina Faso in their second game which, with Congo beating Gabon 1-0 meant Equatorial Guinea needed to beat their great rivals Gabon to go through. The hope was that with all its screens and Cup of Nations decorations, Café Malabo would offer a happy balance of atmosphere and internet connectivity.

Unfortunately, half the bar had been booked out by a baby shower, so the build-up to the game was dominated by kids running about, shaking maracas and hitting drums. As soon as the players left the tunnel, though, the music was turned off and the commentary turned on. The adults at the shower, a couple of dozen young women, belted out the national anthem and settled down to watch the game in a combination of mute anxiety and panicked screams.

It was 0-0 in both games at half-time, then word came through that Congo had scored. For Equatorial Guinea, that changed nothing. Then Balboa burst into the box. Lloyd Palun stuck out a leg, Balboa went down and the referee, Noumandiez Doué of Côte d'Ivoire, gave a penalty. Balboa, under the intensest pressure, drove his kick home. The baby shower went wild, women running about, shrieking, hugging. Then they settled back for 35 minutes agonising waiting. When Iban Edu appeared on the touchline, running his fingers through his carefully coiffed hair, there was a ripple of approval; he's clearly something of a pin-up. He also turned out to be the match-winner, stabbing the rebound into the net with four minutes remaining after Didier Ovono had saved an initial effort from Balboa. The streets were soon packed with cars tooting their horns in celebration.

After Côte d'Ivoire's draw against Mali, Kolo Touré seemed surprisingly bullish. He spoke of the character in the team and how comfortable he felt playing in a back three behind Eric Bailly and Wilfried Kanon who, at 20 and 21 respectively, became emblematic of the rejuvenation of this Ivorian team. Their youth, the fact they hadn't been battered by repeated failure, he said, gave them an optimism that energised the rest of the squad. Needing to win their final group game against Cameroon to be sure of a place in the quarter-final, Côte d'Ivoire finally produced a performance worthy of potential champions, Max Gradel getting the only goal eight minutes before half-time. Cameroon, having looked so bright in qualifying, were flat, only sparking into life after Clinton N'jié came off the bench in the second half — which only served to infuriate the Cameroonian press who had been calling for his inclusion from the start of the tournament.

A 15th-minute penalty from Kevin Constant gave Guinea the lead in the other game in the group. Seydou Keita missed from the spot soon after, but Mali did level shortly after half-time from a back-post Modibo Maïga header. A 1-1 draw meant qualification went down to the drawing of lots.

Dozens of journalists clustered round the lift shaft at the end of the lobby of the Malabo Hilton. For security reasons, two of the three lifts were blocked off with litter bins. In the presidential suite on the fourth floor, a representative of the Guinean and Malian parties each reached into a glass bowl and took a green ball, one marked with a two and one with a three. Aboubakar Baba Diarra of Mali took hold of a ball first, then

Amara Dabo, the financial director at the Guinean sports ministry, grabbed his. Guinea were through.

The word surged through the lobby. Everybody, suddenly, was on phones, on microphones, on Twitter: it's Guinea. The one working lift came down. Dabo, wearing a white Hackett shirt with one red sleeve, one navy, emerged, beaming, and jogged the length of the lobby before he eventually stopped to give a delighted interview. "The god of fortune smiled on us," he said, then broke off to hug a man in an orange and yellow striped shirt and dance with him. He was soon speaking excitedly on two phones at once. Before long he was overwhelmed, standing in a daze, patting sweat from his brow with a folded handkerchief. The lift doors opened again and a CAF official carried out the bowl, returning it to the kitchen, presumably to resume its role in the breakfast buffet.

Finally, out came the Malian delegation, one official weeping, another saying it was "the cruellest way to lose". "Today is a very important day for our country," said Damani Dore, Guinea's sports minister. "It shows when you work hard, and work together, good things can happen. The whole of Africa has come together to fight the Ebola epidemic, including our brothers in Mali. They are a brother country."

Initially the quarter-finals had been scheduled to take place across the four venues, but safety concerns over Equatorial Guinea playing in the tiny stadium in Ebebiyin meant the games ended up being played as double-headers in Bata and Malabo. In some quarters that was portrayed as scandalous assistance to the hosts, but in reality it was probably the only safe option.

Accommodation in Bata was still a problem, but I had no great desire to go back to Chang's, so I ended up spending the first night in an apartment about 10 minutes walk from the stadium. It was not a good decision. The place stank of sour milk and urine, there was graffiti on the walls and, as well as four British journalists, there were a number of local kids staying in the place, who played video games loudly at all hours. When I woke up the following morning, after a fevered and unpleasant sleep during which mosquitos had made a banquet of my left arm, it turned out there was no power and no water, at which I left, resolving to walk around the city begging and throwing money around until I found a hotel. It turned out that, after the Burkina Faso team had left, there'd been spaces in the Hotel de Federaciones, in the stadium grounds. 90,000XFA (£100) for a shower and air-conditioning, with enticing clouds of garlic billowing from the kitchen, seemed like the greatest bargain any man had ever struck.

That was perhaps the hottest, most humid day of a hot and humid tournament. In the press-box, everybody looked wrung out, sweat patches unavoidable. The first half of Congo v DR Congo was understandably half-paced and cautious. Eight minutes into the second, though, Yannick Bolasie struck the bar and the game suddenly took off. Two minutes later Férébory Doré jabbed in a free-kick from the left and, against the run of play, Congo had the lead. Cédric Makiadi smacked a free-kick off the bar, then a defensive error let in Doré again. His initial effort was saved, but Bifouma followed up to make it 2-0. In nine minutes DR Congo had hit the bar twice but had gone 2-0 down. They needed a quick response and they got it: three minutes after Bifouma's goal, Bolasie cut the ball back and Dieumerci Mbokani, whose strength had unsettled Congo throughout, made it 2-1. Jeremy Bokila, having hit a simple chance straight at the keeper, seized on the much harder chance the rebound presented to level with 15 minutes remaining. With the substitute Neeskens Kebano pulling the strings, DR Congo took control. Joel Kimwaki headed in a Kebano free-kick to make it 3-2 with nine minutes remaining and then Mbokani sealed a 4-2 win from Kebano's through-ball in injury-time. It had been an astonishing second half but that, it turned out, was only the *hors d'oeuvres*.

Where can you begin with the second quarter-final? The first half was offensively awful, a game that seemed made up almost entirely of the ball being tossed about so free-kicks could be taken. Tunisia committed 19 fouls in the first half and Equatorial Guinea four, but the most serious incident came when Sipo, the Equatoguinean full-back, spat at Wahbi Khazri. As the second half went on, the foul-rate went down, but behaviour became worse. Both sides at one point seemed to be playing for penalties, while if the Mauritian referee Rajindraparsad Seechurn, who had come to resemble a hapless supply teacher being largely ignored by a troublesome class, had been as strict as he perhaps should have been, three or four Tunisians could have been sent off for dissent

or bad challenges. Ahmed Akaichi, in particular, was fortunate to escape a red card for a reckless lunge at the Equatorial Guinea goalkeeper Felipe Ovono, who perhaps did him a favour by reacting as preposterously as he did.

20 minutes from time, from nothing, Tunisia took the lead, Akaichi sweeping in a cross from the right – after which, of course, their time-wasting became even worse. Equatorial Guinea seemed helpless in the face of it, too naive, too lacking genuine quality, to do anything about it. But then Emilio Nsue ran onto a pass from Iban Edu and drew a fine save from Aymen Mathlouthi and the mood in the stadium changed from resignation to something more optimistic. Deep in injury-time, Ivan Bolado turned in the box near Hamza Mathlouthi and went down. Seechurn pointed to the spot. Replays soon confirmed what had seemed instinctively true: it was never a penalty. Georges Leekens, Tunisia's Belgian coach, later called the decision a disgrace and compared it to the loss of a family member. There's little doubt that history will remember the penalty as a scandal but you could at least see why Seechurn might have given it; there *was* a clumsy movement from Mathlouthi.

The call went up immediately that the game had been fixed, that this was Equatorial Guinea's payback for agreeing to stage the tournament. Perhaps it was, but had Seechurn really been fixing the game, surely he wouldn't have left it so late; he had, after all, had plenty of opportunities to dismiss Tunisians earlier in the game. My personal suspicion is that he simply tired of Tunisia's gamesmanship, his temper got the better of him and he snapped. Balboa, under enormous pressure, swept in the penalty.

Tunisia's discipline deserted them. Still, had they played properly, they would probably have won, but they were too far down the route of skulduggery for that. They had taken a game they should have won and, by cheating and spoiling, had created an environment in which it was suddenly, unexpectedly, possible they could lose. Balboa, a slow-moving, skilful winger, had the game of his life and, 11 minutes into extra-time, Seechurn decided he had been baulked by Aymen Abdennour. The Tunisians protested wildly, barging Seechurn sufficiently that the free-kick ended up being taken about five yards behind where the offence had occurred. No matter: Balboa whipped it into the top corner, a goal marred only by the fact that a green laser-pen had played over the face of Aymen Mathlouthi as he waited on his goal-line.

The game from then on was a farce, Equatorial Guinea time-wasting, Tunisia spoiling for a fight. Seechurn gave two minutes injury-time at the end of the second half, but it was taken up in its entirety by a scrap between the two benches as the Equatoguineans held onto the ball to prevent Tunisia taking a throw. Esteban Becker, the short, dapper, excitable Argentinian manager of Equatorial Guinea, made a point of standing in the corner of his technical area as close to the Tunisian bench as possible, a magnificently provocative gesture, remaining within the laws by such a tiny margin that he may as well have been flicking V-signs. In the end, it seemed Seechurn had just given up. As soon as the whistle went, he was surrounded by Tunisians; one

aimed a kick at him and others threw punches before stewards and police waded in, protecting Seechurn as he scuttled off down the tunnel. When the Tunisians were finally persuaded to leave, bottles were thrown from the stand, the players returning fire. Disgracefully, Sport5, who control the television feed, cut away from the incidents on the pitch meaning there is probably no footage of the clashes. That Tunisia had been hard done by was impossible to dispute; finding sympathy for them given their general behaviour rather harder. It wasn't a game from which anybody emerged with their reputation enhanced. Tunisia were asked to apologise for their allegations that the officials had been biased; when they refused they were banned from the 2017 tournament. Seechurn, meanwhile, was suspended from refereeing for six months.

Not that anybody in Bata cared. Nobody slept that night. The airport the following morning was full of the undead, clad in red shirts and wandering around with glazed eyes and booze on their breath. Most taxi drivers seemed hammered. I shared a terrifying ride to the airport with the British journalist Taimour Lay. When he handed over his phone showing his electronic ticket at the Punto Azul desk, a manager grabbed it and in his drunken clumsiness managed to "archive" the email which, with no wifi in the terminal, immediately became inaccessible. Half an hour of arguing later, Taimour ended up sitting behind the check-in desk as he searched the system for his booking reference.

Back in Malabo things were calmer. Guinea wasted the opportunity the drawing of lots had given them, barely turning up and losing 3-0 to Ghana. Ivory Coast then withstood intense pressure from Algeria to win 3-1 despite having only 40% possession, Wilfried Bony scoring with two excellent headers before Gervinho wrapped up the win from a counter led by Junior Tallo. Renard, who had clearly been irritated by being asked to cover up his lucky white shirt – 15 games unbeaten at that point – with a pink bib, was almost purring afterwards. He knew how significant it was that Algeria, whom he described as the best side in the tournament, were out and that his side had shown the sort of discipline and determination that had characterised his Zambia.

And that, perhaps, was the advantage of taking charge of Côte d'Ivoire when he did: with only four members of the 2006 squad remaining – the Tourés, the left-back Siaka Tiene and the reserve goalkeeper Boubacar Barry – this was the first tournament in a decade when the "golden" tag hadn't been used; that sense of reduced expectations legitimised a more pragmatic response. Although Côte d'Ivoire arguably still had the best squad at the tournament, there was less need for them to assert their goldenness. That said, caution had been François Zahoui's preferred approach in 2012 as well, when the Ivorians went through the whole tournament without conceding a goal; had Didier Drogba not missed a penalty in the final, it would have brought success and Renard might have been remembered as nothing more than the coach who inspired plucky Zambia to play above themselves before greater talent told in the end.

With the exception of December, when he was habitually excellent, Yaya Touré's season has consisted of long patches of indifferent form punctuated by brilliant goals. It was much the same in the Cup of Nations. He hadn't played badly, but he had played lethargically when, 20 minutes into the semi-final against DR Congo, the ball broke to him just outside the box. He struck it ferociously hard and, even though it was nowhere near the corner, Robert Kidiaba had no chance. Mbokania equalised from the penalty spot three minutes later, but the Ivorian menace on the break always looked likely to be too much. Gabriel Zakuani, who had been hit by a medical truck while sitting on a stretcher in the quarter-final, brilliantly nodded a Gervinho header against his own bar and clear after 40 minutes, but two minutes later Bolasie squandered possession and Bony laid in Gervinho to make it 2-1. Sylvain Gbohouo, Barry's successor and a significant upgrade, made a couple of decent saves in the second half before Kanon forced in a half-cleared corner to seal the Ivorians' passage to a third final in nine years, there to face Ghana.

When Equatorial Guinea went out, the hosts' interest ended. Fewer than 1000 fans turned up for the third-place play-off, where there was a notably enhanced security presence, including grenade-toting Angolan riot police. DR Congo won it on penalties, prompting Kidiaba into another of his idiosyncratic celebrations, bunny-hopping around on his backside.

In Bata, the stadium was around a third full for the final. There were perhaps

2,500 orange-clad Ivorians, and maybe 800 Ghanaians – understandably keeping a low profile – but even the free distribution of tickets didn't bring out the locals. Most of the discussion that day was about whether Asamoah Gyan would start, but a couple of hours before kick-off there came startling injury news. Gbohouo was out with a thigh strain which meant Boubacar Barry would start in goal for Côte d'Ivoire. For almost a decade he had been the weak link in the Ivorian side and now, just as they approached the end of the quest, here he was again.

As the journalist Sam Crocker suggested, could it be that Barry didn't really exist? Although he was in the squad, he didn't play in 2006 but then became a regular as the realisation set in that the golden squad may end up winning nothing. Once it was accepted that that generation was gone and that we were in a post-golden age of Ivorian football, Barry disappeared, only to reappear just before the final when thoughts once again turned to possible glory: was he simply a physical manifestation of Ivorian neurosis? After all, does anybody really spend eight years at Lokeren?

It was as though he'd never been away. Within 20 minutes Barry had fumbled a cross and scuffed a clearance straight to Kwesi Appiah who was too startled to take advantage. With his mournful face and untucked shirt, Barry doesn't look like a footballer; his demeanour is that of a sorrowful clown, a Buster Keaton figure, spreading panic and chaos wherever he goes.

But, somehow, he clung on. Christian Atsu, later named player of the

tournament, hit the post, as did Dede Ayew, in a fractious first half in which Gyan and Serey Die should both have been sent off. Ghana had the better of it, but Barry and Côte d'Ivoire battled through to penalties.

Gervinho and Gyan were substituted with a couple of minutes remaining, two players so racked by the trauma of penalties past that they couldn't bear the thought of having to take another one. Three years ago, Gervinho was asked to take Côte d'Ivoire's eighth kick in the shoot-out. He was so reluctant that Kolo Touré volunteered instead, only for the coach François Zahoui to insist Gervinho should take it. He refused, and so Touré, having already begun the tense approach to the penalty spot, had to walk forward again and was rattled enough to miss. Rainford Kalaba then missed, at which Gervinho had to go next and, inevitably, put his kick way over the bar. His sense of guilt was profound, so much so that he refused to watch this shoot-out, instead taking a chair and placing it next to the Ivorian bench, facing away from the action.

Barry, suddenly, was centre stage. Wakaso Mubarak scored. Wilfried Bony hit the bar. Jordan Ayew scored. Junior Tallow missed the target. Ghana led 2-0. But then Barry saved from Afriyie Acquah, Serge Aurer scored, Frank Acheampong missed and Seydou Doumbia thumped in to make it 2-2 after four kicks each.

Barry went down with cramp repeatedly, something that many assumed was feigned and designed to increase the pressure on the Ghanaian takers by making them wait. Maybe it was, or maybe he was simply so worked up he suffered some psychosomatic muscle tension. Ghana's players seemed more worried by his constant talking, although it turned out he was simply praying. There was certainly gamesmanship involved as Dede Ayew prepared to take his kick, as Barry pointed first one way, then the other (which in itself suggested his haplessness, given the whole aim of indicating one side of the goal is supposedly to make the taker think you know which way he's going). Ayew scored and then screamed in fury at Barry, who immediately backed down and apologised.

That was 3-2. Yaya Touré levelled. Everybody was scoring. 4-3. 4-4. 5-4. Then Kolo Touré: given his agonies after missing in Libreville, no neutral wanted him to miss, and he didn't: 5-5. 6-5. 6-6. 7-6. Bailly, a one pace run up, a majestic penalty into the top corner: 7-7. The narrative suddenly had become clear: the press-box buzzed with the realisation of what was unfolding. Barry was going to score the winner: the clown was going to become the king. John Boye scored: 8-7. Serey Die scored: 8-8.

And so to the goalkeepers. Razak Braimah's kick was low to Barry's left. He lunged, got hands to it and pushed it away. He wandered off, as though unaware he was next. He collapsed again with supposed cramp, only increasing the length of time he had to think about the responsibility he faced: by then, Barry seemed so confused he was playing mind-games with himself. He staggered to his feet, shambled to place the ball on the spot. What did it feel like at that moment, he was asked afterwards, to know that with one kick he could bring to an end a decade of near-misses? "I know I am not big in stature or talent," he said, "but I remembered my mother loves me."

Barry scored.

His cramp disappeared. He set off on a crazy run around the stadium. Gervinho, eventually, left his chair. Renard, the first man to win the tournament with two different nations, removed the lucky white shirt and cavorted topless with his players. Barry was the unlikeliest, the most implausible of heroes. Even Yaya Touré, emotionally shattered as he spoke to the media afterwards, seemed shocked. "He has shown," Touré said, "the importance of solidarity." Which perhaps meant simply that a reserve could step in and perform a useful role, but sounded an awful lot as though he was saying: we put up with him for 10 years but now he's done this.

And that, to the delight of CAF, is how this tournament will end up principally being remembered. Not for the rushed preparations, the Seechurn controversy or the violence of the semi-final, but for Côte d'Ivoire winning at last and the improbable redemption of Boubacar Barry.

Home Comforts

Victory in the Asian Cup they hosted seals Australia's place in the heart of the Asian confederation

By John Davidson

Ange Postecoglou pumped his arms wildly at the crowd, willing them on to make even more noise in the deafening Homebush surrounds. Australia had just claimed their first Asian Cup at their third attempt with a dramatic extra-time victory over South Korea. ANZ Stadium was awash with green and gold confetti and Men At Work's 'Land Down Under' blared out of the speakers as a nation rejoiced. It was a special moment for Postecoglou, the homegrown coach who had been in charge for only 14 months but had been slammed in the lead-up to the tournament for his experimental approach and steadfast refusal to alter his plans. The son of Greek migrants who was part-visionary, part-football evangelist, Postecoglou was lapping up every second of an emotionally charged night. He stood alone on the turf, elated, vindicated. It was a triumph, not only for the 49 year old but for the Australian footballing community that had finally come of age and for a nation starting to engage properly with Asia.

For a decade, Australia had been the odd man out in Asia, largely unwanted but desperate for regular meaningful games and footballing acceptance. In 2005, they had left Oceania and joined the Asian confederation (AFC) for a more secure path to the World Cup and a way of guaranteeing higher quality matches after qualifying for just two major tournaments in 45 years. After the success of the 2006 World Cup – at which the Socceroos pushed the eventual winners Italy all the way in the round of 16 before an injury-time penalty from Francesco Totti cruelly knocked them out – Australian football was on a high. Its golden generation of Harry Kewell, Mark Viduka, Lucas Neill, Mark Schwarzer, Mark Bresciano, Tim Cahill and Craig Moore was as its peak and keen for greater success. Australia were members of the AFC and the future appeared bright.

But the country's relationship with its northern neighbours had always been rocky, partly because of its existence as a Western-focused former British colony located at the bottom corner of the southern hemisphere, and partly because of long-standing fears of Asian immigration within Australia and some internal opposition to multiculturalism. In football it would be no different.

Coming off the World Cup in Germany, the expectations for the Socceroos in their Asian Cup debut in 2007 were high. Many tipped the Aussies to walk through the competition in a tournament that was co-hosted by Indonesia, Malaysia, Thailand and Vietnam. After bright performances against Brazil, Croatia and Italy, what could minnows like Oman and Iraq bring? A lot more than the Socceroos could handle, it turned out, as the Antipodeans struggled to deal with the heat, the conditions and opponents that were far more structured and disciplined than they expected. Filled with hubris and arrogance, a squad beset by internal issues and saddled with a caretaker manager who did not command their respect, the Socceroos bombed out. A very lucky 1-1 draw with Oman, thanks to a 92nd minute header from Cahill, was followed by a deserved 3-1 loss to Iraq and a one-sided 4-0 thrashing of Thailand. Australia scraped through to the quarter-finals behind Iraq, but were beaten on penalties by the Asian heavyweights Japan.

The Australians reached the next World Cup in South Africa through the Asian Confederation, but failed to recreate the glory of four years earlier and didn't make it out of their group. They entered their second Asian Cup, held in Qatar in early 2011, with a new head coach and a new plan to win the tournament. More experienced in Asia and with a sprinkling of a fresh blood, the Socceroos got off a better start in Doha. Under Holger Osieck, Franz Beckenbauer's assistant with West Germany's 1990 World Cup-winning side, Australia secured top spot in their group with wins over India and Bahrain and a draw with South Korea. They beat the 2007 Asian Cup champions Iraq after extra time in the quarter-final, then breezed past Uzbekistan in the semi-final, smashing six past the White Wolves. But Japan won the final thanks to Tadanari Lee's 109th-minute volley and the trophy eluded them again. Australia, though, were

learning fast and they were handed the right to host the 2015 tournament as the sole bidder.

After rebuilding at the 2014 World Cup, where no Asian nation made it out of their group, expectation was still high for the hosts even though the Socceroos came into the Asian Cup with one win from their previous 12 matches and a record of one win, one draw and three losses since Brazil. Osieck had been replaced by Ange Postecoglou in November 2013. He had a mandate to rejuvenate the squad: he axed the veterans Neill and Schwarzer, blooding youngsters and trialling 43 players in just 12 months. It was experimentation that the national side had never seen before. The 2014 World Cup was a write-off, nine goals conceded in three straight defeats, but there were signs in South America that Postecoglou's surgery was starting to pay off. But for a moment of Alexis Sánchez brilliance or a vintage Arjen Robben dribble and strike, Australia may have jagged points off Chile and the Netherlands. With a mantra of "judge me on the Asian Cup" fed to the media, Postecoglou had to be ready on his home turf as the pressure ramped up.

Japan headed south confident and secure in their status as Asia's best team. Sure, Iran may have been ranked higher and have performed better at the World Cup, but the Samurai Blue were the defending Asian Cup champions and could call on players at bigger clubs than Team Melli. Keisuke Honda, Shinji Kagawa, Makoto Hasebe, Yuto Nagatomo, Maya Yoshida, Shinji Okazaki... no other Asian side was blessed with a similar array of Serie A,

Premier League and Bundesliga talent. The Mexican Javier Aguirre had taken the reins after the disappointment in Brazil and the expectation was that his experience in international football and La Liga would prove telling with a star-studded squad. Over-confidence and the deployment of a pure goalscorer were the only doubts. Japan had even outplayed Postecoglou's Socceroos just two months earlier, largely dominating the Australians in a 2-1 friendly win in Osaka.

Like the Samurai Blue, South Korea were in Australia with a point to prove after a dismal World Cup. After two defeats and a draw in Brazil, they turned to Uli Stielike, the wily German who had led Switzerland and Côte d'Ivoire but had spent the previous six years coaching clubs in Qatar. The 60 year old set about adding greater structure and discipline, instilling steel into a side blessed with fine technique and speed.

Iran's preparation for tournament had been shambolic at best. While the Iranians had been unlucky in Brazil, pushing Argentina hard before being undone by a brilliant Lionel Messi goal, the wheels had almost fallen off in the six months since. Carlos Queiroz remained Team Melli's coach but doubts persisted about his long-term future after four years in the job. The financing of the team had become a major issue and Queiroz had found it difficult to secure his players for matches leading up to the Asian Cup. Still, Iran had the benefit of a large expat supporter base in Australia and were handed a favourable draw in a group with Bahrain, Qatar and UAE.

It had been feared that the Asian Cup might be plagued by hot temperatures at the height of Australia's summer. But the tournament started in Melbourne in cool conditions, across the road from tennis's Rod Laver Arena, the home of the Australian Open. It was an inauspicious start with a small crowd and a quietish atmosphere at the 30,000-capacity AAMI Park. With a darts event taking over the 56,000-strong Docklands Stadium, games in the Victorian capital were held in the home of the A-League clubs Melbourne Victory and Melbourne City. Australia approached the opening game against Kuwait with apprehension. Would Postecoglou's reformed side fire? Had the leaky Australian defence finally been plugged? Would the people of Australia, a country with four football codes and a myriad other sports all competing for eyeballs, support the competition in numbers? The wait for answers would not be long.

After an opening ceremony that bordered on the farcical, Hussain Fadhel's goal just eight minutes into the match confirmed many fears – the Socceroos' back four was as hard as a cloud. Fadhel's low dive to head the bouncing ball past Mat Ryan, after a mix-up in the Australian box, was perfectly timed but the result of comical defending. The response from the green and gold was swift.

The Australian attack surged forward and Cahill, once the tormentor of defences in the English Premier League, struck. Fed by a cutback from the Swindon Town midfielder Massimo Luongo, Cahill equalised and then Luongo himself headed home to put the Socceroos 2-1 ahead at half-time. A penalty from Mile

Jedinak and a close-range finish from James Troisi in the second half had the hosts humming and the pressure eased. Australia had got the opening win they craved and the Asian Cup had begun in high-scoring fashion.

Saudi Arabia, three times a winner of the tournament, and China met the following night at Brisbane's Suncorp Stadium. The Saudis had entered the tournament shorn of their main striker and reigning Asian Footballer of the Year, Nasser Al-Shamrani. The 71-cap veteran was set to be public enemy number one in Australia, having spat on the Socceroo defender Matt Spiranovic in the Asian Champions League final, but his absence through injury robbed the Asian Cup of this controversy and, crucially, the Green Falcons of their star. China, having failed to qualify for the 2014 World Cup, were starting again under the French coach Alain Perrin.

In the end it was a 12-year-old ball boy who proved to be the difference between the two teams. Stephan White's advice to China's Wang Dalei to dive left as Saudi Arabia's Naif Hazazi stepped up to take a penalty was decisive. Hazazi's shot was saved and Team Dragon won the match 1-0. It was the beginning of a poor tournament for Saudi Arabia, which would include a 4-1 victory over North Korea and a 3-1 loss to Uzbekistan. The Uzbek win condemned the Green Falcons to third spot and elimination while Team Dragon headed into the quarter-finals unbeaten.

On the same evening South Korea rode their luck but saw off Oman 1-0 in Canberra. The Koreans had not convinced and were grateful to the goalkeeper Kim Jin-hyeon, but they would improve with time. Another one-goal victory, over Kuwait, followed, meaning a match against the hosts in Brisbane would decide the winners of Group A.

Iran and Bahrain did battle in Melbourne while the UAE met Qatar in Canberra as Group C got underway. Expectations were high for Qatar considering its petro-fuelled investment in football and its controversial capture of the right to host the 2022 World Cup. The Maroon had beaten Australia 1-0 in October in Doha and were seen as a good bet to make it out of their group. They started strongly, Khalifan Ibrahim getting the opener with a flying volley, but then the Emiratis swung into action, doubles from Ahmed Khalil and Ali Mabkhout, two coming from set pieces, stopping the Qataris in their tracks. It was the start of a great tournament for the UAE and in particular for their emerging attackers Mabkhout and the winger Omar Abdulrahman.

There are roughly 35,000 Iran-born expats in Australia and it seemed that nearly half of them were on hand to see Team Melli in the flesh. Women are banned from attending matches in Iran, but in Melbourne the national team was supported by both sexes with faces painted green, white and red, adding vibrancy to a tournament desperately craving it. Iran finished off Bahrain with goals from Ehsan Hajsafi and Masoud Shojaei. They moved on to Sydney and the Team Melli bandwagon only got bigger. After the defeat of Qatar, Ashkan Dejagah remarked that the raucous atmosphere meant "it was like playing in Tehran". Several of his teammates posed for photos with young women in the stands at full-time. It was an act that drew the ire of the Iranian Football Federation, which stated, "In some of the selfies that our players have taken with the fans we can see they appear next to people whose appearance we regard as being against our moral principles."

For Palestine, football is not merely a game but a way of expressing its existence. Fifa has recognised Palestine since 1998 and this Asian Cup was the first time they had qualified for a major tournament. Ashraf Nu'man's goal against the Philippines at the AFC Challenge Cup final in May 2014 had booked their place and Australia's Palestinian community was ready to party in a big way.

A small but vocal brigade was on hand in Newcastle for Palestine's Asian Cup debut against Japan. Ranked 115th in the world, Palestine had little chance, but that mattered little to the Palestinian supporters. Every clearance, every header of the ball out of danger, was cheered as though they had won the Asian Cup. Straightforward goals from Endo, Okazaki, Yoshida and a penalty to Honda put the Samurai Blue in control but could not dampen Palestine's spirit. Their fans sang and drummed on: just the fact they had it made it this far was an achievement.

Jordan put five past them, Iraq two, but still the Palestinians cheered. Jaka Ihbeisheh's strike against Jordan, Palestine's only goal of the tournament, was a rare highlight on the pitch. As one fan put it, "Support is awareness. If I was a player who came here from a war zone and saw the thousands of people who will be dressed in Palestinian colours, that's more of a victory than actually winning a game."

Australia's third game was their toughest test to date, but one the local community was pretty positive that they would pass. Kuwait had been brushed aside 4-1, Oman obliterated 4-0. Qualification for the quarter-finals had already been secured and a draw would be enough to maintain top spot in the group and an easier path to the final. In contrast, South Korea had laboured to narrow victories. A virus had swept through the Korean camp before the second match, leading Stielike to make seven changes, and the Taeguk Warriors had yet to ignite properly. Could they contain the free-flowing Aussie attack?

Searing heat and a plague of moths greeted the two sides in Brisbane. Postecoglou rested his first-choice front three, bringing in the A-League forwards Tomi Juric and Nathan Burns to lead the line. The Socceroos were bright and positive until they were sucker-punched on 32 minutes. The Aussies pushed forward after the ball was cleared but possession was lost and Lee Jeong-hyeop was left free, giving him enough time to drift into the box unattended and fire a low shot past Ryan.

From there the Koreans shut up shop. Wave after wave of Socceroo pressure marched forward but South Korea would not budge. Kim Jin-hyeon was immense in goal and even Cahill, brought on after

70 minutes, could not save Australia. The Koreans went through in top spot to a meeting with Uzbekistan while the Socceroos stayed in Brisbane to play China. The pressure on the hosts came flooding back, along with the doubts about Postecoglou.

Every tournament has a game than stands out, a fixture of immense entertainment and drama that is remembered for years. This time it was the quarter-final between Iraq and Iran. The war between the two nations in the 1980s killed more than a million people and the wounds are far from healed.

Team Melli went in front after 24 minutes thanks to a thumping header from Sardar Azmoun. But then the referee Ben Williams asserted his influence on the match. After booking Mehrdad Pooladi earlier in the game, he showed him a second yellow card after making slight contact with the Iraq goalkeeper Jalal Hassan when chasing down the ball. Hassan responded by pushing Pooladi, who crashed theatrically to the turf, but that couldn't save him. Williams appeared to forget he'd already booked Pooladi, but the Iraq captain Younis Mahmoud ran the length of the field to ensure Pooladi was sent off. Carlos Queiroz had already slammed Williams for his performance in Iran's win over Bahrain.

Iraq took advantage of their numerical advantage and scored through Ahmed Yasin. Extra-time beckoned. Mahmoud headed in on 93 minutes to put the Iraqis in front, but Morteza Pouraliganji smashed in a header to equalise. The scores were level for just two minutes, as

a bizarre error from Pouraliganji handed Iraq a penalty from which Dhurgham Ismail made it 3-2. But with two minutes left, the substitute Reza Ghoochannejhad popped up to tuck home and send the game to penalties.

The penalties and their aftermath were just as enthralling as the 120 minutes. Both Hajsafi and Abdul-Amir missed their opening spot-kicks, with the next 12 takers all finding the back of the net. Iran's Vahid Amiri was not so lucky, his miss handing the initiative to Iraq. When Salam Shaker fired home, a remarkable upset was complete: Iran were heading home and Iraq would face South Korea in the semi-final. Team Melli appealed for the result to be overturned because Iraq had fielded Alaa Abdul-Zahra, who had failed a doping test in 2014, but their protest was dismissed.

Japan were expected to beat UAE to set up a semi-final with Australia, whom they had eliminated in the past two Asian Cups. But Mabkhout continued his impressive Asian Cup with another goal, his fourth of the tournament, just seven minutes in. The Emiratis packed men behind the ball and Japan surged ahead to respond. The Samurai Blue enjoyed 68% possession and fired in 32 shots to UAE's three. They had 18 corners while their opponents couldn't muster one. Finally, in the 81st minute, Gaku Shibasaki fired in from long range and the game went to penalties.

Penalty shoot-outs can do funny things to players, no matter the experience, their pedigree or individual skill. Keisuke Honda stepped up and, echoing Roberto

Baggio in the 1994 World Cup final, put his shot high over the bar. Omar Abdulrahman, the 23 year old coveted by Manchester City and Barcelona, then had the confidence to deliver a successful panenka. The UAE were ahead until Khamis Esmaeel went high and wild with the third kick. Yohei Toyoda scored to put Japan 3-2 ahead. The two teams traded goals until Shinji Kagawa hit the right-hand post and rebounded across the face of the goal. Ismail Ahmed scored to win it, the cup holders were out and Aguirre was sacked.

The trend of exciting quarter-finals continued. A counter-attacking China frustrated the slow-starting Socceroos in the first half and looked strong until Cahill scored two second-half goals, the first an audacious bicycle kick, the second a trademark header. Uzbekistan held South Korea scoreless until the 104th minute, Son Heung-min scoring twice in extra-time to eliminate the White Wolves.

The quarter-finals failed to match the magic of the previous round, the heavyweights Australia and South Korea playing to form and defeating their weaker opponents. Both the UAE and Iraq were spent after 120-minute efforts against Japan and Iran. Two goals from defenders in Newcastle put the Socceroos into the final, while a strike in each half in Sydney saw the Koreans through. Two weeks after the Taeguk Warriors had upstaged the Socceroos in Brisbane, they met again in Sydney. The best attack in the tournament would face the stingiest defence, yet to concede a goal after five matches.

I clambered off the train at Homebush along with carriages and carriages of merry Socceroo fans. Songs were sung and the mood was festive as the hot sun bore down. A gaggle of Taeguk fans bearing the South Korean flag boarded the steps of the escalator in front of me. One turned back to view the green and gold hordes descending on to the platform below us. "I don't see too many red shirts," he remarked in a concerned tone to his friend.

Sydney's Olympic Park can be a strange place at the best of times. Built for the 2000 Summer Olympics, a vast precinct of stadiums located in the geographical centre of Australia's biggest city, it's a ghost town outside of match days. The 82,000 capacity ANZ Stadium had become Australia's unofficial home since 1999 and was the scene of the dramatic penalty shootout win over Uruguay in 2005 that ended the Socceroos' 32-year World Cup exile. 10 years on, Australia would either create history again or the Koreans would claim another Asian Cup after a 55-year wait.

The final started at a quick pace, both sides a touch nervy but South Korea showing more adventure in pressing the Australians hard. The visitors focused their attack on the Socceroos' left and Son Heung-min almost had the opening goal on 36 minutes. Apart from a Cahill chance, dealt with expertly by Kim Jin-hyeon, it was a half dominated by the Taeguk Warriors until Australia's emerging midfield maestro Massimo Luongo stamped his authority on the fixture. Receiving the ball near the top of the box from Trent Sainsbury, he shifted the ball from his left to his right foot, beating his defender with the turn, and fired a rasping shot past Kim.

South Korea returned to the field emboldened and aggressive. Stielike took off the forward Nam Tae-hee and brought on Lee Keun-ho, altering his 4-5-1 formation as the goal-chase increased. Robbie Kruse limped off and the full-back Ivan Franjic, who had carried a hip injury into the game, also had to be replaced. Postecoglou had already substituted Cahill, meaning his three changes had been made early and his midfield was disrupted, Mark Milligan moving into an unfamiliar right-back role. South Korea dominated but when the three minutes of injury-time were announced, it seemed Australia would hang on.

With 120 seconds left the visitors pulled off a neat one-two and Son blasted past Ryan. The final went to extra-time and the momentum appeared to be with South Korea. Before and throughout the tournament Postecoglou had stressed the importance of his players' conditioning. The Socceroos had decided against playing a friendly just before the Asian Cup kicked off, unlike the other 15 teams, to get more time on the training pitch. His charges had run out of puff in the World Cup but they wouldn't do the same this time.

Juric bamboozled two defenders by the goal-line and let loose a cross-cum-shot. Kim could only push it out to Troisi who bundled the ball into an empty net. The ANZ Stadium exploded. South Korea had 15 minutes to find another goal but it would not come and Australia had the victory.

"I do not agree that we are not champions," said Stielike. "I agree we don't have the cup but the way our players played today, we are also champions of a lot of hearts. There is only one deception, I've been here four weeks and I haven't seen a single kangaroo."

Postecoglou entered the press-conference room with his tie astray and hair ruffled. Accompanying him was Luongo, the baby-faced 22 year old who had been anointed as the star of the tournament. The coach spoke of his personal relief at winning the Asian Cup and insisted this would not be the end for his team but the beginning of a new goal — taking on the rest the world. Asia had finally been conquered and now the Confederations Cup in two years time and the next World Cup were in his sights. "We came into this confederation knowing it would be a huge challenge," he said. "The Matildas won the Asian Cup, then Wanderers won the Champions League and now we've won. The goal for this confederation should be to break the European and South American monopoly on the World Cup. This tournament here, it's a great achievement but it's not the end of the journey."

The Asian Cup had been a raging success, not only for Postecoglou's side but for the whole host nation. Nearly 650,000 people had attended the 32 matches and the goals had rained in. New talents, like Abdulrahman and Luongo, had been discovered, while old heroes like Cahill and Cha Du-ri had bade farewell. Perhaps most importantly, Australia had got behind a tournament that brought it closer to Asia, closer to its future and created new bonds with this vast region.

Blizzard Books

Erbstein: The triumph and tragedy of football's forgotten pioneer

Dominic Bliss

Attention Blizzard fans,
we now do books!

Erbstein: The triumph and tragedy of football's forgotten pioneer, by Dominic Bliss

Ernő Egri Erbstein was one of the greatest coaches there has ever been, a pioneering tactician and supreme man-manager who created *Il Grande Torino*, the team that dominated Italian football in the years immediately after the Second World War. His was an extraordinary life that was characterised by courage and resourcefulness in the face of adversity.

Erbstein was part of the great Jewish coaching tradition developed in the coffee houses of Budapest and, playing in Hungary, Italy and the USA, he moved to Bari to embark on a coaching career that soon became noted for its innovativeness. That he and his family survived the Holocaust was a matter of astonishing good fortune, but just four years after the end of the war, Erbstein was killed with his team in the Superga air crash.

Dominic Bliss, through a combination of interviews, painstaking archival research and careful detective work, pieces together the lost history of one of football's most influential early heroes.

"Erbstein's story, largely untold before today, is one of those tales that makes us realise just how – for better and worse – European history is mirrored in football." – Gabriele Marcotti

"A powerful and moving account of one of football's forgotten heroes." – Anthony Clavane

THE
Blizzard

www.theblizzard.co.uk

90

Representations

"It was a peculiarly offensive smile
and I have not forgotten it."

Homes of Football

The photographer explains what led him to take football as his subject

By Stuart Clarke

People may think I take photographs of everything that moves; my work encapsulates quite a range of subjects under the umbrella of The Homes of Football. Curiously enquirers sometimes ask, "Do you actually like football?' as if I am using football – or perhaps it is using me.

In actual fact, as a photographer I am incredibly fussy; I edit all the time: leaving out is almost as important as putting in. In fact, when I look through the viewfinder (old-school camera) I'm saying "nonononononono…no no…nooo…" to almost everything within that frame. I'm saying, "It's not quite right."

Then eventually, perhaps 15 times in a day, but sometimes just the once, when there comes a moment when it is right, I say "yes". I click. I commit to film. A picture is made. I am decisive. The moment is decisive.

But not wishing to confuse, I am invariably decisive about moments which most people would not think worth being decisive about. Muddled messes of moments. Where a clarity can be sought if one looks for it. Mine is often a delving among the scrap of moment and darkness for something shiny, something beautiful.

When I photograph something there is invariably nothing really much happening, nothing newsworthy. No siege. No hostage taken.

And I like that.

I took this approach to football. A popular universal subject. Something I loved and yet felt peculiarly personal about.

In doing The Homes of Football, I have created my own fantasy league world of decisively taken in-between moments in which I am letting an audience look at each with as much interest as the historic and newsworthy. I am asking them to look away from the narrative commanding the back pages of the newspapers (and sometimes the front) to look at my in-between pages which when strung together take on a sort of narrative; a collection is forged by the association of all these rum, vaguely interesting moments.

Yet perhaps I am using a not particularly secret ingredient to get your interest…

A German writer recently looking on my 'British' body of work with a fresh eye as sometimes only a foreigner can possess, came to the conclusion that whatever I 'Clarke' photographs, there is a cut to the emotional centre of the subject. In essence, Clarke captures passion.

Passion is most evident when I get stuck into my crowd and peopled shots. Less obvious elsewhere: can one really claim a pair of rusting old dilapidated red gates at an entrance to a rusting old dilapidated football ground have "passion"?

...and yet this shot at Doncaster and its stable-mate at Barnsley have become my marquee, cover glam shots. Beauty is at the source of this passion and this emotion, however disguised by me or by convention.

Indeed there is a secondary match going on within what I do: convention versus not-convention. The one is defined by the other. Sibling rivals.

At the National Football Museum I watched Denise of the education department speak to a class of children with learning difficulties from Bolton. She had to be careful about what she included and what she left out. She tasked herself with dressing each of the 12 children in an item from the Museum memorabilia cache. If she left a couple of items over on the rack or left a couple of pupils with nothing to wear (however unbecoming the wear) it would be a source of distraction and confusion.

Denise chose items like rattles, ancient footballs, boots, to give the kids the chance to touch football in a simple and meaningful way. I was spellbound like a child myself at the beauty of the exchange.

For 25 years of approaching stadiums, crowds, matches, occasions, empty stadiums... in coming face-to-face with

people expecting to be photographed and people completely unaware of being photographed and unaware of the power they might portray as a photograph... I am playing a game of 50/50 with your imaginations.

50 is me. 50 is you. I present and you complete photography's magical spell. You pass over the void to share in the emotion, wallow in the moment, run your finger down the fabric, get acquainted with a piece of a football stand as though it's yours to inhabit. The passion and the beauty is yours; my photos say, "You may have overlooked this but you can get a hold of it, now. As I have done.

This is my currency.

From World Cup finals right down to park football... this is all my currency. I am shoulder-barging some other portraits of the game out of the way.

Tripping them up. Undoing their shoelaces and authority and wanting people to look at mine.

I am an exhibitionist, for football. With missionary zeal.

When I look at football – and beyond football, at random stuff in the street or on the TV or in magazines, I could make do without nine tenths of it. Wanting me to handle it, to take a look at it. To buy it. To photograph it.

Actually, I was just being kind, it's more like 999 out of 1000 things that I do not want to seep into me. Contaminate my brain and soul. Heaven forbid: I could end up reprocessing it and serving it up to you as if I am endorsing it. Perish the thought.

Most of everything visual around us we do not need and might be better off without. Emotional clutter.

All the time I'm fighting the churn of 24-hour news, going up the wall screaming, "No no no no no no no," and not seeing a single "Yes" in any of its content. It's a form of hypnosis, porn dressed up as football reporting.

To arms. I get out my camera and try to present my fantasy, my football. I do so competitively so that no one else occupies football's no-man's land, football's vacuum, quite like I do. I want to be a player. A host. There aren't many people having shows and presenting books like I do. Channel 'Clarke' is on air.

I do so to fill the vacuum in my own life created by me saying no to almost everything that doesn't involve a beautiful football.

Thank you for the ball. Sad me... my life is a bit empty when without a ball.

We built a full-sized goal in my back garden when I was seven. Dad built it from found planks of wood, went to the garden centre and bought the netting. He was on the committee of the Berkhamsted Dynamos Junior Football Club. A dad to two of the team.

Dad's dad before him had represented Berkhamsted's senior first team before the First World War and then gone on to create his own team, named after the house he had built, fielding his three eldest sons. His fourth son, 'Dad', my

Dad, was left out for being too young and had instead to mind the back-garden tennis court.

Dad's chance return to football came later. Here he was now building my brother and me a pitch of our own in the back garden. Here he was getting ahead of the neighbours: their kids would all come to us to play. What a host. In 1970 Dad got the first colour TV in the neighbourhood. Come Cup Final Day our house then garden was rammed with kids and dads. Had he not done any of this someone else surely would have. Again, what a host.

Quite a lot of the Dynamos supported Watford but some supported Arsenal and all of them had football at school, five days a week. Except me. I had rugby, fives and Latin homework. I had a school-imposed curfew which meant I couldn't roam the streets after 7pm, even though I lived at home with my family.

Even when the circus came to town I wasn't allowed to go, for in the eyes of the school it would distract. I thought of dressing up as a clown. I worked away at making Watford mine ahead of what Watford might be more easily to the others who could just pop along to Vicarage Road without getting caned. I drew monumental authoritative pictures of the stands and the stadium and then the players. I drew Graham Taylor.

Taylor was unveiled aside my Dad at the Junior Football League End of Season Presentation Night – the new Watford manager. Polite applause. No one in Hertfordshire had seen him before. He was the guest of my dad, the chairman of the League. He sat at our table and inbetween the dishing out of medals and awards he turned to me and my brother, aged 14 and 16, and asked us to jot down our preferred Watford XI, then quizzed us – while signing autographs for boys who hadn't a clue who he was – why we had and hadn't chosen so and so in the XI.

We both made Roger Joslyn captain. We argued passionately to Taylor that 'Jos' always tries, sets an example. (Indeed Roger went on to lead Watford to two promotions in Taylor's first two seasons).

The pictures I drew of Graham Taylor were shown about the club and he subsequently commissioned me to draw some more. Then, Bertie Mee, the former Arsenal manager, at the time vice chairman at Watford, commissioned me to do some of him.

I was paid in tickets and yet more tickets for matches. But I was in for a caning. I simply had to bunk off rugby and fives to get to these matches... and had to dodge the bullets on Monday at school: why I had been absent on Saturday afternoon? How many colds or sicknesses can a boy suddenly get?

When eventually I left school, for good, crayons traded in for cameras, it would be 10 more years before I discovered that my love of Watford could be expanded to include the entire professional football landscape.

I began The Homes of Football.

It's an imperfect storm that brings most things to bear. The Homes of Football began after a visit, a commission, to Liverpool and Glasgow in the same

weekend. I was sent to both by *Time Out 20 20* magazine.

In Glasgow, following the footsteps of the pop group Wet Wet Wet, I realised that in growing up, character traits of each member of the four-piece was shaped by the football clubs down the road and across the nearby water. By peer pressure. In all honesty I felt that in my own growing up I had a choice to support this or that football team – and I chose Watford (with a short flirtation with Chelsea along the way).

In fact I had the choice whether I wanted to support football at all. With the Wets, growing up in Clydebank, its industries dead or in decline, you had to have a football team. It was ingrained in you. It was every other sentence. A way to get through, a way to get battered – in itself part of the code to get through.

I returned from that wet weekend thinking I had to use football as the anchor to an identity-based long-term project. The Homes of Football.

There had also and more importantly been the Hillsborough disaster and I saw 1989 as a coming of age time to tackle the wider implications of that catastrophe – who we were as a nation that we could have that happen?

Four years earlier in the Lake District, seemingly far away from the football, I had been cleaning out the fireplace of the hotel where I was working, when the owner, flicking through the channels on the TV, paused on live coverage of the Bradford fire, learnt of casualties, tutted, flicked channels. With utter disregard. Puffing on a cigar.

I knew then that a flame inside me was lit for this mere game of football.

Not long before that, a vast illuminating light had been turned on as regards football in the neighbourhood. I used to go to Sunderland and stay in a terraced house in Roker rented by some nurses. I walked the streets. Photographing. Anything. One winter's evening in 1984, an almighty Close Encounters spaceship volume of light invaded the bathroom, almost pinning me to the wall, relieving me of my aim.

The floodlights were on at Roker Park across the road!

To prize open the rusty terrace window a mere inch doubled, tripled the Roker roar. Again I was pinned back, put in my place.

But the seeds to The Homes of Football were sown before we had the goals in the garden. Back home. Home being important. In the 1960s we had 'London Children' come to stay, kids who had never seen a field of grass. Around 1967 Joseph arrived at the station with a priest. My mum asked, "Where's your things Joseph?" The priest grimaced, shook his head. Joseph had the T-shirt and shorts he stood up in.

But in the days that followed I learnt that he also had "his Chelsea". Joseph's Chelsea, my mum would say. Some time after he went, I started wearing a blue Chelsea bobble hat and shorts and socks, in bed, even though our family was Watford. I had learnt empathy, aged seven, crucial for the photography career I would pursue. **B**

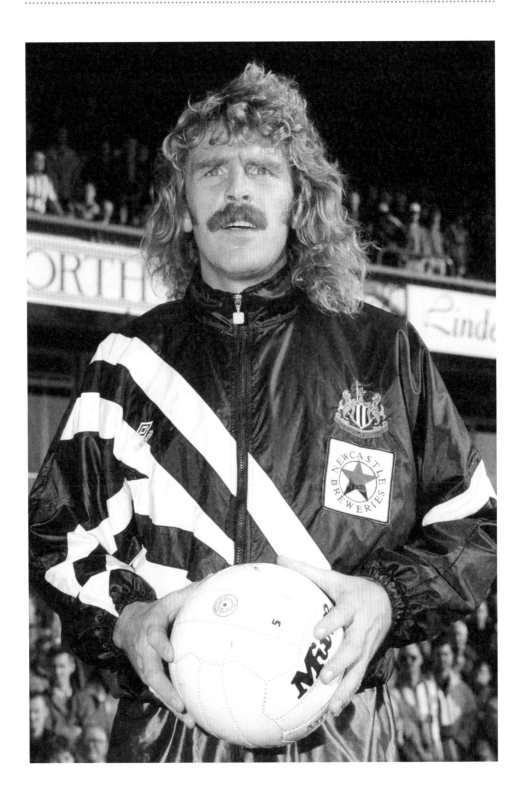

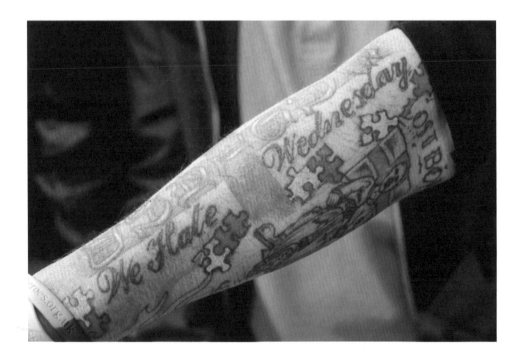

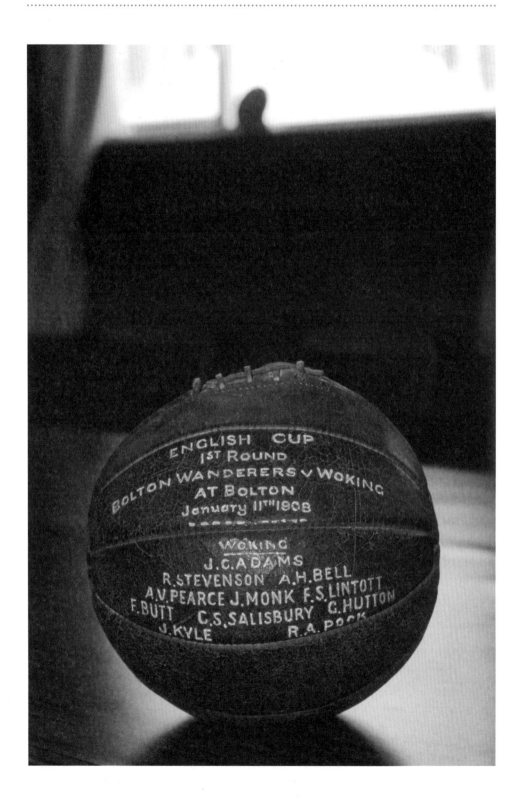

Reel of Fortune

The early days of cinema and the struggle to portray football on screen

By John Harding

"Some say that professional football is a very dull subject about which to write. But that is all a point of view; the national sport of any country must have a wonderful human interest and if there was not something inspiriting and stimulating about Big Football the great sporting public would not throng in their countless thousands to the matches every Saturday." **Sydney Horler (1922)**

"I have proved from experience that the people who go in their millions to football matches are not willing to spend money on buying books dealing with their favourite sport." Sydney Horler (1933)

Very little by way of significant fiction either in print, on stage or on screen has been produced involving Association Football since professionalism was introduced in the mid-1880s. Why this is so, when US (or US-dominated) sports such as baseball, basketball, American football and boxing have inspired such a rich harvest of novels and films remains a mystery.

It's been mooted that because most of the fiction produced in this country before 1945 was by middle-class writers, the latter might have considered the working-class world of professional football unworthy of their serious attention. It's certainly the case that before the First World War the game was the preserve of schoolboy fiction writers in magazines such as *The Boy's Own Paper, Chums, The Boy's Friend* and *The Boys' Realm*.

Early silent films such as *Harry the Footballer* (1911), *The Cup Final Mystery* (1914), and *A Footballer's Honour* (1914) were also simple affairs sharing the same basic plot: the hero is kidnapped prior to a big game, is rescued by his girlfriend and arrives in time to score the winning goal.

On stage, football was the subject of knock-about fun, most notably in Fred Karno's *The Football Match* starring Harry Weldon as the drunk and incompetent Stiffy the Goalkeeper.[1]

In print, only Arnold Bennett in *The Card* (1910) could be said to have dealt with the professional game in any detail, although his use of football is humorous, even satirical and not central to the plot. Horse racing could boast the prolific Nat Gould (1857-1919) with his gripping and entertaining tales of the turf, while cricket

---

[1] *For more on Stiffy, see John Harding's piece in* The Blizzard, *Issue Seven.*

remained beloved of classic authors such as Archibald Macdonell, Anthony Trollope and Thomas Hughes.

In the 1920s, however, the football industry itself underwent significant changes. New grounds were constructed to accommodate the millions flocking to watch a rejuvenated national sport while attractive sporting journals fed an ever-increasing appetite for football news, gossip and photographs. The prejudice against professionalism that had dogged the game since the 1880s faded to some extent as the Jazz Age got into its stride and individual professional footballers became celebrities on a par with actors and stage performers.

It was at this point that two quite different writers, Harold Brighouse and Sydney Horler, chose to utilise the game's gathering appeal to produce football stories aimed squarely at adults, stories that would swiftly be transformed into the game's first full-length feature films. Examining the fate of their endeavours might provide an alternative explanation to that of simple class-prejudice for the failure of football fiction to attract a mass mature audience.

Harold Brighouse was born in Eccles in 1882 and was educated at Manchester Grammar School before becoming a textile buyer in a shipping merchant's office. He produced his first play in 1909 for the Gaiety Theatre in Manchester and became a full-time writer of drama, fiction and journalism. His major success came early in his career with his play *Hobson's Choice* in 1915, written while he was working for the Air Ministry producing propaganda pieces for the nascent air force.

Brighouse wrote plays that often had a Lancashire setting and became associated with what was called the Manchester School along with his friend Stanley Houghton, whose great dramatic success was *Hindle's Wake*. They both wrote about the daily lives of ordinary Lancashire people, not always in a flattering way. Nevertheless, Brighouse rejected the idea that the overriding theme of the School's work was grey and gloomy, like the Manchester weather. Instead, he and Houghton were writing "human comedies"and Brighouse's *The Game*, written in 1914, would fall squarely into that genre. "[It] is...aimed at making people laugh,"he said in an introduction to its eventual publication in 1920.

The Game's story line is a straightforward one. A star professional centre-forward for Blackton Rovers FC, Jack Wetherall, is placed in an invidious position when his club's chairman first sells him to a powerful rival, Birchester United, and then immediately attempts to entice him into throwing a crucial match between the two teams that would ensure the survival of his former club. The matter is complicated by the fact that Wetherall is about to marry the same chairman's daughter – against the wishes of his own mother. He refuses to be bribed, even when it is made clear that permission to marry said daughter is dependent on his acquiescence in the crooked arrangement. During the crucial game, however, he breaks his arm and has to leave the field. With Blackton leading, it appears to many that the injury has been contrived and that he is indeed throwing the game, despite his earlier refusal. Indignant, he forces his way back onto the pitch and heads the winner for Birchester. The final act sees his mother relentingly agreeing to the marriage and all ends happily.

The play was performed briefly in Liverpool in 1914 but the onset of war spelled an end to theatre-land for its duration. In 1920, however, on the back of his worldwide success with *Hobson's Choice*, Brighouse re-worked *The Game* for a London premiere prior to a nationwide tour. Simultaneously, a prestigious British film company was busy turning it into a major feature film but the film would eclipse the stage version in certain crucial respects.

When *The Game* opened at the King's Theatre, Hammersmith in September 1920, the reviews were lukewarm. The *Manchester Guardian* found the acting "curiously amateurish" while "the dialect spoken on the stage has no local habitation". The principal problem for a number of critics, however, was the central character, Jack Wetherall.

Brighouse had created an "erudite professional footballer" who wanted to improve his mind by reading classics such as Ruskin, Carlyle, Browning and even Plato. His fiancée, on the other hand, being an educated middle-class girl, eschewed such effete strivings, insisting that the excitement of football was more to her taste. Why, she asks him, do you want to waste your time on such boring subjects as literature and philosophy when you have the thrills and spills of professional football to enjoy? It's an interesting clash of the classes with the heroine having the majority of the good lines, but Jack ultimately comes across as something of a mother's boy, a lion on the football pitch but a lamb when it comes to making love to a

high-spirited, liberated young twenties flapper. Set in the context of what the *Observer* saw as a traditional melodrama, this complicated tug-of-love seemed out of place. *The Stage* reviewer concluded that, while there was much to please the average playgoer, "those who go with memories of *Hobson's Choice* will feel a twinge of disappointment."

As the curtain fell in Hammersmith and *The Game* set out on its tour of regional theatres, less than a mile away in his Richmond studios the film-maker George Berthold Samuelson was busy putting the finishes touches to his celluloid version. It was to be a "Samuelson Super Production", clearly designed to exploit football's burgeoning popularity.

Samuelson was a pioneer of the British film industry and his version of Brighouse's play would be one of a number of sporting movies his company would make in the early 1920s. Without the finances to employ top film stars, Samuelson relied on a regular group of players when casting for the film. These included the strikingly attractive Maudie Dunham to play the girlfriend along with the experienced actors Haidee Wright as the disapproving mother and Tom Reynolds as the player's uncle. Where the question of Brighouse's incongruous thinking footballer Jack Wetherall was concerned, however, Samuelson made an astute move by selecting a prominent professional player called Harold Walden for the role.

Walden was no ordinary footballer. Born in India where his father was serving with the Cheshire regiment of the British Army, he lied about his age in order to enlist in his father's former regiment when he was only 14 years old. Upon leaving the army he was signed by Bradford City but under FA rules he was not allowed to turn professional for 12 months. He was thus free to play as an amateur for the Great Britain team at the 1912 Olympics where he scored six goals in one match and a total of eleven in the tournament, establishing a British Olympic scoring record which remains unbeaten. After further army service in the First World War he briefly joined Arsenal before returning to Bradford where he ended his playing career. By then he'd started a new life on the music hall stage as a variety performer. He developed an act called "The Anaemic Footballer" in which he came on stage sporting a kiss curl above a pallid white face wearing the claret and amber shirt of Bradford City and carrying a small football. His outsize long shorts were worn at half-mast and his football boots looked much too big for him. He would launch into some simple comic patter before singing one of the musical pieces he'd created for the ukulele, such as "Only Me Knows Why," which became his signature tune.

When the film was released, Walden turned out to be the star-turn. Although the *Bioscope* claimed that, "Mr Harold Walden scores more by his prowess on the field than by his histrionic talents," everyone else felt that he was perfect for the part. Walden was helped by the fact that, it being a silent film, he wasn't burdened with the task of delivering lines or adopting any sort of accent. The *Kinematograph Weekly* commented, "Harold Walden makes a quite unusual hero – a nervous young man who allows himself to be made

love to – but his performance suits the part," and the *Times* critic agreed: "The part of the footballer hero is very well played by an heroic footballer, Mr Harold Walden, and this idea of employing somebody who really knows something of the kind of part he is called upon to play seems worthy of encouragement provided, of course, that he knows how to act as well."

The change of emphasis from the stage play was even more obvious in the re-titling: *The Game* became *The Winning Goal* as the focus switched from the confines of the theatre to the open spaces of the football arena. For the film's climactic football match, directed by Samuelson using a megaphone from the centre of Brentford's Griffin Park ground, the company employed no fewer than 22 top-class professional players. These included seven of that season's title-winning West Bromwich Albion team, including the League's top-scorer Fred Morris; two from the seasons's FA Cup winners Tottenham Hotspur, plus the popular international stars Dickie Bond, Sam Hardy, Alf Quantrill, Frank Barson, Harry Hampton and Ted Vizard. The Chelsea and England centre-forward Jack Cock also starred. Owing to his good looks and tenor voice, Cock had already appeared on the music-hall stage many times; in fact, during his playing days, he was known for singing as he entered the pitch, a device that appealed to many female admirers in the stands.

By and large the film appears to have been a success. "Brilliantly cinematographed," said the *Biograph* while the *Times* enthused, "The football match is unusually well done and the employment of professional players who know their business has meant the absence of stupid details which make some football films impossible. "It was, "a real football match on a real football ground with a real football crowd and real football teams." By contrast, however, the *Burnley News* critic dismissed the football scenes as "necessarily farcical".

It's hard to assess its overall quality as no copies remain but Samuelson was not noted for subtlety. In fact, his cinematic style was already considered out-of-date and his fondness for spectacle was regularly undermined by cost-cutting and poor technique. Although the *Kinematograph Weekly* declared it, "a winner without any doubt", the same critic still felt that the film lacked "visual appeal" and that the climax was marred by "the irritating intrusion of close-ups". Brighouse himself was certainly not impressed, restricting himself to the simple comment in his biography that Samuelson's creation had been "workmanlike".

Brighouse once said that he was more interested in "the investigation of character"rather than "the unfolding of a story". In *The Game* he had afforded the professional footballer his debut as an acceptable dramatic hero: Jack Wetherall was a flawed individual with aspirations beyond the field of play and preyed upon by others whose demands conflicted with those aspirations. His determination to "play the game" and resist the temptations offered (winning the girl and saving his old club) arose from a sense of his own integrity as a professional player. Ironically, however, Brighouse discovered that the character had to be played by a *real* professional in order for it to be successful.

By coincidence, in this same year of 1920 a very different writer was trying his luck with the same subject, only this time in prose. Sydney Horler's *Goal!* was published with little fanfare by the newly-formed Odhams Press as part of their Popular Library series which comprised cheap hard-backs aimed squarely at adults. Other titles in the series included *Behind the German Lines, The Girl Who Stopped The War* and *White Snow: The Confessions of a Cocaine Taker By A Young Actress*. The reviewer for *John O London's Weekly* declared Horler's novel, "the first work of fiction entirely devoted to our great national pastime of football", adding, "I should not be surprised if football novels have a great vogue. It is significant that the film companies are already beginning to exploit the game to some purpose."

Horler was a 32-year-old London-born journalist who'd spent the years after leaving school at 14 working on a variety of publications ranging from the *Bristol Evening News* to the boys' magazine *The Captain*. By a twist of fate, he'd also found himself during the First World War working in the same Air Ministry department in London as Harold Brighouse but had spent his time sorting out photographs rather than writing propaganda.

His first piece of adult sporting fiction written in 1919 was based on tennis. It appeared in the *Strand Magazine* and led to an offer from the *News of the World* to write one based on boxing. However, being married by this time and with no job, he needed to find steady work. Horler later wrote, "At that time I was casting around in my mind for a regular source of fiction material. I hadn't seen a professional football match since my school days but Lady Luck now led me to the ground of a professional football club once again [to Craven Cottage to watch Fulham play Bristol City]. Directly I saw the scarlet jerseys of the team whose fortunes I had so passionately followed as a youngster something like 20 years slipped away from my shoulders as I became a schoolboy again. Then came the inspiration: no-one, apart from boys' comic writers, had ever turned England's greatest national sport, professional football, into fiction. So I resolved to have a shot at the thing myself..."

In fact, Horler had already contributed football stories to those same boys' comic papers. In 1919 he'd written a six-part serial for *Chums* entitled "The Ginger Genius", followed in November the same year by another serial for *The Boys' Realm* called "The Lightning Left" featuring a player called Rex Hartley. What he was now trying to do was lift the juvenile football narrative onto an adult plane.

His literary inspiration was a US short-story writer called Charles E van Loan who in the immediate pre-First World War days had perfected a formula that was to make his fortune. Writing mainly about baseball, he created fiction using a combination of insider information, humour and intrigue. His central character, Buck Parvin, would become a national institution. Horler, while readily admitting that he did not possess a fraction of Loan's abilities, hoped to follow suit. He wrote, "I imagined I could get some of the humorous angles and human interest twists [from soccer] which my mentor had turned to such wonderful use in writing about baseball."

Unfortunately, humour (of the intentional sort, at least) was one of those literary qualities Horler did not possess. When Horler obtained a contract to supply the *Burnley Express* with a series of football stories in 1922, the newspaper adverts described Horler as, "The Nat Gould of Football," and he would soon emulate Gould where sales and productivity were concerned.

Goal! was written in lodgings in Weston-super-Mare in February 1920 and its plot establishes a template that Horler would stretch and manipulate many times in subsequent novels before it finally came apart at the fictional seams.

The hero Richard Marr, a penniless son of a once wealthy man, meets Johnny Bell, an old international who'd trained him when Marr was playing centre-forward for the Oxford University team. Bell suggests Marr takes up playing football for a living, so he signs on for lowly Hollywood Football Club, who are in debt to a shady businessman called Fairfax Stopford. The latter is only funding the club in the expectation that Margery Kirkby, a pretty young supporter, will marry him. When he realises that Margery and Marr are becoming amorously connected, Stopford threatens to bankrupt the club by calling in his loans but the club's supporters rally round and pay off the debts. The team, with Marr now starring as centre-forward, then embarks on a Cup run during which Marr defies the opposition of Margery's guardian to him as a suitable husband for her while simultaneously thwarting Stopford's underhand efforts to prevent him from playing in the final. Hollywood win the Cup, Marr gets the girl and Stopford goes to prison.

Horler recalled that Odhams had been "wildly enthusiastic about its chances" but although it brought him a tremendous amount of publicity and paved the way for innumerable magazine stories, the book did not sell as readily as he had hoped.

Nevertheless, Horler's football fiction continued and over the six years that followed he produced six novels including *The Legend of the League*, *Life's a Game*, *Love, the Sportsman*, *McPhee, a Football Story* and *The Ball of Fortune* all of which would be serialised in the *News of the World*. He also penned several syndicated short stories, wrote a football column for the *Daily Mail* and worked on two film adaptations, all devoted to what he called "Big Football" – i.e. the burgeoning professional game.

Despite his professional and personal interest in football, however, Horler struggled to develop storylines that more than scratched its surface. Instead, he introduced ever-more outlandish incidents in order to intrigue the reader, a technique designed specifically for newspaper serialisation where the reader must be hooked from one week to the next.

A comparison between *Goal!* and two of his football novels that followed soon afterwards will demonstrate the point. In *Goal!*, the only aggravation comes when the hero is knocked out by paid thugs in an attempt to prevent him playing in the final. Two years on, the hero of *The Legend of the League* is knocked out twice, once on the pitch, a second time in the course of being kidnapped. His love-interest is also kidnapped and

threatened with sexual assault and being sold as a white slave while the villain is finally tied to a chair and flogged. There is also an attempt to fix a match by bribing the keeper of the hero's team. A year later in *The Ball of Fortune*, the hero is knocked out twice, pricked with a hypodermic needle (twice if one counts a suspicious nail in his football boot) drugged, kidnapped and chloroformed, while his friend is also kidnapped and almost executed by hanging before being saved. Add in the fact that the heroine's father is being blackmailed by a "good-time girl" known as 'Cocaine Connie' and it's obvious that football is becoming secondary to more sensational themes.

It would be *The Ball of Fortune*, however, that would be turned into a full-length feature film in 1926. Made for Booth Grange's Mercury Film Service production company in Leeds, the action sequences featured the full Leeds United team plus their trainer and were shot at United's Elland Road ground. Even one of the club's directors had a minor role.

The story-line runs as follows. A penniless amateur footballer, Dick Huish, finds himself forced to turn professional when his legacy is squandered by his scheming relatives, the Brighursts. His cousin Daniel Brighurst has designs on Dick's sweetheart, Mary Wayne, who happens to be the daughter of the chairman of Dick's new club. The Brighursts subsequently try various ways of eliminating Dick and also attempt to blackmail the chairman, but are foiled by a combination of Dick's determination to find out the truth concerning his father's lost fortune and the sleuthing of a local lawyer who befriends Dick. The *Yorkshire Post* reviewer summed up the denouement: "There are half a hundred other complications but in the end the hero not only saves his team from relegation to the Second Division by a brilliant bit of work on the field but also comes into his own."

The cast was by no means second-rate. Mary Wayne was played by a petite blonde actress called Mabel Poulton who was well used to portraying feisty or mischievous characters. She would later star with Ivor Novello in the hit film *The Constant Nymph* and cause a stir by insuring her eyes for £30,000. Dick Huish was played by James Knight, who'd begun his stage career touring music halls as a wrestler. An all-round sportsman, he was a handsome and athletic-looking hero. John Longden, who played a heavy who tries to drug Dick, would subsequently feature in five films directed by Alfred Hitchcock, most notably as the male lead in *Blackmail* in 1929. Dorothy Boyd played Cocaine Connie, "a girl who belonged to that growing army who have surrendered their souls to the drug fiend." She would also be cast by Hitchcock in his feature *Easy Virtue* (1928). Nevertheless, just as with the film version of Brighouse's *The Game*, a real-life professional footballer who would turn out to be the *The Ball of Fortune's* star attraction.

Billy Meredith was the best-known footballer in Britain in the 1920s even though he'd begun his career in 1894. A star player for Manchester United and Manchester City before the First World War and a Wales international since the 1890s, Meredith was still playing in the early 1920s and almost reached a Wembley Cup Final in 1923 at the age of 49. Suspended for bribery in 1906, a

founder member of the Players Union in 1908, a peerless ball-player and the darling of cartoonist's everywhere with his trademark toothpick and bandy legs, Meredith was a living legend if ever there was one.

He had already featured in Horler's fiction in *The Legend of the League*, albeit thinly disguised as Billy Millington: "With one action he not only swept the ball forward, but brought it under control – here was ball pedipulation of the highest class – and with that loping run familiar to football audiences England-wide, blazed a trail to the corner flag...". He also features in the novel of *The Ball of Fortune* as Sam Toucher, an ageing wizard of the wing who is instrumental in providing the crosses for the hero Dick Huish to bang into the net.

Hugh Croise, the film director and a much respected cinema veteran, however, discarded the pretence for the celluloid version and Meredith played himself. As such he would be prominently featured on posters and in adverts. He was also on hand for the movie's trade showing at Manchester's Piccadilly Picture Theatre in May 1926 while an assortment of his memorabilia was displayed in the windows of the film's northern distributors. The resulting curious crowds caused an obstruction on the pavement when the display was unveiled, providing a tremendous publicity boost for the film that was trumpeted as, "a sensational football feature in six reels" and which was well-received up and down the country.

Croise appears to have captured the football action far more successfully than any previous director (the film's advertisements declared, "See Billy Meredith's Wonderful Touch-Line Runs"), certainly surpassing those featured in the film of Brighouse's play *The Winning Goal*. The *Yorkshire Evening Post* film critic commented, "How often have we laughed when we were not intended to laugh at the way supposedly British games were reproduced on the American films? Football has figured in these and now, almost for the first time, we have a really satisfactory football film. I am glad to learn that it is being booked with far more than the usual success all over the North of England. The one and only Billy Meredith takes a principal part."

Like Brighouse, Horler wasn't impressed by the film version of his story. In 1932 he wrote, "Two of my stories when seen on the flickering screen were almost, if not quite, the worst exhibitions of cinematographic art that has ever been inflicted on the public."In *The Ball of Fortune*, he commented, "the only decent piece of acting was accomplished by an amateur," while he considered Mabel Poulton" not my idea of a screen heroine".

Horler had harboured grand ambitions where the cinema was concerned. His American mentor Loan had overseen a series of wildly successful silent film comedy shorts while seven of Nat Gould's novels had been made into films between 1916 to 1920. Other contemporary novelists such as Edgar Wallace, Arnold Bennett and, significantly, Harold Brighouse, had been invited to Hollywood (the real one, not the fictional football club). Horler revealed in his autobiography in 1933: "Some years ago when I sat in the office of the scenario editor of British

International Pictures, he told me that they had been looking for some time for a football subject to hand over to their producer Hitchcock. 'What about my own stories?' I returned. He smiled. It was a peculiarly offensive smile and I have not forgotten it."

By then, however, Horler had all but abandoned football fiction as a genre. It was, he declared, "an unprofitable fictional subject." In 1927 the *News of the World* publisher Emsley Carr had suggested that he write a straightforward thriller, ditching the sporting context. He subsequently produced *The Mystery of Number One*, which was a great success. Henceforth, Horler would join the ranks of those million-selling low-brow authors such as Edgar Wallace, John Buchan, Sax Rohmer and Angela Brazil, all of whom dominated the bookshops and commercial lending libraries during the inter-war years.

His favourite fictional antagonists were no longer wicked club directors and scowling full-backs but fanatic Germans and Fu Manchu-type megalomaniacs, many of whom were given sobriquets such as 'the Disguiser', 'the Colossus', 'the Mutilator', 'the Master of Venom' and 'the Voice of Ice'. It was an impressive list that included mad scientists, American gangsters, vampires, giant apes, ape-men from Borneo, venal dwarfs, slavering 'Things', a man born with the head of a wolf and, perhaps his crowning achievement, a bloodsucking, man-eating bush.

Horler explained: "The vast wealth of action and excitement from which 'shockers' can be fashioned is limitless whereas in football such opportunities are soon exhausted."For someone who came to depend on ever more unlikely scenarios with which to keep his readers interested, one can see his point.

Horler was always honest about his achievements. Unlike Brighouse, he maintained that he wasn't interested in writing "psychological" novels. "Give me a pretty girl, a likeable young man, a Bentley car and a spot of trouble round the corner – then I'm working at my trade." It's hardly surprising, therefore, that he struggled to create a significant fictional football hero.

Over the years, the best he managed was an eccentric trainer called Angus McPhee, "an uncouth angular being with woollen gloves, an unbelievable hat and the general air of a non-conformist pastor", described by his publishers as the first real character in football fiction. However, McPhee was neither funny nor glamorous enough to be memorable and when Horler eventually came up with 'Tiger' Standish, a football-playing amateur sleuth, the stories in which he featured would contain little if any professional football. It was the real Billy Meredith, either thinly disguised or in person, who afforded Horler his biggest football fiction successes. Horler needed Billy Meredith just as Brighouse needed Jack Cock and Harold Walden for their work to capture a mass audience. And therein perhaps lies a clue as to why so few writers have utilised professional football as a setting.

The national game serves up, on a weekly basis, as much fantasy, drama, wish-fulfilment, startling coincidences, heroic failures and last-minute denouements as anyone seeking release

from the everyday world could possibly wish for. Fiction simply cannot match it. What's more, the serial saga that is professional football continues to be populated by an array of larger-than-life individuals whom writers of fiction have struggled for a century to match.

Brian Glanville, considered by many to be the best writer of football fiction since the Second World War, produced two novels featuring fictional players, the first being the centre-forward Gerry Logan in 1965, the second the goalkeeper Len Rawlings in 1976. Fine period pieces though they are, neither character registers today on either the literary or the football psyche.

Other notable writers in recent years have used the game in various ways. Barry Hines's *A Kestrel for a Knave* (1968), BS Johnson's *The Unfortunates* (1969), JL Carr's *How Steeple Sinderby Wanderers Won the FA Cup* (1975) and John King's *The Football Factory* (1996) are all excellent novels, but none of them deal directly with the game and none feature those who actually play it.

The outstanding success of David Peace's *The Damned United* (2006) underlines the point. The plot concerns a young, headstrong manager taking over a title-winning side from a legendary and much-loved predecessor but failing as the players reject his attempts to impose his purer version of the game on them and the club. This might not seem particularly inspiring but because it is squarely based on Brian Clough's calamitous few months as Leeds United's new manager, both football fans and those with little interest in the game bought the book in their hundreds of thousands. As modernist fiction, of course, Peace's book is much more than a simple retelling of the facts: it's a heightened version of reality, or as one critic put it, "a fusion of history and fiction creating a hypo-history, a story under the surface of the known."

Nevertheless, it's arguable that had Brian Clough been re-christened Billy Wilson and Leeds United re-titled Headingley Hotspurs, neither book nor film would have succeeded or even caught the imagination to the extent that they did.

In Ken Loach's film *Looking For Eric*, Éric Cantona plays himself as imagined by Eric Bishop, a long-suffering postman. The ever-enigmatic Cantona says at one point: "I am not a man: I am Cantona," a surreal example of how the professional footballer can assume mythical status. The football we watch and particularly the players we idolise are more than they appear to be. Whether dead or still living, they are the fantastic creations of our own imaginations and as such will continue to usurp the best efforts of writers as diverse as Sydney Horler, Harold Brighouse and Brian Glanville.

Scripted Drama

The long wait for football to be taken seriously as a literary subject

By Stephen O'Donnell (with Lee McGowan)

"The author of the best books written about English culture since the War..." reads the blurb on the cover of John King's landmark 1996 novel The Football Factory, a rampaging yarn about a gang of miscreant Chelsea supporters strutting their stuff around a succession of English cities and football stadiums and offering an uncompromising portrayal of the dark motivation of the archetypal English 'hoolifan'.

It's a bold assessment of a bold novel, offered by King's contemporary and fellow Jonathan Cape stablemate, the Scottish novelist Irvine Welsh. The *Trainspotting* author has himself occasionally wandered onto the football fiction turf, most notably in *Maribou Stork Nightmares*, in which the protagonist Roy Strang is assessed for his 'casual' credentials by a group of fellow Hibs supporters on a train to Motherwell. But King's book is explicitly set in a world which takes football and the environs of fandom as its main setting and it explores attendant issues with the kind of trenchantly opinioned voice that one is unlikely to find replicated in national newspapers or on Sky Sports News HQ. Welsh's comment is undoubtedly calculated to make the greatest impact for a debut author signed up by the same publisher, but even so – "the best books written about English culture since the

War"? We're talking about a football novel here. How did it ever come to this?

We're used in our culture to separating schoolboys at a very young age into one of two groups, sporty or academic. From then on, it seems, never the twain shall meet. It has certainly proved very difficult for these two apparent polar opposites to be subsequently reconciled in literary fiction. To be sure, football fiction in this country has a fairly dreadful reputation; even at the best of times publishers are extremely wary of the whole genre – if indeed an established genre can seriously be considered to exist at all – and these are by no means halcyon days for the publishing industry.

On novels about football Mark Jensen, co-owner of the largest sports bookshop in the world, The Back Page in Newcastle-upon-Tyne, is quoted as saying, "The only one people come in and ask for is *The Damned United*. I'm not sure whether football novels don't sell well because not many are published or whether not many are published because they don't sell well." The suggestion of an answer to that dilemma can be found in the recent demise of at least one specialist publisher.

In 2010, Know the Score Books, an established outlet, went out of business after becoming entangled in multiple legal cases against several of its own authors, whom they claimed owed them money. However, slow sales of sports books in an era of recession was the primary cause of their collapse. When I approached Simon Lowe, the company's MD, about my novel *Paradise Road*, he refused even to accept any sample chapters from the book. Football fiction doesn't sell, he told me, bookshops don't know which shelf to place it on. Is it fiction, is it sport? What about *The Damned United*? I countered. That was the exception which proved the rule, I was informed, and it could be explained in one word: Clough. Football fiction, it seemed, was dead on its feet.

Yet stories about football have been around as long as the game itself. In King Lear, Shakespeare has the Earl of Kent kicking Oswald and calling him a "base football player", but nevertheless, 400 years later, the number of serious titles that could be filed under the heading 'football fiction' would struggle to make up a bookshelf. This is of course in marked contrast to the plethora of non-fiction football books which are put out annually by a variety of publishers, the best of which readers of *The Blizzard* will be fairly familiar with. Many of these non-fiction titles would meet the scrutiny of the highest academic and journalistic standards, and given this, no matter how cerebral the concept of a literary novel about football might appear, the lack of fiction pertaining to the game would appear something of an anomaly.

Nick Hornby, who did much to make football writing acceptable to the literary elite with his memoir *Fever Pitch* (1992) has argued that there is enough

excitement in the real game already and therefore no need or appetite to produce fiction in this context. Larger-than-life characters and dramatic twists and turns are part of football's existing narrative, whereas any fictional scenario constructed around the kind of events which occur in sport on an almost weekly basis would no doubt stretch the bounds of credibility. It's certainly an interesting point; sport is unscripted drama – this is an important part of its enduring attraction – so in attempting to construct a plot around a game of football an author might be seen as undermining the sport's appeal and its essential nature. How often has a television commentator or analyst been heard uttering the cliché "you couldn't have scripted it" to describe a particularly dramatic conclusion to a game? As so often with clichés, they're only clichés because they are true.

In the sixties, the sports journalist Brian Glanville, author of such noted football titles as *Goalkeepers Are Different* and *The Rise of Gerry Logan*, noted that football was a working-class game and therefore unsuitable as a subject for treatment in a literary context. Whether or not the remark was true at the time, football since the sixties has changed almost beyond recognition, and society itself has changed perhaps to an even greater degree to the extent that although the observation seems crass 50 years after it was made, nevertheless it might not be too politically incorrect to concede that maybe Glanville had a point – or at least to acknowledge that it was perceived as being unsuitable for literary consideration. Up to that time if a young working-class lad wanted to read stories about football he would have little choice but to do so in the dubious literary forums of comic books and club almanacs.

I have to admit that, even as a young boy (who loved football, playing it, watching it, reading about it), I found the football comics of limited interest; to me they were puerile and jejune and in no way reflected my fascination with the game itself. *Roy of the Rovers* was first published in 1954 and it had the virtue of espousing what were seen at the time as the traditional British values of fair play, never-say-die spirit and strong moral character.

By the time of the Sky era, however, these values seemed absurdly quaint and *Roy*, after being transferred around a variety of different outlets, finally hung up his boots in 2001. Over the 40-plus years of publication the eponymous hero Roy Race went from teenage prodigy to player-manager (and ultimately owner, after the strip moved to *Match of the Day* magazine for a brief period in the late 90s), winning every conceivable trophy on the way – usually against the odds or after a highly improbable comeback – and even surviving a terrorist bomb in the Middle East, which killed half his teammates. Rovers has its devotees as well as its rivals and imitators, such as *Hotshot Hamish* and *Mighty Mouse*, both of which moved to the *Roy of the Rovers* comic in 1985. This form of football comic was mercilessly lampooned in Viz's *Billy the Fish*, an absurd strip about a goalkeeping fish with a human head, complete with mullet, who kept nets for Fulchester United (Roy, lest we forget, played for Melchester Rovers) and who floated in the air above his goal-line, while offering semi-useful advice to his teammates. The saying goes that imitation is the sincerest form of flattery, but I'm not sure if the same can be said of the spoof. Sadly or otherwise, the era of the football comic has come to an end.

Serious writing taking football as its main subject goes back to the Victorian era and its emergence can be traced back almost as far as the game itself. Before the First World War, journals and magazines such as *The Boy's Own Paper*, *Chums*, *The Boy's Friend* and *The Boys' Realm* told short-form tales, aimed at the public-school boys who had grown into those who had founded and codified the game in the relatively recent past and who were the game's early pioneers. The stories in these journals were fairly basic, with predictable and hackneyed plots; the hero is kidnapped before a big game, is rescued by his girlfriend and turns up just in time to score the winning goal. In 1910 Arnold Bennett decided to incorporate real-life professional players into his novel *The Card*, but his use of football in the novel is as a humorous aside, and not central to the plot. It would take the advent of the 1920s and the subsequent transformation and growth of the game in this period for football fiction to undergo its first serious development.

Football's popularity soared at this time as the game finally went mainstream and its transformation from upper-class pastime to the working man's ad hoc expression of local and cultural identity was complete. The old attitudes faded into the past, resistance to professionalism was finally ended and to accommodate the increased levels of attendance new stadiums were constructed, including Wembley, most of which were in use practically unaltered until the Hillsborough disaster, when the Taylor report finally rendered them obsolete. Between 1920 and the mid-fifties, paperback series such as the Aldine Football Novel (88 volumes) and Amalgamated Press' Football and Sports Library (564 volumes) fulfilled supporters' needs to read football stories. The transition to serious literary fiction proved difficult however.

As John Harding writes in this issue, the pulp novelist Sydney Horler wrote 20 football novels in the same period, but serious literature concerning football was rare. The English 20th-century novel has occasionally concerned itself with the plight of the agitated working class. In the 1950s this type of writing found its apex in the so-called 'angry young men' movement, led by the playwright John Osborne, whose *Look Back in Anger* became a seminal work in what later became known as the 'kitchen-sink drama', and the novelist Kingsley Amis, who achieved overnight success with his 1954 debut *Lucky Jim*.

These works represented a considerable advance, in a literary sense, from Horler and his contemporaries, and there were some attempts to incorporate football fiction into this era of post-War working-class self-expression. Alan Sillitoe is another name often associated with the literature of this period and his 1959 short story 'The Match', from the celebrated anthology *The Loneliness of the Long Distance Runner* is typical of the genre. Set in the Midlands, it offers a bleak critique of the socio-political conditions of the time, while the author tantalises the reader with some fine

prose descriptions of a live football match: "Suddenly the man with the ball spurted forward, was seen to be clear of everyone as if, in a second of time that hadn't existed to any other spectator or another player, he'd been catapulted into a hallowed untouchable area before the goal posts..." The story also made the link between football and domestic violence, the scar of many a derby match and a particular blight on the Old Firm game in Glasgow, as police statistics have shown. 'The Match' also hinted prophetically at a more general hooligan tendency, which was to become more prevalent in the game. Though short it stands as a high-water mark in football-related writing from this time.

Sadly, it doesn't have too many rivals. Noted exceptions are Robin Jenkins's *The Thistle and the Grail* (1954) and *The Hollow Ball* by Sam Hanna Bell (1961), both of which offer a profoundly philosophical critique of football's place in culture and society. Mention should also be made of the young adult fiction of Michael Hardcastle, but still, very few serious titles set in the world of football emerge from this era. Again this would appear anomalous, particularly when one considers that the US literary giants Richard Ford and John Updike were incorporating baseball and other sports into their work. And even rugby league produced a noted text when in 1960 former Leeds player David Storey penned *This Sporting Life*, which Peace has acknowledged provided the literary inspiration for *The Damned United*. Perhaps this is the greatest disappointment in the fragmented history of football fiction: that a period so apparently suitable for including treatment of such stories, ripe as it was with the kind of intellectual disillusionment which invariably produces so much great literature in other contexts, failed to offer anything more than a tantalising glimpse of what the imagined 'Great Football Novel' might look like. We can perhaps see this lack of football fiction emanating from the fifties and early sixties as the wider context for Glanville's assertion about the game being unsuitable for treatment in literary form.

And so we come down in the past three decades. King's novels (he followed up *The Football Factory* with two sequels, *Headhunters* and *England Away*) can be seen in the tradition of *The Match*, and indeed due regard is paid to Sillitoe in King's acknowledgements page. One of the main differences between the two writers is that there is little, if any, implied criticism of the protagonists' behaviour in King's work. The reader is compelled to accept his characters as they come and we can see this uncompromising approach as a reaction against the middle-class embracing of the game, which flourished post-Italia 90, post-*Fever Pitch*, and out of which the Sky era later grew. In a literary sense this is a very modern technique employed by King. The reader ultimately has to decide for himself about the characters' lifestyle choices, there is a noted absence of preaching in any sense and this lack of truth or moral certainty is a characteristic of what might be described as postmodern art in its various forms.

Other works to have followed the King model in treating the concerns of the post-Thatcherite English urban male include Kevin Sampson's *Awaydays* filmed in 2009, and Dougie Brimson's

The Crew (1999), which, along with his non-fiction work on hooligan culture, provided the inspiration for the movie *Green Street* (2005). Peace's novels are, by contrast, set in the world of football itself, rather than around the periphery of fandom, and despite the apparent temptation to wax lyrical about what Shankly might have made of the modern game for example, they do not offer much social criticism or cultural observation. Thus we might establish, despite the obvious difficulty in genre labelling with so few titles to consider, that modern football fiction can be separated into two categories: the Peace/King divide.

Peace takes us into the world of football itself and employs an imagined literary voice in the head of real characters (Clough, Shankly) operating around the margin of real events, which are often meticulously described and come complete with a raft of statistics concerning dates, goal scorers, attendances etc. Because he deals with real characters in real settings while still writing what is undeniably recognisable as fiction, it is hard to think of a purer voice in the entire history of this genre, and if one is asked to consider the apex of what modern football fiction represents, then Peace will surely be considered its archetype.

What King has done, however, is what the best writers of any age have attempted since Homer: he has investigated his own culture and offered a literary representation, which is based partially on his own experiences and developed using the full force of his creative imagination. Despite the obvious differences – Scottish/English, left-wing/

right-wing, Catholic/Protestant, Celtic/ Chelsea – I was aiming for something similar in my novel *Paradise Road*. It is the story of a rejected ex-footballer trying to make a living as a joiner and the book examines the role of young working-class men in a post-industrial landscape, where the manufacturing and heavy industries which used to sustain their communities have been almost completely replaced by the ever-expanding retail and service sectors.

How have these and other changes affected the traditional relationship between a working man and his football club? All the issues are there – sectarianism, declining standards in Scottish football, the power and role of the media – so we can see that by asking questions which affect modern football we are now considering some of the most important issues that society has to deal with as a whole. *Scotball*, my second novel, is different in that it is narrated by an English-teaching

university graduate, late of the financial services sector, and is set in the world of sports-related media. By changing the background of the narrators in this way, I hope to have covered a range of viewpoints in the two novels and portrayed a wider section of the community than would otherwise have been the case if the protagonists had both been from a similar upbringing.

Thus, hopefully, we have arrived at a situation where novels about football, regardless of what one thinks of their literary value, are undeniably at the cutting edge of literary fiction, because they portray and attempt to explain not just the narrow footballing context in which they are set but also the society in which modern football takes place and ultimately the world around us. They capture the zeitgeist and we see our cultural predicament reflected back at us through them. Perhaps this is what Irvine Welsh was alluding to, when he described *The Football Factory* in such gushing terms. Ⓑ

Blizzard Books

Johnny Cook: The Impossible Job

Iain Macintosh

124

Theory

"...a 105-day reign at Wimbledon
in which he banned jeans and
won one match."

Echoes in Eternity

Of all the great managers, which has been the most influential in inspiring future generations?

By Paul Simpson

Velvet Underground's status as one of the greatest rock groups ever rests securely on their trailblazing genius and the legend that every one of the 30,000 fans who bought their debut album, *The Velvet Underground & Nico*, launched their own band. It's a seductive idea, first suggested by Lou Reed in conversation with Brian Eno. Actually, the album sold around 50,000 copies in two years and, though it didn't inspire 50,000 new bands, the Velvets have been acknowledged as a seminal influence by the likes of Beck, David Bowie, Bryan Ferry, the Buzzcocks, Joy Division, Morrissey, Nirvana, Orange Juice, The Pretenders, REM, Jonathan Richman, Patti Smith, Sonic Youth, Talking Heads and U2.

So what has all this to do with football? Over lunch, the editor of *The Blizzard*, Jonathan Wilson, and I debated whether any football managers had been as inspirational. As Arsène Wenger has been managing for 30 years, why weren't more of his former players in the dugout? The examples that immediately sprang to mind were Tony Adams, whose managerial career fizzled out after underwhelming stints at Wycombe Wanderers, Portsmouth and the Azerbaijani club Gabala, and David Platt, whose very name still makes Nottingham Forest fans wince. For a manager nicknamed the Professor, Wenger didn't look to have galvanised many of his students.

Later, I brainstormed the point with Philippe Auclair — although, to be fair, Philippe's brain did most of the storming. Ferguson's record as managerial mentor begins with his first transfer. In 1974, as East Stirlingshire boss, he signed the 24-year-old inside-forward George Adams. After his knee gave out, Adams managed the Highland League team Fraserburgh before helping Ferguson develop the Aberdeen side that disrupted the Old Firm's duopoly of Scottish football in the 1980s. Arguably Adams's greatest success came when, as Ross County's director of football — with his son Derek as manager — he led the Staggies to the 2010 Scottish Cup final. (The Adamses left County last August).

Adams was the first of 41 names on Auclair's list. Some had achieved fame (Steve Bruce and Gordon Strachan), others infamy (Paul Ince and Clayton Blackmore, whose reign at Porthmadog lasted only four months in 2007), and many a bit of both (Roy Keane, Mark McGhee, Alex McLeish, Bryan Robson, Ole Gunnar Solskjær.)

Fergie's *enfants* span Europe — with Jordi Cruyff technical director at Maccabi Tel Aviv, Henning Berg coaching

Legia Warsaw, Laurent Blanc at Paris Saint-Germain and Andrei Kanchelskis managing Jurmala in Latvia.

Closer to home, Ferguson's players have managed, assisted or trained at 33 clubs in England, 13 in Scotland, three in Wales and one apiece in Northern Ireland and Ireland. At the time of writing, Strachan and McGhee manage Scotland, Keane coaches Ireland with Martin O'Neill and Gary Neville is part of Roy Hodgson's England coaching staff.

Five of Ferguson's 41 protégés have won league titles: Berg (Legia Warsaw), Blanc (PSG), McLeish (Rangers), Solskjaer (Molde) and Strachan (Celtic). A decent strike rate even if it's hard to know whether Blanc's successive Ligue 1 triumphs owe more to PSG's budget or Ferguson's inspirational example. Similar caveats must apply to McLeish and Strachan, as the Old Firm have, between them, won 99 out of 118 Scottish titles.

The process by which players move into the dugout is full of incongruities. Great players – Diego Maradona, Bobby Charlton and Hristo Stoichkov – often turn out not to be great managers, whereas inferior footballers – Ferguson, Jack Charlton and José Mourinho – flourish. One known unknown we must factor in is the randomness of personal choice. Widely tipped as a future Liverpool boss while winning three European Cups as an elegant central defender, Alan Hansen told me he never wanted to manage: "I looked at Kenny Dalglish and Bobby Robson, their passion for the game was an addiction, they couldn't live without it. I knew I never felt like that." Yet Hansen's view is no reflection on

Bob Paisley, who signed Hansen from Partick Thistle.

Before we delve deeper to see if any other manager can match Ferguson's record as mentor, it is necessary to add some historical context. When Ferguson moved into management in 1974, part-time at East Stirlingshire for £40 a week, the game was much less lucrative, broadcasters usually only supplied football punditry for special events (FA Cup finals, internationals, World Cups and so forth) and the principal career options for retiring footballers were: opening a sports shop, running a pub and becoming a manager.

The financial imperative to coach is less urgent today, when many players retire as multi-millionaires or join the lucrative pro-celebrity circuit that surrounds the game. British football was also much more parochial, less globalised, in the early 1970s. The route from player to manager was simpler – no need for those Uefa coaching badges.

So measuring how much of Wenger and Ferguson's impact as mentors reflects their personality, coaching style or inspirational quality – and how much is driven by the economic revolution that has transformed football since the 1970s – is hardly straightforward.

Wenger could well have influenced more *enfants* if he had stayed in France, where his approach is still admired, and not moved to England, where the rosy glow from his scientific revolution at Arsenal in the late 1990s has faded somewhat. Ferguson's style – or the media portrayal of him as a ruthless, crockery-breaking, hairdryer-treating autocrat – seemed a more natural fit for British managerial mores and a football industry so steeped in the past that players still call managers "gaffer", a term for a factory foreman in Victorian times.

It's also true that some clubs simply have more clout than others. As the FA's serial evasions during Ferguson's reign attest, Manchester United are the most powerful club in England. Any player with United on his CV can be reasonably confident of becoming a coach. The same principle applies in the Netherlands and Spain where the massed ranks of Johan Cruyff's players who became managers owes an unquantifiable something to the superpower status of Ajax and Barcelona.

Deciding who influenced whom can be tortuous. Ferguson's most influential mentor was Jock Stein, who once tried to buy him but never managed him. Although Pep Guardiola was coached by Fabio Capello, José Antonio Camacho, Javier Clemente and Cruyff, the mentor he hails as "my maestro" is Juan Manuel Lillo[1] , for whom he played for six months at the Mexican club Dorados de Sinaloa in 2006.

With such caveats in mind, how does Wenger's record compare to Ferguson's? Of the 200 or so players the Frenchman has used at Arsenal – many of them still playing at some level – 22 have become directors, coaches, assistants and trainers. Yet the only one presently managing a league club is Fabián Caballero, the Argentinian striker who made three

appearances for the Gunners in 1998-99 and coached Deportivo Recoleta in Paraguay's fourth tier before stepping down late last year.

Apart from that, there are a few assistants (Steve Bould, Arsenal; Dennis Bergkamp, Ajax; Giovanni van Bronckhorst, Feyenoord; Scott Marshall, Aston Villa; Sylvinho, Corinthians) sporting directors (Marc Overmars, Ajax; Edu, Corinthians), the Manchester City reserve team boss Patrick Vieira, the Latvia Under-17 team coach Igor Stepanovs and Ömer Riza, player-manager of the Isthmian League Division One North side Cheshunt. And then there's Rémi Garde, who won the French Cup with Olympique Lyonnais in 2012, and is enjoying a well-earned break after three years of trying to reconcile finite budgets and infinite expectations at Lyon.

This odd list doesn't tell the whole story. Some of Wenger's *enfants* have been unlucky or daft. Once a defensive coach at Blackburn, Nigel Winterburn was collateral damage as Paul Ince's managerial career imploded. Two of Wenger's *enfants* from Monaco were just as unfortunate: Sonny Anderson's reign as coach of the Swiss club Neuchâtel Xamax, then owned by a Chechen oligarch, lasted two games in 2011. Enzo Scifo managed the Belgian club RE Mouscron, which went bust in 2009. The promising coaching career of the former Arsenal defender Nelson Vivas ended abruptly in October 2013: he quit as manager of the Argentinian club Quilmes after running into the stands and punching a vocal fan three times.

---

[1] *For more on Lillo, see Sid Lowe's interview with him in Issue One of* The Blizzard.

At Monaco, Wenger did inspire some trophy winners. The defensive midfielder Claude Puel was Wenger's manager on the pitch then. Now coaching Nice, Puel won Ligue 1 with Monaco in 2000 and 10 years later led Lyon to the semi-finals of the Champions League for the first time in their history. The low point of Rámon Díaz's CV is an unpaid stint as Oxford United boss in 2004-05, but the former Monaco striker has won six league titles and the 1996 Copa Libertadores as River Plate boss.

Wenger's other notable protégés from Monaco are Glenn Hoddle, a half-decent England manager who also helped transform Chelsea from flashy underachievers to perennial contenders for honours, and Jürgen Klinsmann, who has reached the last four of the World Cup with Germany and the last 16 with the USA. The "very technical and fast-paced game" (Klinsmann's words) played by Wenger's Monaco obviously influenced his Germany side. Eight of the players managed by Wenger at Nancy between 1984 and 1987 became coaches but only the defender Albert Cartier, now in charge of Metz, has enjoyed an enduring, successful career.

So in this heavyweight contest between Ferguson and Wenger, the Scot still has the edge, but how do they compare with other coaches?

A painstaking plotting of the *enfants* of Europe's managerial greats suggests that Ferguson's record stands alone in England. He certainly inspired more players to greater effect than Don Revie. None of Revie's protégés won a league title as manager, although Jack Charlton did steer Ireland to four successive qualifications for major tournaments and the last eight of the 1990 World Cup.

Big Jack owed his start, at Middlesbrough in 1973, to Revie's example. Invited for an interview, he handed the panel a list of a manager's responsibilities drafted by his old boss and left the room, giving them 25 minutes to make up their minds.

Charlton's managerial ruthlessness – urban legend suggested, erroneously, that he used his dogs to keep players in line – is often attributed to his former boss but he was also, in Revie's words, a "one-man awkward squad". Charlton was no Revie clone: his tactics as Ireland boss were, he insisted, "influenced by watching Northampton Town when they won the Second Division" in 1966. For all his tough guy image at centre-half, Charlton never really subscribed to the Peckinpahesque "if they move, kill 'em" streak in Leeds's play under Revie. His teams were combative, but not brutal.

Leeds United's post-Revie history suggests that the mechanism by which managers pass on their magic to their players is deeply unpredictable. Between 1980 and 1988, four Revie greats – Allan Clarke, Eddie Gray, Billy Bremner and Norman Hunter – managed Leeds to little effect. Yet some club chairmen remain impervious to such disappointments. In 2006, the Sheffield Wednesday chairman Dave Allen hired Brian Laws as manager, saying, "I like him, he comes from the Clough camp. I'm a great admirer of the Clough camp." Although Laws played at right-back for five years for Clough at Forest, such service didn't stop Wednesday firing him within three years.

As manager of Hartlepool United, Derby County and Forest, Old Big 'Ead inspired a legion of players to coach. Not all were successful – Gary Megson's nickname as a player, 'Suitcase', also encapsulates his managerial career and Peter Withe is best remembered for a 105-day reign at Wimbledon in which he banned jeans and won one match – but Richie Barker (an African Champions League winner with Zamalek in 2006), Frank Clark, Alan Durban, Trevor Francis, Paul Hart, Roy Keane, Roy McFarland, Stuart Pearce and Colin Todd have all enjoyed respectable careers. Sean Dyche, who spent a year with Clough but never played for him, has led Burnley into the Premier League, possibly making him less of a 'ginger Mourinho' and more of a 'ginger Clough'.

The most successful members of Clough's camp are Martin O'Neill (who won two League Cups with Leicester and three league titles with Celtic, whom he led to the 2003 Uefa Cup final) and, ironically, Dave Mackay, who succeeded Clough at Derby in 1973, winning the league in his first full season.

As indebted as O'Neill is to Clough, he had a rambunctious relationship with his mentor. As Tony Balfe, the Grantham Town chairman who made O'Neill manager in 1987, said, "Martin seemed to believe that no matter what he did, Cloughie would find fault with it." O'Neill's nickname at Forest – 'The Squire' – reflected Clough's suspicion that the player was, Balfe said, a "bit of a smart arse".

One of Clough's favourite Forest players and O'Neill's assistant at Wycombe, Norwich, Leicester, Celtic and Aston Villa, John Robertson felt the two

managers shared "an innate ability to get players to want to play for him", a willingness to dish out bollockings when necessary, a philosophy of how football should be played and a gift for simplifying the game's complexities. Yet, in his autobiography, Robertson noted, "I genuinely don't think there was any considered attempt by Martin to manufacture that likeness."

As populous as Clough's camp is, they haven't won as much silverware as the heirs of Bill Shankly and Bob Paisley. The most notable recruits in the Red army of coaches are Kenny Dalglish (one of only four managers to win the English league title with two clubs: Liverpool and Blackburn), Kevin Keegan, white-shoed Jimmy Melia (who led Brighton to the 1983 FA Cup final), Gordon Milne (who won three Turkish titles with Beşiktaş), Graeme Souness (three Scottish titles as Rangers player-manager and cups with Liverpool and Galatasaray) and John Toshack (a La Liga winner with Real Madrid in 1990). And then there's Phil Neal, a four-time European Cup winner whose 11-year-career in management is best remembered for winning the Associate Members Cup with Bolton and the alacrity with which he said, "Yes, boss" to the England manager Graham Taylor.

Yet neither Ferguson nor Shankly nor Paisley have shaped a nation's football culture as profoundly as Jock Stein. The great Scottish manager has inspired at least 46 of his former players to take significant roles in coaching. That tally doesn't include players he capped as Scotland boss (the most notable of those, in a managerial sense, being George Burley, John Grieg, Mackay, McLeish, Maurice Malpas, McGhee,

Souness, Strachan and Paul Sturrock). Nor does it reflect his impact on many managers who never played for him. As Pat Nevin wrote, "Sir Alex Ferguson says he was the biggest influence on him and Craig Brown, Walter Smith and Jim McLean say much the same."

Judged purely on silverware, Stein's most successful protégés are Dalglish, the Lisbon Lions' skipper Billy McNeill (who won four league titles as Celtic boss) and David Hay (a league champion with Celtic in 1986 and with the Norwegian side Lillestrom in 1989). Other managerial stalwarts to emerge under Stein include Roy Aitken, Tommy Burns, John Gorman, Lou Macari and Pat Stanton, Ferguson's first assistant at Aberdeen. At Dunfermline Athletic, where Stein won the Scottish Cup as manager in 1961, seven of his players have filled the hot seat with Harry Melrose steering the Pars into the top flight in 1979. In contrast, the full-back Freddie Pethard, who spent 1969 at Celtic without breaking through, later managed the Torbay Youth Offending team (he worked for the probation service; he wasn't himself an offender).

The student Stein would probably be proudest of is Ferguson, briefly his assistant as Scotland manager in the 1980s, whose haul of 49 trophies – including 16 league titles (three at Aberdeen, 13 at Manchester United) two Champions Leagues and two Cup Winners' Cups – makes him the most successful manager in British football history.

One of the few coaches whose influence on a nation's football culture can be likened to Stein's is Albert Batteux, who led Stade de Reims to the European Cup final in 1956 and 1959 and developed

an attacking playing style hailed as "champagne football". In 31 years as coach, Batteux won nine French titles (five with Reims and four with Saint-Étienne) and led *les Bleus* to the semi-finals of the 1958 World Cup. When France won Euro 84, they were managed by Michel Hidalgo, a former Reims midfielder who had scored in the 1956 European Cup final. In 1998, France won the World Cup coached by Aimé Jacquet, a former defensive midfielder Batteux coached at Saint-Étienne.

Four of Batteux's *enfants* have coached France – Hidalgo, Jacquet, Just Fontaine and Jacques Santini – and six have won league titles as managers: Jacquet (three times with Bordeaux), Santini (Lyon, 2001), Bram Appel (PSV, 1963), Robert Herbin (four times with Saint-Étienne, whom he led to the European Cup final in 1976), Pierre Sinibaldi (four with Anderlecht) and Jean Vincent (twice with Nantes). Other Batteux old boys to prosper in the dugout include Georges Peyroche (French Cup winner with PSG), José Anigo (Uefa Cup runner-up with Marseille in 2004) and Victor Zvunka (a French Cup winner with Guingamp). Jacquet was also a guiding spirit behind Clairefontaine, one of Europe's most productive football academies.

Rinus Michels had a similar transformational impact to Batteux and Stein. He was the perfector of Total Football, who won four Eredivisie titles and one European Cup at Ajax before steering the Netherlands to the 1974 World Cup final and winning Euro 88. By developing Ajax's revolutionary play – and shaping Cruyff's philosophy of football – the General became the intellectual godfather of the modern game. Cruyff is the only one of Michels's charges at club level to win European silverware as coach: the Cup Winners' Cup (Ajax, 1987) and the European Cup (Barcelona, 1992) yet Velibor Vasović (Red Star Belgrade, 1988) and Arie Haan (Anderlecht, 1986) have won leagues. It is virtually impossible to disentangle the influences of Michels and Cruyff but the Dutch Euro 88 squad included Frank Rijkaard (a Champions League winner as Barça coach in 2006) and Ronald Koeman (who won three Eredivisie titles: two as Ajax coach and one at PSV). One of Michels's most passionate admirers was a young Italian football fan called Arrigo Sacchi.

Few coaches have inspired as many players to coach as Cruyff. Finding a player in his Barcelona squads between 1988 and 1996 who didn't manage is the exception, rather than the rule. Two of his *enfants* have won the Champions League as Barça coach: Rijkaard and Pep Guardiola (2009 and 2011). Apart from Rijkaard and Guardiola, three other Cruyff protégés have won league titles as coaches: Ernesto Valverde (Olympiacos in 2009, 2011 and 2012), Óscar Garcia (Maccabi Tel Aviv, 2013) and Ronald Koeman. Although he loves to cast himself as a Camusian *étranger* in European football, Cruyff has also inspired the likes of Bakero, Danny Blind, Albert Ferrer, Gheorghe Hagi, Michael Laudrup, Robert Prosinečki, Stoichkov, Marco van Basten, Johnny van't Schip, Aron Winter to coach and Frank Arnesen, Txiki Begiristain, Jordi Cruyff and Andoni Zubizaretta to become directors of football.

Guardiola learned a lot from Cruyff, partly by constantly questioning his mentor — as his former teammate Garcia recalled, "He wanted to know everything." While acknowledging the Dutch master's influence, Guardiola insists he is his own manager, declaring once, "Cruyff didn't make me." Sometimes, you learn as much from a mentor's flaws as their strengths. After Barça's complacent build up to the 1994 Champions League final, which Milan won even more comprehensively than the 4-0 scoreline suggests, Guardiola ensured that his players kept completely focused before the 2009 and 2011 finals.

The only German coach who comes close to Batteux, Cruyff, Michels and Stein as an inspirational influence is Hennes Weisweiler, architect of the legendary Borussia Mönchengladbach side of the 1970s. The most famous of Weisweiler's alumni are Jupp Heynckes (who has won the Champions League twice — with Real Madrid and Bayern), Berti Vogts (Euro 96 winner with Germany), Winfried Schäfer (an African Cup of Nations winner with Cameroon in 2002), Christoph Daum (who has won five league titles: three in Turkey, and one apiece in Austria and Germany), Marcel Koller (who won the Swiss league with FC Gallen and Grasshoppers and now coaches Austria) and Horst Köppel (a German Cup winner with Borussia Dortmund in 1989).

Weisweiler was too inspirational for his own good. He trained hundreds of coaches at Cologne's German Sports University between 1958 and 1970. One of his students, who played for him at Köln, was Zlatko Čajkovski. The Croatian won the German championship with Köln in 1962 and, as coach, laid the foundation for the Bayern side that won the European Cup Winners' Cup in 1967 and competed so thrillingly with Gladbach in the 1970s. Managers in the top three tiers of German football are still obliged to study in Cologne at the Weisweiler Academy, as it is now known. In the academy's 44th class were Jürgen Klinsmann and Joachim Löw.

Yet Klinsmann and Löw also bear the imprint of a much more obscure figure: a construction engineer called Helmut Gross. Building bridges by day and managing amateur teams by night, Gross was the first German coach to teach players zonal marking and ball-oriented defending – at Geislingen in the fourth division in 1981. One of the youth players there was Markus Gisdol, whom Gross signed to coach Hoffenheim in 2009 and now manages the first team. In 1989, Gross took charge of VfB Stuttgart's youth set-up, laying the foundation for a system that has since unearthed such talents as Mario Gomez, Sami Khedira and Timo Hildebrand. Among Gross's colleagues at Stuttgart were Löw, Rainer Adrion (later Germany Under-21 coach) and Thomas Tuchel, manager of Stuttgart's Under-19 team, whose success at Mainz led to him being reductively dubbed the 'German Mourinho'.

In the words of the *Frankfurter Allgemeine Zeitung*, Gross "founded a highly innovative coaching philosophy in the south-west of Germany", where many of the country's most successful recent coaches – Klinsmann, Löw and Jürgen Klopp – have come from. Now 66, Gross advises Ralf Rangnick, sporting director of Red Bull Salzburg and RB Leipzig. In the late 1980s, shortly after Rangnick and Gross met, they

became obsessed with Sacchi's Milan, buying the most expensive video player on the market and watching tapes of the Rossoneri's matches so often the machine wore out.

In some ways, Giovanni Trapattoni's record as a mentor is the antithesis of Gross's. In a mostly glorious 41-year career as coach, Trap won every major Uefa club trophy and managed Juventus, Inter and Bayern. Around 50 of his *enfants* become coaches. Although his *enfants* include Michel Platini, Dino Zoff, Cesare Prandelli and Lothar Matthäus, only three of his former players – Antonio Conte, Ramon Diaz and Walter Zenga – have won the league as coach. Some of Trapattoni's former charges, such as Klinsmann, Prandelli and Zoff, have thrived as managers but many – notably Dietmar Hamann, Paolo di Canio, Fabrizio Ravanelli and Mario Basler – have crashed, burned and given up.

The influence of Ferguson, Wenger, Revie, Clough, Shankly, Stein, Batteux, Michels, Cruyff and Weisweiler manifested itself in similar ways: they made their name at one or two clubs where, during enduring golden eras, they instilled their values in their players. In contrast, Marcelo Bielsa has never coached a club for more than two years. His longest managerial reign came with Argentina, from 1998 to 2004. Cesar Luis Menotti and Carlos Bilardo may have won the World Cup with the *Albiceleste*, but Bielsa has probably inspired more players to coach.

Let's start with his Newell's Old Boys squad that reached the 1992 Copa Libertadores final. 10 of the 23 players to feature in that campaign became coaches: Eduardo Berizzo (now at Celta Vigo), Alfredo Berti (Newell's), Fernando Gamboa (Club Atlético Colón), Fabián Garfagnoli (a youth coach at Tiro Federal in Rosario), Juan Manuel Llop (most successfully at the Argentinian club Godoy Cruz), Ricardo Lunari (Millonarios), Gerardo Martino (Argentina), Mauricio Pochettino (now at Spurs, assisted by his Newell's teammate Miguel D'Agostino), Julio Zamora (Sportivo Huracán in Peru). Bielsa casts such a long shadow over Newell's that their past four coaches have all played for him: Lunari, Berti, Martino and now Gustavo Raggio.

Bielsa's first major tournament as Argentina boss was the 2002 World Cup. His squad for the finals included Juan Sebastián Verón (now an unpaid sporting director at Estudiantes), Matías Almeyda (managing Banfield), José Chamot (assisting Almeyda), Germán Burgos (assistant at Atlético Madrid) and Diego Simeone (who has won the Europa League twice and La Liga once in three years as Rojiblancos coach).

The most remarkable aspect of Bielsa's legacy is that his most successful students – Martino, Pochettino and Simeone – have applied so much of his teaching.

Bielsa's manager on the pitch at Newell's, Martino won the Primera Division with the Old Boys in 2013, with a team whose high tempo, quick vertical passing style and collective pressing and defending came straight out of Bielsa's play book. At Southampton, Pochettino adopted his mentor's principles, looking to have at least one man spare when building from defence, varying the play with vertical passes, and using an attacking midfielder with three players ahead of him in the final third. During Atlético's run to the Champions League final, Simeone's side were Bielsaesque, playing with collective resolve, industrious intensity and an eye for the telling long pass.

Guardiola has long admired Bielsa's style, commenting on the Argentinian's Athletic side, "They all run up ... then they run down again. Up, down, up, down, it's fascinating." Once, when Guardiola toured Argentina, he and Bielsa talked football for 12 hours at an *asado*, with the Argentinian using salt pots, ketchup bottles, chairs and tables to demonstrate his theories. On the same trip, Guardiola met Menotti and Ricardo la Volpe, then manager of Mexico, and was particularly struck by the latter's emphasis on defenders starting attacks and his insistence that they practise this so intently "they understand each other as if they were lovers".

Guardiola never enjoyed such free-ranging discussions with Arrigo Sacchi, but that didn't stop him learning from him. His move to Brescia in 2003 was spurred partly by his belief that Sacchi's Milan had made Serie A the most tactically intriguing league in Europe.

Sacchi's attacking 4-4-2, with its emphasis on pressing, shape and work-rate, destroyed *calcio's* defensively-minded tactical orthodoxy. The former shoe salesman's most distinguished alumni from Milan are two Champions League-winning coaches (Rijkaard and Carlo Ancelotti), three national coaches (Roberto Donadoni, Italy; Marco van Basten, Netherlands; and Dejan Savicevic, Yugoslavia) and Ruud Gullitt, who taught Chelsea to play "sexy football" and won the FA Cup. Many of Sacchi's *enfants* have moved into coaching – Franco Baresi was briefly technical director at Fulham – but few have done well.

Among the notable Azzurri capped by Sacchi are Conte, Gianfranco Zola and Roberto di Matteo. Sacchi welcomed Conte's appointment as *Azzurri* coach, while sounding as if he was praising himself: "Antonio's philosophy of football is modern. He has great abilities to instruct as well as an elevated sensitivity that allows him to correct things like the small mistakes players make in training."

Yet Marcello Lippi is clearly the greatest influence on Conte. In his autobiography, the former midfielder admits he learned about motivation and preparation from his mentor. One humiliating episode showed him that players must never put their interests ahead of the team's. When Lippi moved him from central midfield to the flanks, Conte bemoaned the switch in the *Gazzetta Dello Sport*. Incensed, Lippi assembled the players and admonished Conte for his egotism. Conte's emphasis on the collective good is one of the most striking aspects of his managerial style so, the message clearly hit home.

In Ukraine, Valeriy Lobanovskyi, who built, honed and drilled Dynamo Kyiv, still casts a long shadow. Career paths were very different in the old Soviet sports system so it is hard to make direct comparisons with the likes of Batteux, Ferguson, Michels and Stein, but his *enfants* can still be found in dugouts across Ukraine.

Seven of the eight men to have managed the national side since he left

in 2001 played for him: Leonid Buryak, Oleh Blokhin, Oleksiy Mykhailychenko, Yuriy Kalitvintsev, Andry Bal, Oleksandr Zavarov and present incumbent Mykhalo Fomenko. (The exception is Myron Markevych, who quit after four games in 2010.) Three of his protégés have won the league as Dynamo Kyiv boss: Fomenko, Mykhailychenko and Anatoliy Demanyenko.

If you look at Lobanovskiy's three great Dinamo sides – the teams that won the Cup Winners' Cup in 1975 and 1986 and reached the Champions League semi-final in 1999 – 34 of the players have become coaches, youth coaches or scouts. Yet the most notable – apart from those already mentioned – are probably Oleh Kuznetsov (who helped Blokhin steer Ukraine to the quarter-finals of the 2006 World Cup), Serhiy Rebrov, (a Ukrainian Cup winner with Dynamo Kyiv), Anatoliy Konkov (who has managed Shakhtar and Ukraine) and Sergei Baltacha (now a youth coach at Charlton Athletic, who managed Inverness Caledonian Thistle from 1993 to 1995 but is probably best known in the UK because of his tennis-star daughter Elena, who died of cancer at the age of 30 in 2014).

Assessing the impact of the coach known to his players as 'the Colonel' is particularly problematic because so many of his *enfants* stayed in Ukraine. There are only two proper trophies at stake – the league and the cup – and, since 2003-04, the Shakhtar coach Mircea Lucescu has won 13 of them. Lobanovskyi's intellectual influence is finally waning with Dinamo and Ukraine are departing from his model without developing a distinct identity.

To an extent, every successful manager is metaphorically standing on the shoulders of giants but only they can know how much of their success is owed to which particular giant. Rock stars, poets and football managers are all reluctant to identify their influences, insisting on their originality. Given the battering managers' egos take, such delusions – their equivalent of Steve Jobs's "reality distortion field" – may be a professional necessity. Almost 20 years ago, I interviewed a Scottish Premier League manager who told me he didn't want to talk about tactics because he had, he insisted, spotted something in midfield nobody else had. His subsequent career does not suggest this secret knowledge has yielded any enduring competitive advantage.

So we are left counting numbers. If we do that, it's clear that Batteux, Bielsa, Clough, Cruyff, Ferguson and Paisley/Shankly all inspired many of their players to become managers – and Wenger not so much. This is certainly not conclusive proof that Ferguson is a better manager than Wenger but it is truly mysterious.

The Arsenal boss is renowned – even ridiculed – for telling players to go out and express themselves. So why have so few of them successfully expressed themselves in the dugout?

Fishing in a Small Pond

Ralf Rangnick explains the philosophy behind Red Bull's investment in Salzburg and Leipzig

By Ben Lyttleton

Ralf Rangnick chuckles at the memory of the moment he fell in love with English football. He was a 21-year-old student on a year abroad at Sussex University, as part of his degree in English and PE at Stuttgart University. On 10 November 1979 he went to the old Goldstone Ground and watched Brighton & Hove Albion lose 4-1 to Liverpool. "I remember the Brighton fans singing, 'Seagulls! Seagulls!' despite the score-line," Rangnick said. "And the Liverpool fans responded: 'Seaweed! Seaweed!' Scouse humour, huh?"

Rangnick played for the local non-league side Southwick FC and before his first game, against Steyning Town, he turned up two hours before kick-off ready for a warm-up routine. His teammates appeared 10 minutes before kick-off. After his debut, he ended up in Chichester hospital with three broken ribs and a punctured lung, but even that did not put him off. He played 11 times for Southwick, a short period that moulded him as a coach. "The most important thing for me was the amount of coaching we did on the pitch," he said. "There was hardly a situation where we didn't spur each other on, doing some coaching among ourselves or motivating each other. That was totally inspirational for me."

Rangnick took the lessons into his coaching career, which began as a youth coach at Stuttgart. He first appeared in the German consciousness after appearing on the TV show *Das Aktuelle Sportstudio* on 19 December 1998, talking up the merits of a flat back four in front of a magnetic tactics board. He earned the nickname 'Professor', but it was not a complimentary one. At the time he was head coach of second division side SSV Ulm and as most teams then played three at the back, he was dismissed as an eccentric without a successful playing career behind him.

In the 2014-15 Bundesliga season, coaches like Roger Schmidt (Bayer Leverkusen) and Marcus Gisdol (Hoffenheim) were feted for their tactical smartness: it was no coincidence that they shared the same coaching instructor as Rangnick, Helmut Gross, at the Württemberg academy. "He was years ahead of his time, talking about ball-oriented spatial coverage and pressing opponents back in the mid-1980s," said Rangnick. "The next step is to transfer those theories onto your players."

When SSV Ulm won promotion, other clubs took Rangnick seriously and in 1999 he was appointed by Stuttgart.

He flopped there: in part, because he was not used to working under a sports director. It was a similar story at Hannover 96 and Schalke, but everything changed when he took charge at third-division Hoffenheim in 2006. This time, he had control of the club from top to bottom and his time there – consecutive promotions and consolidation in the Bundesliga – was the most successful of his career.

He resigned in January 2011 and was all set to take a year out before Schalke persuaded him back three months later: he went on to win the German Cup and a place in the Champions League semi-final (beating Internazionale 7-3 on aggregate in the quarter-final) that season. He left in September, citing exhaustion, and has since admitted he should have seen out that sabbatical year in full.

That did not put off a succession of English clubs – including West Brom, Everton, and Brighton – getting in touch with him, but with no luck. In summer 2012, Rangnick was drinking coffee with a friend when he received a phone call from Gerard Houllier. "Hi Ralf, I'm just with Dietrich Mateschitz [the founder and owner of the Red Bull energy drink company] and we wondered if you were around," said the Frenchman. "We're going to jump in a helicopter and visit you this afternoon."

Rangnick was persuaded to join Mateschitz's team, and since then, he has been sports director of Red Bull Salzburg and RB Leipzig. The two 'brand-owned' clubs have caused controversy, for differing reasons, in their respective regions but the switch upstairs has suited the German. He still thinks like a coach, but having a certain distance allows more clear-headed decision-making. "I'm convinced that emotional thinking, either in the euphoria of success or crisis, causes the biggest mistakes in football. Coaching brings you to those extremes every day."

Rangnick certainly looks healthy when we meet on a wintry afternoon in Zurich. He is about to address delegates at the International Football Arena conference, hosted at Fifa House, where he would explain his past, his philosophy and his future. He may still love the English game, but a job coaching there seems increasingly unlikely now.

● *How would you sum up your first two years at Red Bull?*

A lot has happened. In Salzburg, in the first official Champions League game against [the Luxembourg champions] FC Dudelange, we lost after two legs [4-4 on away goals]. After 20 minutes you could see from the stands that it was not a good game. For me it was impossible to lose, but it happened; we made a lot of changes to our squad and staff after that. Last season we won the double; we didn't qualify for the Champions League [losing to Fenerbahçe just before they were banned from the competition] but we did well in the Europa League. We were very unlucky to lose to FC Basel in the round of 16.

We have an exciting squad, with some young players who are on the list of bigger clubs. The development is good, we have the kind of squad we were trying to get, and that experience against Dudelange accelerated the process.

What about RB Leipzig?

Leipzig started in the fourth division with an average attendance of 2,000 fans, and now we are in the top six in the second division after two consecutive promotions. The average attendance is now 30,000, and recently we played against St Pauli in front of 40,000 so the development there is amazing, especially in terms of the public interest.

What's the philosophy driving you?

The difference between us and other clubs is that when we sign or scout new players, we are fishing in a very small pond. We only interested in players aged between 17 and 23, as from our experience, when you are 23 you are no longer a talent. If you look at other clubs and their development, you can see that players start their careers earlier than 10 years ago and finish earlier too. So we are only scouting those players. The maximum age is 23. The second difference is that in both clubs, we try to implement and play the same style of football and of course between the two clubs, we make use of synergies that can be developed out of those two factors.

Does that make it even more important that you hire the right people?

What I did at the start of working with both clubs was to spend five weeks in Salzburg and another four in Leipzig to get to know the people who were in place at the time. Were the right people there? I'm convinced that you have to have the right man or woman for the right job and we tried to do that, to keep the right ones and change others. Some of the positions we didn't have at all: for example, we now have a sports psychologist in both clubs, a nutritionist responsible for players' diet at both clubs. I tried to use my network, especially the one I used in Hoffenheim, and there are many people that I have worked with before who are with us.

What has been the local reaction to the presence of Red Bull in Salzburg and Leipzig? Are fans happy that you have been successful or is there a backlash against the commercial element of the club?

It's different in the two cities. When Red Bull came to Salzburg in 2004-05, the former Austria Salzburg club was bankrupt so Dietrich Mateschitz bought the club. At the time, they decided to change almost everything: the name of the stadium, the colours of the jersey, the badge. Had I been there then, I would have persuaded them to do it more moderately. We know that football is an emotional business and supporters identify themselves through those things. There are three things you cannot change when you buy a club in England and those are the three things. That was why in the beginning, the Austria Salzburg fans more or less left the club and it was hard to win other fans back. Then we started playing some good attractive games in the league and Europe and the stadium sold out. There are only 10 top-flight clubs in Austria, and six are small, more or less village clubs. In Germany you might have no more than three or four like that. But in Austria it's six out of ten and if you play them four times a season, or five times if there is a Cup tie, then that is not very exciting [for fans].

Leipzig was different. The club existed in the fifth division in 2009, and at the time the people in Leipzig didn't know what to do with this new club. In the end, all the traditional clubs in the city went bankrupt, and when Mr Mateschitz started this venture, people were very apprehensive. There has been big progress in the last two years and that's why I say the development in attendances is amazing. Even away from home we had 600 fans who travelled just before Christmas five hours by coach to Sandhausen. In Leipzig, the team has been accepted. There are young players that no one knew whom we have discovered and the fans in the city acknowledge the way we play and it works well together.

Describe the style you're trying to bring to both teams.

When Mr Mateschitz called me, the average age of the two squads was 29. In fact, it was almost 30 at Salzburg and 29 in Leipzig. The players they were signing were signing their last contracts. When he asked what I would change I said, "The commercial slogan says, 'Red Bull gives you wings'. The target market [for Red Bull] is 16-25, and young people don't identify themselves with 30 year olds, so you need players the same age or slightly older." So we have changed the average age in Salzburg to 24 and in Leipzig it's similar. We have reduced the average age of the whole squad by four years in the last two seasons.

You did something similar at Hoffenheim, didn't you?

Yes, at Hoffenheim the average age when we won promotion to Bundesliga was

21.9; it was actually younger than the club's Under-23 team. But for us [at Red Bull], it didn't make sense to have an old team if the product is aimed at 16-25 year olds.

How important is it to play in a way that suits the Red Bull brand? Does Mateschitz have a vision of how he wants his teams to play?

Mr Mateschitz said to me when we first met in 2012 that he's not a football man but he has a vision and this is what I like most about him. It was the same as F1 six years ago; in one of his rare press conferences he said I want to win the F1 title and at the time Ferrari and Mercedes laughed at him. They thought he had drunk too much Red Bull. We all know what happened: they won the title four years in a row. I explained how I would try to develop the two clubs; to sign young unknown talented players and to play an attacking, high-pressing and quick transitional football, because that is more suited to the Red Bull brand than a defensive, apprehensive and counter-attack and cautious game. And he thought that sounded good. After Dudelange he was not amused; he thought, "What are you doing?" Since then, he has realised we didn't do too much wrong in the last two years and he trusts that we are doing the right things with the money he gives us.

So how does the team play in a Red Bull way?

Here are the principles: one, add maximum possibility to the team and act, don't react. So you need to dictate the game with and without the ball, not through individuals. Two, use numerical superiority and let the ball run directly whenever possible, with no unnecessary individual action and with no fouls. Three, use transitions, switch quickly. Try to win back the ball within five seconds with aggressive pressing. After winning the ball back, play quickly straight away, play direct and vertically towards the opponent's goal, surprise the disorganised opponent to get into the penalty area and shoot within ten seconds of winning the ball back.

At Hoffenheim, we did research and showed that the likelihood of scoring is within eight seconds of winning back the ball. In training we have a countdown clock and the target is to score within 10 seconds. Jürgen Klopp has said that the best playmaker is 'perfect counter-pressing'. So four, the more a team sprints (i.e. the more the players sprint) faster to win back the ball then there is a greater likelihood they will score a goal once they have won it back quickly.

⚫ You used to love zonal marking...

When I was an Under-19 coach at VfB Stuttgart, in the early 1990s, we developed zonal marking even though in the 1990s, Germany was famous for playing with a libero. But in the last few years Barcelona changed football again. Zonal marking is not special, but pace in transition has changed football. You used to hear people say this team needs a player to slow things down, put his foot on the ball, but that won't work now, it's no longer possible. Due to Barcelona, also Mainz, Freiburg, Borussia Dortmund and Swansea, it has influence on everything. It's a way to educate young players. The players are no longer individual circus artists. Johan Cruyff

once said that the team with the best 11 individuals will always win but Dortmund have shown that's not true. Tactics play a more important role than five years ago.

⚫ What happened to the tactics against Dudelange?

I think we must have some kind of Champions League curse. That first experience with Dudelange was a disaster because it should never have happened. Looking back, I don't know if our whole development would have been so rapid if we hadn't lost that game. Last year we dropped out against Fenerbahçe, and that was very unlucky: we were the better team in both legs but there was something lacking; we did not have enough experience when we were 1-0 up at home and conceded late on. Again we were 1-0 up in Istanbul and lost 3-1. This year was the year when everyone thought, "If we don't make it this year, we never will make it." We were 2-0 up against Malmö, Kevin Kampl had missed a few one-on-ones and then they scored in the last minute. It was a long ball, the goalkeeper thought it was his ball, a defender headed it out of his hands and the ball fell to the striker and it was 2-1. But conceding an away goal in the last minute, it's like conceding two goals... Then we had problems we had with Sadio Mané before the second leg and, looking back now, that was decisive: he didn't turn up the day before, he didn't show up for training as he was so desperate to leave and he was afraid no-one would come up with the right offer, so he didn't play. We had another two or three players injured and we lost that game 3-0, and deservedly so. We didn't perform on the night.

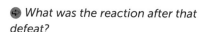

⊕ What was the reaction after that defeat?

We were almost paralysed for three or four weeks. It took me at least five or six days to get back to normal business and take something useful from that experience. We lost three games in a row in the league, which has never happened before, but then finally we turned things around. We beat Dinamo Zagreb 5-1 in Croatia and beat Celtic 3-1 at Celtic Park, so we did get back to playing Red Bull football again.

⊕ So the target next year is obvious: Champions League group stage?

I don't know. Mané left, Kampl left. We have young players ready to take the next step. This is the normal result of the change in our transfer policy: because we sign players who are signing their first or second contracts so when they are ready for the next step, we have to let them go, if you get the right offer. Our next players must be in the pipeline already. Our reserve team has the youngest average age in Europe, 19.3, and they are second in the league and hopefully some of them will be in the first team next season. We will probably make the Champions League when no-one thinks we will qualify, when we are underdogs. Before Malmö, no-one thought we would lose to that team. We saw ourselves as clear favourites in those two legs. That made losing more difficult.

⊕ How can an Austrian club compete at that level?

FC Basel in Switzerland shows how to do it. The advantage they have, even though they have been successful in

recent years, is that no matter who they play, they are underdogs. I would be convinced that with the team we have in Salzburg, although it sounds strange, if we had qualified [for the group stage], we would have had a chance of staying in the competition after Christmas. Now our ambition is to go as far as possible in the Europa League – we were top in our group – and hopefully go further than last season. We have two strikers who can score 30 goals this season – Jonathan Soriano and Alan – and a young Belgian, Massimo Bruno, who is set for the top. But we can look at what Basel have done in the last 10 years; they have been doing a great job. What is possible in Switzerland must be possible for a club like ours.

⊕ What's been the reaction from the rest of German football to the success in Leipzig?

Supporters of big traditional clubs don't like us, as they fear we might take away one of their places. But officials of the other clubs have realised we do things in a special way. For example, we were the only club in the second division who didn't sign a player from another second-division club and we did the same last season with third-division clubs. Experience-wise, our players have the lowest number of minutes played at first or second division level. This has been acknowledged. We have to differentiate between other fans who emotionally don't like us, the media and other sports directors and coaches, as they realise we do it in a different way. Some people try to reduce it by saying we have more money available, which is true, but the question is, how do we use that money? What are we doing with it? We have invested in the staff to get best possible people to work with the players and then we try to give them blue chips, highly talented young players who can be trained in those surroundings and developed into top-class players. Joshua Kimmich is a good example. He was an Under-19 player at Stuttgart that not many people knew and Stuttgart themselves thought he should play in the Under-19 team although they had a reserve team in the same league as ours. We found a solution with Stuttgart and he joined our club. Not only did he play every game last season, but he was one of our best players. He was in the Under-19 Germany side that won the European title and has been called to the Under-21 squad. [In January 2015, Bayern Munich signed Kimmich for €7.5m on a pre-contract agreement.] Yussuf Poulsen is another example: a striker we scouted for six months in Denmark and we persuaded him to join us in division three and he's still with us too.

Do you get frustrated with the debate about traditional clubs?

Football clubs are now businesses, whether you like it or not. There is a German second division side near the top of the league, Ingolstadt, which is owned by Audi. The difference between them and us is that their average attendance is 7,000 and ours is almost four times that. I am convinced that if we get to the Bundesliga, our stadium will be sold out every home game. We will also be one of the teams that brings the most away fans

with them. That's another reason why it won't be bad if Leipzig gets promoted.

If Leipzig are promoted to the Bundesliga, life will be more complicated for you. Can you be sporting director of two top-flight clubs?

No, but that was clear from day one. If they are both in the top divisions, then I can only be sporting director of one of them, for two reasons. Theoretically, both clubs could qualify for Europe and we want both clubs to be able to play in European competitions. It would not be possible if I was sports director for both clubs. I'd have to decide and it's clear I would then focus on Leipzig. Time-management right now is difficult, with Leipzig in the second division. I cannot be in both places at the same time.

How valuable is it to have gone through something similar with Hoffenheim?

Of course it's valuable to have that experience, to know what's important, which screws to use – but every season and every team is a different situation. You have to prepare each team properly – we have the experience to know what to do in special situations, if the pressure increases, and if we don't win for three or four games in a row, the coach knows he has a sporting director who understands what it's like. We are pretty proud that in two and a half years, we've not sacked a single coach in either team. Okay, we lost Roger Schmidt to Bayer Leverkusen but that's part of the DNA of our job: if we allow our players to take the next step I can't tell the coach that he has to stay as well. We have to be ready to have the next coach as well.

You spent years as coach and being hands-on with the players, so on a personal level, how do you cope having taken a step back? Are you tempted to coach again?

No, because I appreciate what I can do in my current job. It's very difficult to imagine where another club can offer me the same conditions I have now, and it's a great privilege. For the first three or four months, it was pretty difficult. I still think and watch games as a former coach. It was not easy to see the line that I should not cross, but there were some situations, maybe after Dudelange I crossed that line, but now I know where the line is. I can give the coach advice and pass on a note at half-time, but then it's up to them. They are the ones with the responsibility and they have to decide what to do. Physically and mentally I have never been in as good shape as I am today. So I do not really think about doing something different. I currently have a very high job satisfaction. **B**

Pedestrian and Backward

How Ron Greenwood tried to instil a Hungarian approach at Arsenal

By Jon Spurling

Trying to bring success to Arsenal throughout the wilderness years of the late 1950s and 1960s was arguably the toughest managerial assignment in football. The former Arsenal goalkeeper George Swindin – who'd forged a fine reputation as an up-and-coming manager at lower-division Peterborough in the mid-1950s – took over at Highbury in 1958. He reflected, "I tried all sorts of new combinations on the pitch, and experimented with new systems, but I was always some way from the right mix."

Swindin embraced the progressive tactics that were espoused by his assistant manager and first-team coach Ron Greenwood. A journeyman defender with Bradford Park Avenue, Brentford, Chelsea and Fulham, Greenwood subsequently coached at Eastbourne United and Oxford University and the England Youth team. In December 1957, he moved to Highbury, where he would later declare himself to be "utterly horrified with the pedestrian and backward nature of Arsenal's training methods."

For Greenwood – who was there at Wembley in November 1953 – the England v Hungary game proved an epiphany: "It showed beyond all doubt that football can be a game of beauty and intelligence, a lovely art

as well as a muscular science." In his 1984 autobiography *Yours Sincerely*, Greenwood – a Chelsea player at the time of the Wembley defeat – spoke of how he quickly became "entranced" by Hungary's approach to the game. Whether it was Ferenc Puskás "flicking the ball up a couple of times, catching it with his instep and returning it to the [centre] spot" or the pace with which the Hungarians passed the ball – "They kept the ball on the ground and they fizzed it about" – Greenwood recalled shutting "everything else out and concentrating on the play".

Most bewitching of all for Greenwood was Hungary's remarkable exploitation of "space, how to make it and how to use it... The man with the ball always had good, simple alternatives and one reason for this was the fact that they were not hide-bound by numbers. Their players were free agents." Greenwood pointed out that many teams attempted to copy Hungary's use of triangular movements but, as he explained, this often proved an ineffective tactic because the triangles were static. Puskás and co deployed *moving* triangles, "so the size, angles and direction of their triangles were constantly changing". Greenwood also noted that the Hungarians were adept at playing the ball to a marked man, "to give him the choice of pushing the ball back or trying to turn his opponent, something else we had not seen in those days."

Greenwood, whose coaching career lasted for over 25 years, later admitted that he'd "never witnessed any team, before or since, master the concept of space better than Hungary did that day." Puskás "dictated the shape and pace of the game around him, and had an acute sense of the angles and distances on the pitch." Kocsis, the Hungarian inside-right, "was brilliant in the air and had an almost other worldly sense of where others were on the pitch." The midfield trio of Bozsik, Puskás and Hidegkuti were a formidable trio who "imposed themselves on a game, creating space, using it and promising to make the ball their personal possession."

The defender remained captivated by the Magical Magyars for years afterwards, and devoted an entire chapter (entitled "Revelation") to the England v Hungary game in his autobiography. He was obsessed by the concept of space, both in football and beyond. When he arrived at Highbury in late 1957, it had already been more than four years since Arsenal had last won a trophy. Greenwood accepted that he was none too popular with several of the players because the manager Jack Crayston gave him *carte blanche* to alter the training techniques and tinker with the team. He later suggested that his previous club Eastbourne was more technically advanced than the ailing Gunners. Arsenal, he claimed, were "set and stodgy in their playing ways." The wing-halves Cliff Holton and Peter Goring had been banned from crossing the halfway line. The lively inside-forward Jimmy Bloomfield had been instructed

to deliver long balls to the forwards. "It wasn't playing to his strengths," claimed Greenwood. He despaired at the brutal treatment meted out to the winger Joe Haverty in training sessions. "The club's methods were unbelievably traditional. The past was always part of the present," he admitted. "Long balls, square passing, not exploiting pace. It was monotonous. They were crippled by fear." That was about to change, as Greenwood began to experiment with new routines. But not before he revealed to his new charges his fascination with the cosmos.

The space race was well underway. The Soviets had launched Sputnik 1 in October 1957 and four months later the first US satellite, Explorer 1, blasted into orbit. Greenwood was captivated. Cliff Holton, who Greenwood claimed was "sarcastic", recalls the new coach discussing (or at least trying to) with the players "the possibility of life on other planets, and how none of us knew what lay out there in space". Holton admitted to giving Greenwood "short shrift" on the subject. Peter Goring remembered the future West Ham boss bringing in a copy of *Time* magazine and speaking of how "within 15 years, an American or a Russian will walk on the moon. Imagine that. Space travel will open up our minds." But not the Arsenal players' minds, it appeared. While Greenwood spoke of the need for a more "systematic and scientific approach to coaching", and deplored "the lack of education and intellectual curiosity amongst British footballers", Goring claimed Greenwood's "head was slightly in the clouds, like he wasn't fully on earth." Ultimately, that proved to be his undoing at Highbury, but not before Arsenal's players, initially at least, lapped up his training techniques.

With Jack Crayston clinging onto his job by his fingertips, Arsenal were trailing Manchester United 3-0 at half-time in February 1958, before Greenwood reminded his team at the break to put into practice the work they'd completed on overlapping runs in training. "The side had been quaking in their boots, and reverted to type against United, knocking the ball long, which was meat and drink for United defenders," explained Greenwood. "I insisted that they turn this around at the break, and they did." His players, delivering pinpoint crosses and ripping down the wings, rallied superbly, narrowly losing 5-4 in the Busby Babes' last match before the Munich air crash. Jimmy Bloomfield, who went on to manage an aesthetically pleasing Leicester City side in the early 1970s, reckoned, "If you could bottle what Ron delivered at half-time that day, you'd have the perfect team talk; inspirational and tactically astute."

Greenwood introduced one-touch and two-touch training sessions. He deployed the use of shadow play in games, whereby players were drilled in the shape and layout of the team – minus the ball. He worked with goalkeeper Jack Kelsey (it was initially Kelsey's idea) on honing the traditional defensive wall at free-kicks. Kelsey advocated the wall standing on one side of the goal, while he covered the other side. It was a tactic which Arsenal used at the start of the 1958-59 campaign, before other teams cottoned on to it by getting a player to shape to take the kick, run over the ball and be played in by the next player. "We had to ditch it," admitted Kelsey, "but we liked the fact that Ron gave it a go." There were "moving triangle" passing sessions,

doubtless inspired by the Hungarians, and Greenwood even used radios and walkie-talkies in an attempt to vary training techniques. In 1958–59, Arsenal finished a much-improved third. Although they were 11 points behind the champions Wolves, there was genuine optimism that they could launch a title assault during the following campaign and counter the rising threat of their north London neighbours Tottenham, who were becoming a potent force under Bill Nicholson. "Their game was wonderful; quick, intelligent and adaptable. Beautiful to watch. I felt that all teams should aspire to play in such a beautiful way as Tottenham," said Greenwood years later.

In August 1959, both Swindin and Greenwood were interviewed in the *Observer*. The interview was headed, "Space the secret." Their comments appeared to usher in a new and forward-thinking era in Arsenal's tactics. "We've got to change or be left behind," explained Swindin. "We've thrown away the defensive concept. To attract the public the game has got to be entertaining and in football, goals are entertainment." Naturally, Greenwood went on to discuss the Arsenal players' use of space. "The halves must be the springboard of all your attacks. They must use all the space between them and the forwards so that by moving the ball intelligently they can dominate the field." Swindin waxed lyrical about his coach, claiming, "Before Ron went to Highbury, David Herd had no conception of blind-side runs, and now he can sit behind us in the stand and see the entire position for laying on a blind side run before it is set up." Swindin insisted that Arsenal's youth sides were playing "superb one-touch football" and that Arsenal had evolved into "a team of thinkers". To summarise, Greenwood concluded, "The secret of football is space-creating and using it – give and go all the time – there's no other way of keeping the ball *and* making progress. But it must happen in the player's brain."

But the brave new world at Highbury never came to fruition. Geoff Strong recalled, "Ron quickly became too hypothetical. On one occasion he was talking to us about rotating positions and being clever without the ball. It got very, very technical and there just wasn't the quality of player to run with what Ron said. Players kept being switched around too. It was chaos. I turned to young Gerry Ward and asked him if he grasped what Ron was trying to teach us. 'Not a bloody clue,' came Gerry's response. We switched off when he spoke in the end. We felt that he was trying change too much. It got awkward. One of the directors told me that Ron 'wasn't an Arsenal man' and that his days were numbered."

Greenwood, who also served as England Under-23 manager during his time at Highbury, delivered lectures on the use of space on the football pitch throughout the country, but more earthly concerns began to scupper his plans in N5. He labelled Swindin "... impetuous. George will say anything to the press to create a headline, whereas I'm far more wary of which journalists I speak to." There were concerns over injuries. In the 1960-61 campaign, Swindin and Greenwood used 30 players in the League and FA Cup, an unwieldy number whatever the injury situation at the club.

There was also the knotty problem of moulding the squad to fit the new tactics. Swindin's final throw of the dice had been to sign George Eastham from Newcastle in December 1960 for a whopping £47,500, but he lost the striker David Herd who, with an average strike rate of a goal every other game, was one of the best – if most underrated – players in the First Division. Herd exercised footballers' newly earned right to depart at the end of their contracts and went to Manchester United.

Eastham turned down Arsenal's £30 per week offer in late 1961 only for the Arsenal manager to cave in and offer an improved deal. Swindin struggled to control events both on and off the pitch. Days after Tottenham completed the Double in 1961, Greenwood went to West Ham as manager and a year later Swindin was dismissed. The final straw for Greenwood, it seemed, had been Arsenal's parsimony when they tried to lure Denis Law from Huddersfield: "The kind of system that I was aiming for at Arsenal required the purchase of top players, who were willing to think through the issues, and the board decided to be frugal and conservative when they could have landed Denis. It's a decision they came to regret."

So was this another in a catalogue of missed opportunities at Arsenal, a club with a historical penchant for advocating retrenchment and caution when a more expansive approach could have paid dividends? Swindin certainly felt aggrieved at the board's reactive approach to a more monied era in the game, and failure to embrace a new approach on the playing side. "Ron and I wanted a more attractive game, more like Tottenham's. Whenever I approached the board about signing new players who could play that style, they weren't interested. They felt that sticking to tried and tested Arsenal methods was the way. One director told me, 'Don't take too much notice of what Tottenham are doing, George. We'll do things the Arsenal way.' They were bloody-minded about it."

Swindin himself claimed that Greenwood was "probably too technical for the average footballer at Arsenal back then," but Greenwood's tactical nous (Geoff Hurst later claimed that "Ron's ideas on the game, in particular on passing and movement, were a revelation to us and turned us into a highly attractive team") and insistence that his players exploited space on the football pitch to its maximum served West Ham United – and indirectly England – well in the mid-1960s. Many of the training ideas he espoused at Highbury were met with a far more receptive ear in East London as the Hammers won both the FA and Cup-Winners' Cups.

In contrast, the sixties never swung at all for Arsenal, and the club went from bad to worse under Billy Wright. It wasn't until the arrival of Dave Sexton at Highbury in 1966 as a coach under the new manager Bertie Mee that the club began to lay down the tactical blueprint of the pressing game and zonal marking which suited the group of players they had at the time and, crucially, fitted better with the club ethos of defensive solidity and tradition. Don Howe would later adapt Sexton's system to great success as Arsenal won the Fairs Cup in 1970 (a year after Neil Armstrong walked on the moon – Greenwood was out by four years in his prediction) and the Double in 1971.

Arsenal's dismal decade which preceded their short burst of glory could have taken an entirely different course if Ron Greenwood's fascination with space exploration (in all its guises) had been treated in a rather more enlightened manner both among players and directors at Highbury in the early 1960s.

150

Sierra Leone

"Our word is our honour – at least,
that is what our mothers taught us."

The Player

How Kei Kamara divides his time between his MLS career and his work in Sierra Leone

By Firdose Moonda

"Ebola, Ebola, Ebola."

20,000 voices in the stands joined in a jeering chorus. "It hurt," said Kei Kamara, Sierra Leone's star forward. "It really, really hurt."

The Leone Stars were not supposed to be met with such a hostile reception. The match — a qualifier for the 2015 African Cup of Nations against the Democratic Republic of Congo — was supposed to be a home game for them.

But their country, along with Guinea and Liberia, was banned from hosting internationals because of the presence of the Ebola virus within their borders. Sierra Leone could not find an alternative venue so they conceded home advantage to their opponents and played in Lubumbashi instead.

Amid waves of verbal attacks from the stands, Sierra Leone could not hold out on the field. The DRC dominated proceedings and scored twice in the second half, leaving Sierra Leone with two defeats from their opening two matches and little chance of making a first Cup of Nations appearance since 1996. But Kamara and his teammates had other things to think about.

The team donated their match fees from the defeat to hospitals in need of supplies

and began to think of other ways they could contribute to the relief effort. Michael Lahoud, the Philadelphia-based midfielder who made his international debut during qualification for the 2014 World Cup, joined forces with Dr Thila Kunkel, an assistant professor of sport at Temple University in Pennsylvania, to start the #kickebolainthebutt campaign.

"The idea behind it was similar to the Ice Bucket Challenge and he was looking to raise funds," Kamara explained. The entire national team became official backers of the project. They saw no other choice. "We have to be ambassadors against Ebola as well now," Kamara said. "For so long we had to spend our time convincing people there was more to Sierra Leone than civil war, child soldiers and blood diamonds and now we have to persuade them we are not a country that is all about disease either."

The reputation of an entire nation is not an easy burden for anyone to bear but it is one Kamara has carried since he was a teenager. He left his homeland in 1998, as the civil war was still raging. He had mixed feelings: leaving would reunite him with his mother, Fatima, who had received refugee status in the United States. Staying would allow him to be with the rest of his extended family, those who were either still formulating escape routes or had none at all. Because Kamara had the opportunity to do the former, it was the only realistic choice.

He first found himself in the Gambia, where he spent 18 months waiting for his application to enter the USA to be considered. Once he was cleared, he travelled to California. He was 16 years old at the time and that is where he believes his story truly began: "By then I had reflected on where I had come from and where I was going."

With the knowledge that his homeland could easily be swallowed in the flames of its own fury, Kamara joined the almost 250,000 people seeking a different future somewhere else. That Kamara was not a footballer; he was simply a refugee.

"I was too small to play football," he said. "My older brothers played football but it wasn't really something I did. They were much better than me anyway."

Once he got to his new home, he did not have much choice. Football was one of the few things that did not feel foreign to Kamara and he started dabbling in it at school. Having learnt the game by jostling with those bigger, stronger and faster than himself, Kamara was better than he thought he was. Much, much better.

His talent earned him a scholarship to college and took pressure off his mother, who worked a minimum-wage job to fund his education. It also increased the expectations on him to juggle academics with on-field performances but Kamara took the increased responsibility in his stride. "I

just stuck to the programmes," he said. "I knew I had to keep my grades up and I also had to play well to be able to stay in school. It was a good challenge and I wouldn't want to change that. I'd go to school all day, go back home to do homework and then be back at school in the evening for soccer. It motivated and pushed me to where I am today."

Kamara's career officially began at California State University Dominguez Hills, where he spent his sophomore season. Impressive showings there led to two seasons with Orange County Blue Star in the USL Premier Development League, the top-level men's amateur competition in the country. But his big break came when he was drafted as the ninth overall pick by Columbus Crew in 2006.

Being selected so early in the process confirmed Kamara's stock had risen. "It was a real shock," he said. "I wasn't one of the known kids and I was from a second-division school. It felt like it came out of nowhere, even though I considered myself a really hard worker. When it happened that way, I was just really proud."

Things moved swiftly for Kamara as his profile grew and he went from Columbus to San Jose to Houston and ultimately to Sporting Kansas City. He was a Major League Soccer professional and knew he had been given an opportunity few from his homeland would ever have the chance to take. "It is not easy living in Africa," he said. "The chances of success are greater in the United States than back there. It made me wish it was easier for people to come over here but it just isn't."

He was also earning an MLS professional's salary and he was careful not to hoard it but to plough it back into the place that he thought needed it most. Kamara became involved with Schools for Salone, a Seattle-based non-profit organisation founded by a Peace Corps volunteer, backed by prominent figures such as the Sierra Leonean philanthropist Joseph Lamin and the former child soldier turned author Ismael Beah.

The organisation's focus was on a subject close to Kamara's heart: they aimed to build schools and libraries in Sierra Leone. Kamara's partnership with them extended to building his own school – the Kei Kamara School in Freetown. His involvement in the project took him back home, where he was also starting to come to the attention of the national footballing authorities.

Despite residing in the United States, Kamara remained a citizen of Sierra Leone and he was eligible to play for their national team. He received his maiden call-up in September 2010, ahead of the 2012 Cup of Nations qualifying campaign. Simply reaching the competition would have been considered a massive achievement and Kamara wanted to be part of a team that could do that.

He made his debut in Cairo, in a 1-1 draw against Egypt. Sierra Leone's next match was against South Africa at home and would be crucial in the context of the pool: Egypt had won the previous three titles but political turmoil had set them back, meaning South Africa seemed the most likely qualifiers. It was the first time Kamara had represented his country

in front of his own people and he was determined to make the most of it.

He maximised his time in Sierra Leone, training with the national team and visiting his school project. That was where he met Dave LaMatinna and the film crew of Copper Pot Pictures. They were shooting a documentary about the Schools for Salone foundation and the last person they expected to meet on the way was an international footballer. But when they did, it was just the person they wanted. "We had always been interested in soccer stories and wanted to produce some of our own but we had nothing on our reel," LaMatinna said. "So when we found out who Kei Kamara was and that he was involved in the Schools for Salone project, we thought we could do a short film on him and that would give us something to show people going forward. We asked Kei if we could follow him around for a little while and put something together. And he said yes."

What was supposed to be a few hours of shadowing a sportsman to make a snippet of showbiz news turned into a several sessions of shooting and a sizeable amount of material. The crew were drawn into the Kamara story in every way. "We found that he had an amazing way of being confident without being cocky," LaMattina said. "We had great balance. Obviously confidence comes with being a professional athlete but his confidence in his abilities never overshadowed his kindness. He is an intoxicating guy. He was so accessible and welcoming that we thought all footballers were like that."

After tracking Kamara at training, observing his interactions with colleagues and countrymen, they understood that a short segment would not do justice to what they had witnessed. "We knew the story we had could not be done in seven or eight minutes, so we made it into a 22-minute short film," LaMattina said.

The end result is an artfully painted portrait of a man who leads a charmed double life. One half of it is the American dream, the other an African adventure. To tell them together is almost as difficult as living them but the film *Kei* does it.

It juxtaposes scenes of Kamara's MLS career with his fortunes at international level, pitting success against struggle. Kamara was regarded as a hero in Kansas, where the stands were brimming with supporters brandishing banners reading "We Love Kei," and he was on the scoresheet often. With Sierra Leone it was much more difficult. Although their stadiums were also full and the fans always cheered, they very seldom had anything to cheer about.

Sierra Leone drew against South Africa, for instance, and failed again to qualify for the Cup of Nations but they can hardly be blamed for lagging behind. "The civil war impacted everything about the country's infrastructure and football did not escape," LaMattina said. "They are doing the best they can with what they have."

That is also obvious from the film where the quality of the surfaces in US club football - pristine and smooth - is contrasted with pitches in Sierra Leone that are often pocked with puddles and patches of sand. The only thing that does not change between the two places is

Kamara himself. "He loves life, he loves his teammates and he is just happy to be able to play soccer to make a living," LaMatinna said. "Most of his time, he plays on one of the biggest stages in the world but that does not mean that he forgets Sierra Leone. He loves his country - that is best illustrated by the fact that he remained a citizen - and he wants to do well for them. He wants to be involved with them."

That relationship extended to the film as well. Copper Pot's agreement with Kamara was that the proceeds from the mini-documentary would go towards the Sierra Leone schools' project. The documentary screened at the Bermuda International Film Festival and London's Kicking and Screaming Film Festival. Importantly, it was also shown in Sierra Leone, where people were starting to put a face to Kamara's name. "When I first went back there, some people may have heard of me, but they didn't really know what I looked like," Kamara said.

The relative anonymity allowed Kamara to move around undetected at home at first but any chance of that happening after January 2013 has vanished. That was the month when Kamara understood what it really means to play with the big boys.

He was signed on loan by Norwich City. The previous season, Kamara had scored 11 times in 33 appearances and his style of play had begun to combine the speed and accuracy that came naturally to him with maturity and subtlety. He was only the third player from Sierra Leone to appear in the Premier League. "It's where every footballer wants to be and I was no different," he said. "It was massive for me and I knew it. I had a smile on my face from minute one. People would ask me why I was always so happy and I would tell them that I was living my dream."

For football fans in Sierra Leone, Kamara's move to the Premier League provided the recognition they needed to reassure themselves of the richness of their own resources. Almost overnight, they became Norwich City fans and purchased the Canaries jerseys en masse. The club's matches were broadcast in cinemas in Freetown and in their third week of watching the audience had reason to celebrate.

Kamara came off the bench in the 58th minute in a match against Everton, with his team a goal down. With an early touch, he headed just wide. "That rare chance seemed to lift the home crowd and bring much-needed belief," the match report on the BBC website said. Six minutes from time Kamara met a Robert Snodgrass corner and powered home for an equaliser. Grant Holt struck even later to give Norwich an unlikely win.

That remained Kamara's only goal for the club.

He appeared 10 more times for Norwich that season, in which they were relegated. Kamara had impressed, though, and was signed by Middlesbrough. Again, it did not put him in the same league as the likes of Didier Drogba and Samuel Eto'o, or even Mohamed Kallon, whom Kamara regards as Sierra Leone's greatest player, but it was another step. Kamara didn't go any further in English football but that was something he was always prepared for.

"He knew it could all end tomorrow," LaMatinna said. And one tomorrow it did.

His contract was cancelled by mutual consent in August 2014 but Kamara felt little sadness. "It was an experience to go out there and taste that level of football," he said. "I tasted it."

Although he was out of contract, he was not out of heart. "I knew he would bounce back because he is the type of player whom anyone would want in the team," LaMatinna said. "He may not be a superstar but if he is on your team, you will do well."

For a while, Wolves considered signing him. Kamara trained with them for a few days and the manager Kenny Jackett described him as having "done OK," but stressed that any long-term relationship would depend more on administration than ability. "He would need a work permit because he is a Sierra Leone international," Jackett said.

The citizenship he clung to so fiercely ended up costing him in the end. The paperwork proved too bothersome and Kamara was not signed. He returned to the United States to look for a club and his search forced him to pull out of Sierra Leone's Cup of Nations qualifiers against Cameroon in early October, something he was loath to do but on which his long-term professional future depended.

Shortly before chatting to *The Blizzard*, Kamara signed for Columbus Crew - the MLS team who had picked him. For some that may be seen as a move back, but for Kamara, it's something of a homecoming. "As much as I enjoyed the Premier League, I respect the Major

League and the players who are here so much that I had no hesitation in coming back," he said. "The only thing was that I couldn't play for the national side. I had to stay here to solidify my next career move. But I hope the guys can do well. The task at hand is big."

Sierra Leone held Cameroon to a goalless draw — a decent result in itself — but one which meant their chances of appearing at the Cup of Nations in 2015 all but disappeared. Qualifying for tournaments in the future is unlikely unless there is a dramatic upsurge in what Sierra Leone have available to them and Kamara knows it. "We need preparation to be a lot better," he said. "That has always been our biggest problem."

That is only on the field. Sierra Leone has far bigger problems off it and it's those that Kamara is more driven to solving. In the immediate term, he wants to do something about Ebola, having witnessed its horrors first-hand. "I could not believe what I saw when I went back," he said. "The disease had spread so much and there was such fear. The problem was that people didn't believe that it existed at first. I just hope first-world countries can help get things sorted out and that we can do our bit as well. We know that

it's not something we can control so all we can do is to fight together."

Once that battle is won, Kamara wants to turn back to the bigger picture of promoting Sierra Leone in a more positive light and he has a plan for how to do it. "I'd like to be a movie star," he said. "Seriously. I do a bit of television work at the moment but I want to do something to represent Africans and tell a story that the world should know." He references movies like *Captain Phillips*, a story about Somali pirates holding hostages, and *Machine Gun Preacher*, on Somali orphans, as the kind of stories he would like to tell not because of the desperate situations they show but because they tell of people's attempts to change them.

Does all that mean Kamara will one day return home for good? Even he is not so sure, especially now that he is recently married and thinking of starting a family in the States. "I can never turn down my country but going back permanently is not something that is in my plans right now," he said. "I just know that I love going home, I will keep going and I enjoy going home every single time." That he still considers it home says everything about where his heart is.

The Coach

Johnny McKinstry on the challenges he faced as coach of Sierra Leone

By Greg Lea

Johnny McKinstry was a teenager when he committed to coaching as a career; at 29, he has already worked on three continents. He spent two and a half years with New York Red Bulls then, in 2010, his curiosity and ambition took him to Sierra Leone, where he became the Academy Manager of the Craig Bellamy Foundation, a charity set up by the former Wales striker to help underprivileged youngsters reach their potential through football.

When Lars-Olof Mattsson resigned as coach of the Sierra Leone national team in March 2013, McKinstry, armed with his Uefa A Licence, 10 years coaching experience and a growing knowledge of the country, threw his hat into the ring. One stunning presentation to FA bosses later, he was appointed caretaker manager and impressive performances in World Cup qualifiers against Tunisia, Cape Verde and Equatorial Guinea were enough to earn a permanent contract.

McKinstry's first full qualifying campaign was for the 2015 Africa Cup of Nations. Aggregate wins over Swaziland and Seychelles in the preliminaries saw the Leone Stars reach the group stage where they were victims of a tough draw and grouped alongside Cameroon, Côte d'Ivoire and DR Congo. Early

defeats to the latter two spelled the end for McKinstry: despite having taken Sierra Leone into the top 50 of Fifa's rankings for the first time, he was sacked last September.

It's unclear whether the prospect of non-qualification was the motivation behind the Sports Ministry and FA's apparently joint decision, but missing out on the continent's foremost competition should hardly have come as a surprise. Sierra Leone have only participated in two previous Cups of Nations, in 1994 and 1996, and they failed to make it past the first round on both occasions.

History, moreover, was far from the only thing against McKinstry and his charges. In May 2014, just four months before the group stage was scheduled to begin, the Ebola epidemic that had broken out in Guinea the previous December reached Sierra Leone. Around 1100 people had officially contracted the disease by the time of the first qualifier against Côte d'Ivoire, with countless more thought to have been suffering without medics being aware of their condition. Curfews were imposed, expats fled and the country went into lockdown. Working in such an environment is presumably not covered on the coaching courses run at Uefa's plush headquarters in Nyon.

⊕ *You arrived in Sierra Leone in 2010 as a coach at the Craig Bellamy Foundation. How did that opportunity come about and what were your first impressions of the country?*

I'd spent a couple of months in Ghana back in 2006 with the Right to Dream Academy in a small town called Atimpoku. They were hired as the consultants by Craig's people and because of my past experience over there, the Foundation knew of my interest in Africa. In the middle of 2009 I was approached with this proposition of a new project in Sierra Leone. It was a dilemma because I was very happy out in New York with the Red Bulls, but it just seemed like a really good challenge.

I didn't know anything about Sierra Leone before I arrived. I even had to look it up on the map, which shows my ignorance; I'm ashamed of that years later. People said to me "why are you going there?", because the only thing they knew about Sierra Leone was conflict. [Up to 300,000 people were killed in the civil war from 1991 to 2002].

It's so unfair for Sierra Leone to have to go through another national disaster at the moment. It's a fantastic place and the people are amazingly warm and friendly. I've finished my time over there now, but I know I'll have a lifelong relationship with the country.

⊕ *How did you convince the FA to hire you when the national team job came up? You were trying to become the youngest coach in international football in a continent where the older man tends to be a hugely venerated figure.*

I'd actually shown an interest in the job years ago, before the Swedish guy [Lars-Olof Mattsson, McKinstry's predecessor] was hired, but that never went anywhere. The word on the street in 2013 was that they wanted a Sierra Leone-based coach. It was assumed that that meant a native, but as soon as I heard those words I thought, "Get me in a room with the decision-makers and I'll show them there's not even a decision to make".

I met with some senior figures from the FA and Sports Ministry and made a presentation to them. I basically put together this dossier and handed out a copy to everyone in the room, highlighting where I thought Sierra Leone were at and what I would do to make improvements. It just shows the importance of being prepared and knowing your stuff.

⊕ *Did you experience any hostility from local coaches, fans or the media?*

There was never any hostility, no. I think the big difference was that I'd lived in the country for three years: the man on the street who likes football – which is basically everyone in Sierra Leone – would have either known who I was or the work of the Craig Bellamy Foundation. It wasn't like I was a total stranger. Some managers in Africa, like my predecessor, fly in for games and then leave again. That was a big difference for me. The other thing was the inclusionary approach I took with regards to my staff. One of my assistant managers, my fitness coach and my goalkeeping coach all worked in the Sierra Leone Premier League. I'm a big believer in coach education and it was great to be able to take on the ideas of some of the local guys.

⇨ *The average age of the squad went down significantly during your tenure. Was that a conscious decision?*

Yeah, we brought it down from about 29 or 30 to 23. I thought the team was very slow and I wanted to play with speed and take the initiative. Any team of mine has to play the way I want it to play, so a lot of youngsters came in.

⇨ *And which way is that exactly?*

Football is entertainment. Of course winning is paramount but I think you should try and do that with a certain style and panache. People pay hard-earned cash to watch the sport, which is even more apposite in a country like Sierra Leone where there's not a lot of money going around. I used to ask the players, "When you were 10 years old, did you dream of collecting the ball off the keeper and punting it forward 80 yards? No, you wanted to keep possession, you wanted to have fun." One of the little sayings we had was "football for the brave". I told the guys that they had to be courageous and cherish the ball. We gave the players the confidence to play like we knew they could. It was as if we'd literally taken the shackles off them; it was an overnight change.

⇨ *What was the build-up to the first Cup of Nations qualifier against Côte d'Ivoire like?*

Frustrating. That match was in September, four months after the first Ebola case in Sierra Leone. Logistics in Africa are never easy but this was a nightmare. Six days before the game, I was under the impression that it could still be called off and it wasn't until the Tuesday [four days before kick-off] that we got the go-ahead. The Sports Ministry still wanted us to wait, but I went completely against that. We had to get out there and start training. We were really unlucky not to get a result. People thought I was crazy when I said we could go to Abidjan and beat them, but we very nearly did. [Sierra Leone took the lead through Kei Kamara and missed a golden chance to go 2-0 up, before strikes from Seydou Doumbia and Gervinho gave the Elephants the three points].

⇨ *Your home game with DR Congo was then moved to the Congolese city of Lubumbashi. That can't have been easy.*

Home advantage is huge anywhere in any sport. In football, the home team wins about 50% of the time. In Africa, the statistics show that the home team wins 65% of games and the away team only 5-10%. To give up home advantage was a devastating blow. It was the right decision and there was no other solution, but it was still a real disappointment. I thought we could beat all three sides in Sierra Leone, which would have given us enough points to qualify. When you've got 30,000 Sierra Leone fans cheering you on, that's a hostile atmosphere. Sierra Leone have an incredible home record, but that was all lost.

It took us 48 hours to get to DR Congo. The lads were sat at Casablanca airport for 12 hours and then at Kinshasa airport for another nine without anywhere to stay. We were never going to play well after that. Our legs were gone from the first minute.

The most infuriating thing was that I'd foreseen this happening. On the plane back from the preliminary game with Seychelles in April, I'd penned a letter to the Sports Ministry telling them that CAF would move our home matches and that we should contact Morocco and enquire about playing our games there. For whatever reason, that was completely disregarded. As far as I'm aware, there was no contact with the Moroccan government whatsoever. I don't understand it. Guinea [who have also been heavily afflicted by Ebola] played their home games over there and qualified for the tournament. It was completely avoidable and it really frustrates me.

⊕ Did you ever experience any discrimination from other countries about hosting your team?

We had regular temperature tests at hotels, scans as we landed at airports, that type of thing. I completely understand countries looking out for their own interests and their own people, but you've got to remember that none of the players had even been to Sierra Leone since the outbreak. The lads were thinking, "They're only treating us this way because we're Sierra Leonean." Mentally, that had an effect. In our 'home' game with DR Congo, you had 17,000 Congolese fans chanting 'E-bo-la' for 90 minutes. It was intimidating and distressing for the players. They felt shunned.

⊕ What was it like living in the environment at the time on a human level?

It sounds strange to say, but it didn't really affect my day-to-day life. At the [Craig Bellamy] Foundation, we had a 15-acre site about an hour outside Freetown which was completely self-sufficient, with its own generator and water system. Every couple of weeks I'd go out in the van and go to the bank, stock up with food and supplies and everything. It was essentially a self-imposed lockdown and there weren't any people coming and going. Ebola's a disease of contact, so if you remove the contact you remove the danger. For the country, it was horrendous. People were worried, the economy took a huge hit, the currency plummeted. International visitors probably went up, but it wasn't the type of international visitors we wanted. It was an extremely difficult time.

⊕ How do you get the players to focus on football in such a situation?

The players knew they were role models for the country. Football in Sierra Leone is a huge part of the national psyche: if the national team does well, people have an extra spring in their step. We thought that if we could progress the team and win matches, we'd put a positive spotlight on Sierra Leone at a time when there were only negative things being written about the country. We wanted to show that there is more to Sierra Leone than Ebola. Some of the players took things into their own hands. Michael Lahoud, an American citizen, started the "Kick Ebola in the Butt" Twitter campaign, and George Davies, John Kamara and Rodney Strasser did great work with the "I'm a Sierra Leonean not a virus" stuff. In our small way, we wanted to bring awareness to the situation.

⊕ So in a way the national team took on even greater importance at that time?

Yes, I think so.

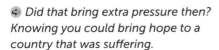
Did that bring extra pressure then? Knowing you could bring hope to a country that was suffering.

Ever since I took the job, I told the players that they were more than just footballers. Anyone who pulled on that Sierra Leone jersey was an ambassador for the country. Even prior to Ebola, Sierra Leone was in the bottom five of the UN Human Development index. It's a beautiful country but it still has a long way to go. If the people are happy, though, things like social mobility become a lot easier, so I was always drumming into the players that they could make a real difference through football. Maybe if that hadn't always been our mentality, Ebola would have brought extra pressure. But our way of thinking had always been that football was more than a game, so I think it was very easy for the players to get on board with that after the outbreak.

Do you think you could have qualified but for the off-field distractions?

Oh, 100%. Sierra Leone have a really good team. People will perhaps see that as rose-tinted glasses but I knew the players we had coming through, many of whom were with Premier League and Bundesliga clubs. Our aim was always to qualify. It was certainly a difficult draw: all three of our opponents participated in the competition proper in January. We had a lot of respect for Côte d'Ivoire, Cameroon and DR Congo, but we also thought they could all be beaten. The off-field stuff certainly had a massive impact. If we could have given our entire focus to football, who knows?

Given all those complications, the fiendishly difficult qualification group and the fact that you lifted Sierra Leone to their highest ever position in the world rankings, did you think your sacking was unfair?

I don't think there was any logic behind it on a football level, but we'll never really know the reasons. I've heard one or two stories but I don't really want to go into them.

So if it wasn't a decision based on football, was it politics?

I think there was more than a footballing reason, let's put it that way. The most disappointing thing was how it was done. I'd been at the FA talking about arrangements for the Cameroon game that morning; two hours after leaving the headquarters, I got an email from the person I'd been speaking to earlier that day saying that they'd be dismissing me. I expected better than that.

Sierra Leone have only ever been to two Cups of Nations. What's the country missing?

In terms of ability, nothing, but the civil war had a huge effect. A decade of fighting meant everything stopped: there was no league, no football development, no renovation of facilities. We also missed out on all the Fifa regeneration programmes that started to come in in the late 1990s, when Africa truly came onto the footballing global stage. If the conflict hadn't happened, there's no reason why Sierra Leone couldn't be like Senegal or Mali today. Nigeria and Ghana have huge populations so will always be ahead, but

Sierra Leone could definitely have been regular Cup of Nations participant.

⇨ *Do you think Ebola may similarly set Sierra Leonean football back long-term?*

It'll affect Sierra Leone in all walks of life, but the people are very resilient and have experience of dealing with these existential, national crises. I don't fear for Sierra Leone because I know how tough they are. There's no doubt it'll delay things, however. Investment and tourism will be damaged, which will weaken the economy and in turn decrease the amount of money that can be spent on non-essentials like sport. It's really disappointing. When are Sierra Leone next going to play a game? They can't play friendlies because of the outbreak, so they'll slide down the world rankings and lose the cohesiveness that comes with playing together regularly. All that momentum we built up will have been lost.

⇨ *Will an African team ever win the World Cup?*

The talent is there, no question. If you look at the amount of professionally-run football academies – Ghana has three or four, Nigeria, Ivory Coast and South Africa too, the North African countries – it's only going to get better. That tactical gap with the top European and South American nations should also be bridged in the next decade because the coaching is getting better and better. Guys like Stephen Keshi and Kwesi Appiah are truly excellent managers.

The biggest problem in African football is the planning. I've spoken to coaches from all over the continent and it's the same story everywhere. The administrators think that you can just turn up on the day to play a game of football. Unless that preparation element is sorted out, you're never going to win a World Cup. Ⓑ

The Football Supporters' Federation

By Fans, For Fans

 **INFORMING**

 **SUPPORTING**

 **CAMPAIGNING**

- www.fsf.org.uk
- Free Lions Magazine
- The Football Supporter Magazine

- Legal Advice and Support
- International Fans' Embassies
- Case Work and Consumer Advice

- Local Campaigns
- National Representation
- Football Supporters Europe

The President

How Isha Johansson has risen to lead the Sierra Leonean Football Association

By Joanna Howarth

Sierra Leone has been in the news for only tragic reasons recently. I lived there for just two months, but during that period the laid-back, inviting and stunningly beautiful country captured my heart. Sadly, this isn't the Sierra Leone that a lot of the world will ever know, instead visualising Ebola, blood diamonds and a horrific civil war when they think of the country.

Football is what I will think of when reminiscing about my time in Sierra Leone, having moved there to volunteer for a footballing charity during the World Cup and qualifiers for the African Cup of Nations. As I learnt quickly, football is central to the nation, uniting everyone from street children playing with stuffed plastic bags to men playing on their local dirt pitch every weekend.

I volunteered for the Craig Bellamy Foundation, a charity founded in 2009 by the former Wales, Liverpool and Manchester City forward. There are two sides to the charity – an academy and youth development league. The Academy is based in a small fishing town called Tombo; it takes in the most promising footballing talent from across the country, offering five-year scholarships to boys aged 11 and 12. Alongside this runs a nationwide Youth Development League that more than

2,240 children take part in every week; to be part of the League, they must attend school full time. If they achieve this, the Craig Bellamy Foundation will pay their annual school fees. It's only £11, but this is still far beyond the scope of too many families, particularly for girls.

During the 2013-14 League, school attendance among those involved in the league averaged 96% for girls compared with the national average of 33%. Boys and girls in the league also deliver monthly outreach projects on topics such as HIV, malaria, cholera and Ebola to their communities, and learn about 'Fair Play' to reduce youth violence.

One of the girls who takes part in the league is 16-year-old Fatmata. She has realised through the Youth Development League that "education is a lifelong investment". The combination of education, community development and football has persuaded Fatmata's family to support her football – they have seen their daughter mature into a community role model who advises younger girls on the risks of teenage pregnancy, applies herself academically and dedicates herself to her passion: football.

Fatmata is incredibly enthusiastic about the schooling she and her teammates now have access to – many of her friends' parents are regularly unable to afford school fees, meaning that the CBF League academic scholarships are providing them with an uninterrupted education for the very first time. When asked what she takes from involvement with the CBF League, Fatmata's immediate response is "pride". The confidence she draws from her achievements on the pitch, in the classroom and in the community has helped her develop the self-awareness to recognise the fundamental lack of gender equality in Sierra Leone, and the self-belief that she can be a part of changing it.

And she has an excellent role model to look up to. Sierra Leone has one of the world's only two female football federation presidents, Isha Johansen.[1] A serial entrepreneur and household name in Sierra Leone, Johansen went head-to-head with Mohamed Kallon – often considered Sierra Leone's most famous footballer, having played for Internazionale – to become Sierra Leone Football Association president in 2013.

Isha Johansen is the owner and CEO of Sierra Leone National Premier League club FC Johansen. Founded in 2004, the original aim of the club was to use sport to provide hope to young people. She is a woman with integrity, opinions and courage.

⇨ *Describe your journey to becoming the first female president of the SLFA.*

Sincerely, I never mapped out a journey or a strategy towards becoming

president of the SLFA. I grew up in a household where my father more or less ran a football club – East End Lions. He was a professional senior banker, but his intense passion for football resonated in our home. I grew up with my two brothers and being the only girl in the family then, what choice did I have but to be a typical tomboy.

FC Johansen happened to be my walking billboard and the legacy that spoke volumes for me during the campaign. Everything that I achieved for the club and ultimately the country is what was used in the presidential campaign and I guess it was a refreshing, rewarding and inspirational aspect to the campaign. The FC Johansen story is one of success above the odds; it's a story that shows that honesty, integrity, patriotism and hard work will always reap worthy benefits.

⇨ *What has been your proudest moment as president?*

There are a couple that really stand out. The day I heard my name being announced on national and international media as having made history as the first female FA president in Sierra Leone, and the second in the world, is up there as an incredibly proud moment.

But most recently, a day that stands out was when I was able to secure a country that would allow the Sierra Leone national team to play our home match for the Africa Cup of Nations qualifiers. Almost all other nations had turned us down [due to Ebola]. DR Congo came

[1] *The other is Lydia Nsereka of Burundi.*

to our rescue in a very emotional and difficult time.

⇨ *What are your greatest challenges as a woman in a male-dominated sport?*

I honestly do not see my challenges as stemming from the fact that I am a woman; remember I am not a newcomer into football administration in Sierra Leone. The challenge is not being a woman, but for others, dealing with a woman with firm principles on morals and work ethics.

I also believe that men in general are slowly coming to terms with the fact that there are some very determined and most importantly efficient women in our society. I would never advocate for giving a woman a top position simply because she is a woman. She has to earn it and be given the opportunity to earn it just like any other candidate in her position.

⇨ *While women's football has developed a lot over the past decade, there's still a long way to go to make it a level playing field in terms of salaries, sponsorship and coverage. What do you feel needs to be done to help achieve gender equality in football?*

Developing women's football in Sierra Leone – both in terms of administration and the game of play itself – has a long way to go. This SLFA administration has one main school of thought and that is that we have to put in structures if we as a nation are going to go anywhere with this beautiful game. Women's football is going to have to be introduced in schools so we get them young. We have already started running young coaches programs with a few female coaches on

board. We have four C-licence female coaches and a few female referees also. This is a far cry from what has existed in the past. It is going to be a long road to success, but this we are prepared for, as long as we are all committed to starting from basics and not to try to invent any shortcuts for it simply does not work that way. I am hopeful that gradually people are beginning to understand this.

⇨ *You are a great role model to a lot of women in Sierra Leone – in terms of your entrepreneurial spirit, career history and the respect you have gained among your peers. What would your advice be to them in achieving their goals and dreams?*

Every woman knows that the one thing we cannot afford to comprise is our integrity. That is what makes us women; that is what stands us apart (I hope) from most men. Our word is our honour – at least, that is what our mothers taught us. If you strongly believe that a certain path is one you chose to go down, and you chose that path because you honestly believe you can bring about the change that is needed, and most importantly you chose that path because it is your choice and not the choice of others for their gain, then go for it regardless.

⇨ *You've done a huge amount for youth football in Sierra Leone – what do you feel football offers young people?*

Football is a great sport for our kids, both boys and girls, and hopefully we will see more girls participating in football in the not too distant future. However football should, and under this administration will, be used to educate both academic and social skills as well as behaviour.

Most of the challenges we face with grown players and even some club administrators arethe lack of social skills and behaviour. Football is not just about ball skills – at least not anymore. Football is a whole new mindset and social behavioural aspect. We have had cases of our African players who, talented as they may be, have struggled in European clubs. It is because there is a breakdown of social and behavioural skills.

I hope that one of the biggest legacies I can leave behind after my tenure of office will be that of the 'Dawn of a New Era' of football in Sierra Leone. This applies to the new breed of players and the new mindset of administrators in Sierra Leone football.

◈ *The sports minister Paul Kamara has called you an 'Iron Lady' before – a title also applied to the UK's first female Prime Minister, Margaret Thatcher. Who is your global female role model and why?*

I had a lot of respect and admiration for Margaret Thatcher irrespective of her political stance. She was firm and decisive, but most importantly she took responsibility for her actions rightly or wrongly.

My role models? I admire women who are able to stand up for what they believe in, I admire creative women, women who are not afraid to break barriers, women who are not afraid to be the first in whatever they set out to do regardless of whether they succeed or fail, women who are not afraid to fail and if they do fail, women who will be ready to dust themselves down, stand up and be ready to take on the challenge again. That kind of woman is my kind of role model woman.

It is hugely apparent that football has the potential to be a positive vehicle for change in Sierra Leone, not least among girls and women. The understanding that football and education can go hand in hand, is having life-changing consequences for so many girls like Fatmata, providing them with the platform they need to become tomorrow's role-models and leaders.

While Ebola has tragically put a halt to so many activities, including football and schooling, it hopefully won't be too long before the start whistle can be blown again. Crowds will resume to watch matches, children will return to school, families will piece themselves together again and the spirit of the country will return. Ⓑ

GOALS ARE OVERRATED... THE BEAUTY IS IN THE STRUGGLE.

Exclusively available online from **www.theblizzard.co.uk** and **www.goalsoul.net**

THE BLIZZARD BY GOALSOUL
A PARTNERSHIP BORN OF FOOTBALL

In celebration of our most popular design, The Blizzard and goalsoul have decided to release 'Goals are overrated...' across three stunning new colour combinations.

The Blizzard by goalsoul partnership is a commitment to style and substance in equal measure. Our stunning and original graphic tees look and feel great. Lovingly hand screen-printed on 100% combed-cotton and shrink-resistant fabric — you can be sure of the highest possible quality, durability and wearability.

170

Greatest Games

"...several fully grown adults
spent the afternoon behaving like
teething bairns..."

Rangers 2 Celtic 2

Scottish Premier League, Ibrox, 17 October 1987

By Scott Murray

The grand old football clubs of Rangers and Celtic have got tangled up in some ludicrous scrapes over the years. In 1909, plans to complete the Scottish Cup final were abandoned when fans of both sides, sensing a second money-spinning replay had been cynically contrived, burned down the ticket booths at Hampden using cheap whisky as fuel. The infamous full-scale pitched battle between fans and polis at the 1980 final palls in comparison, though only just. In 1999, the referee Hugh Dallas was quantitatively eased to the floor by a targeted injection of the pound sterling.

And in 2011, Lennon and McCoisty stood on the touchline making sweet music in the keys of eff and cee, a full and frank exchange of views, eyeball to eyeball, nose to nose, which led to questions being asked in parliament.

There are others, too, plenty of others, but let us cut to the chase, because nothing compares to what happened at Ibrox on 17 October 1987, a brouhaha of the highest order, and arguably the best-remembered match in the entire history of Scottish football. Domestically, any road. The game, fair's fair, isn't seared on the national consciousness with a waxy seal of quality like the Lisbon Lions triumphing over Inter, or Rangers winning the Cup-Winners' Cup, or Aberdeen lifting the same trophy after seeing off Real Madrid, or any of Dundee United's many glorious victories over perennial losers Barcelona, or the national team's rare sweet successes against England and regular bittersweet failures against England. But all of those contributions to the Scottish canon occurred on the continental and international stage. Domestically, when it comes to the bread and butter of the league, this is almost certainly the one. Whether we like it or not.

Whether it deserves to be *celebrated* is another matter altogether. Its fame endures simply because several fully grown adults spent the afternoon behaving like teething bairns, flailing around in a style rarely seen outside the playground playpen. And of course the depressing sectarian undertones – never too far from the surface at the best of times – are impossible to ignore or argue away. But it's well worth another look, not least because – to paraphrase the old music-hall joke – at a couple of points during the fight, a half-decent football match broke out. And in any case, it'll be a sorry day when the guilty pleasures of a widescreen slapstick skirmish such as this can't raise at least a wry eyebrow, maybe even a smile.

This didn't appear out of nowhere, a thorny rose blooming amid a vacuum. There was a century's worth of animosity, of course, but the roots of this particular stramash were less than two years old.

Rangers – specifically Graeme Souness's Rangers – had been working up to something like this.

It was the culmination of a perfect storm of nonsense. In March 1986, Rangers and Celtic drew 4-4 at Ibrox and the home manager Jock Wallace danced into the executive lounge after the match to perform a loud impromptu rendition of "The Sash My Father Wore". Members of the board were less concerned with the tedious sectarian triumphalism than the fact their manager was so happy after a farcical high-scoring draw in which his team failed to hold onto a lead against 10 men. More ambition was required. And more ambition, with the old-school Wallace shipped out in favour of fashionable new player-manager Graeme Souness, was what they got.

Perhaps too much ambition. For the former Liverpool midfielder Souness arrived with the intention of taking "one of the biggest clubs in British football" back to the top. They hadn't won the league title in eight seasons. They'd only won three of the last 22 titles, an unthinkable return for a club historically considered as one half of an effective duopoly. Their state-of-the-art Ibrox stadium was more than half empty most of the time, so abject were the team. It would take plenty of effort to haul Rangers back into position and Souness was certainly not afraid of getting his hands dirty. A fact that would become very apparent very quickly.

Souness's steely determination would be a factor in driving Rangers to their desired success, but also to excess. His team would become the cartoon baddies of Scottish football, desirous of playing football in the right style – how could they not, with absurdly talented winger Davie Cooper and statesmanlike midfield glider Ian Durrant in the team – but fully prepared to mix it if needs be. Souness had once observed that the all-conquering Liverpool team of which he was the linchpin was programmed to play, but was primed to fight if required. And that they'd win, whatever method of engagement the opposition chose. It was a philosophy he wasn't ready to reconsider any time soon.

The Souness rebrand began when it began. He made his debut as both player and manager against Hibernian at Easter Road on the first day of the 1986-87 season, and picked up a booking after 23 minutes for a needless tackle on Billy Kirkwood. Momentarily regaining his equilibrium, Souness sashayed down the middle of the park 11 minutes later, dropping a shoulder with insouciant ease to make himself a little space. Sheer class. At which point he was charged off the ball by the Hibs winger Stuart Beedie. The red mist came down once more and by way of retribution he raked his studs down … well, Beedie's leg, hopefully? But sadly he was mistaken. Confused by a second player sporting Beedie's thoroughly contemporary mullet, Souness instead opened up George McClusky's knee, a wound that would require nine stitches. The new Rangers manager was sent packing. He sauntered off with a chilling, borderline psychotic calm, leaving a 21-man melee going off in his wake. Eight other players, four on each side, were booked.

After the game, which Rangers lost 2-1, journalists wondered whether Souness would be fining himself for letting the team down. "That's not my way of discipline." He also announced that he wouldn't be fining any other players who happened to get themselves sent off. Conversation over. (Though it wouldn't be the last time he would have to field the question during the campaign.) Souness was banned for four matches, fined £5,000, put on a disciplinary notice by the SFA and informed by Scotland's solicitor general, Peter Fraser QC, that prosecutions would be advised for on-field offences. A harbinger, albeit one that was breezily ignored, with extreme prejudice.

Rangers were knocked out of the Uefa Cup in December by Borussia Mönchengladbach, somewhat unluckily it has to be said, on away goals after thoroughly dominating the German side at the Bökelbergstadion but failing to score. Cooper and Ted McMinn sparkled on the wings in their very contrasting styles and both were kicked from pillar to post for their troubles. But Rangers were also putting it about. Ally Dawson was extremely fortunate not to walk after eight minutes for a knee-high lunge on Michael Frontzeck. "At the time, I thought an early dismissal would have been too drastic," recalled the referee Alexis Ponnet. "I hoped things would calm down. I was wrong."

Souness was lucky to escape a red card for a comprehensive clatter on Thomas Krisp, who was left lying on the touchline like a pile of dirty washing. Stuart Munro was sent off for kicking the left-back Andre Winkhold during a tussle, while Cooper, aggrieved at being hacked to the floor one time too many, walked for dissent. Cooper claimed he asked the referee if he was afraid of booking Germans, and that Ponnet replied, "I am

German" before sending him off. Ponnet, who was in fact Belgian, insisted Cooper called him a "dirty German", a dubious observation which earned him a second yellow, thoroughly deserved for offences against basic geography, if nothing else.

At the final whistle, Terry Butcher had to be restrained for raising one or two discursive matters with Ponnet. "I have refereed a lot of Scottish matches in my career, but I have never seen one like this," the beleaguered official later sighed. "Both teams went out not to play football, but to kick each other." Souness, however, was perfectly content with his team's behaviour and once again confirmed that he would not be disciplining anybody, certainly not in financial terms. The argumentative Butcher was singled out for special praise, suggesting his actions "reflected the way he has come to be involved with the club". Another ominous harbinger, as Butcher would later further illustrate his newly discovered fierce loyalty to Rangers during an interview in which he famously announced "Celtic! You hate 'em so much!" and revealed that he'd thrown his favourite Simple Minds cassette out of the car window upon discovering that the singer Jim Kerr was a regular at Parkhead. (Whether Butcher had been enjoying the contemporaneous bombast of "Alive and Kicking" era Simple Minds, or mining the group's early, subtle, krautrock-tinged experiments in new pop, has never been satisfactorily ascertained.)

Rangers were fined £5,300 for that farce, and another one was quick in coming. In mid-January, Souness's team allowed themselves to get awfully het up by a struggling Hamilton Academical side which had won just two of their 27 league games that season, were

propping up the Premier Division in some style and as a result had been suffering the ultimate indignity of being patronised week in, week out on national television by Jimmy Greaves. The tone of a performance of wanton lunacy was set when Butcher slid in recklessly on Bobbie Barr, out of control, both feet in the air, studs up. On STV, the commentator Jock Brown nonsensically argued that Butcher had "taken the ball cleanly", a dismal soundtrack for grim viewing; there's a point at which Barr, prone and clearly in shock, opts to look down and check on the state of his leg, before being deafened by an inner monologue screaming "AW NO!" He leans back in anguish, his fate sealed. Barr was stretchered off, a clean break.

The new signing Graham Roberts was fortunate to escape a red card for kneeing John Pelosi in the kidneys, but did eventually walk after shouldering Albert Craig to the floor, a yellow apiece for those party tricks. Durrant then flipped the hapless Craig into the air like a greasy fried egg and stomped off for his early bath. Exactly what Souness had said to his men before the game is sadly not on the record, but it must have been quite a spiritual rouser. Whether the rhetoric was well-timed or not is for others to judge, but it should be noted that this particular fixture had been rearranged, crowbarred into the schedule so Souness could sit out another suspension, with a view to picking from a full complement of players for an upcoming game with Aberdeen. The best laid plans... Again, Souness said no action would be taken, instead blaming the referee for letting things spiral out of control.

Hamilton gained revenge less than a fortnight later by knocking Rangers out of the cup at Ibrox, a shock of Berwickian proportions, Adrian Sprott and all that. Rangers responded to that grievous insult by thrashing Hearts 5-2 at Tynecastle, ending the Jambos' 32-game unbeaten home run. A fine response befitting an increasingly impressive football team, though for the record Souness, Dave McPherson, Jimmy Nicholl and the already-risible Roberts were fortunate to escape reds for challenges various, all merely seeing yellow instead.

But it's easy to knock. And Souness's approach was working. Rangers had been a thundering irrelevance since the advent of the eighties, but now they were in with a shout of their first title since 1978. Souness had also wasted no time in lifting his first silverware: within a couple of months of his debut, Rangers had won the 1986 Scottish League Cup after a tempestuous 2-1 victory over Celtic during which Mo Johnston was sent off, responding to his dismissal by ostentatiously crossing himself for the comedic benefit of the Rangers support.

The elusive title was landed at Pittodrie, though few remember the firmly planted Butcher header that sealed the deal. Souness ensured his season would be bookended by red cards, two absurd lunges on Aberdeen's Brian Irvine earning another spectacular dismissal. But this had been some effort by Souness and his men in the period between those particular atrocities. On the BBC, the savagely under-rated Archie Macpherson hailed an "incredible achievement", opining that, having seen Wallace's Rangers a mere 12 months previously, "they looked as though they could never

win anything within the next five years... and here they are, having won two of the three domestic trophies". The Rangers chairman David Holmes – the man most piqued by Wallace's myopic Sash celebration, and thus the prime mover in the Ibrox revolution – spent most of his post-match interview with Macpherson running through detailed plans for the immediate and effective absorption of carbonated French wine.

The champagne rush didn't last long. The outgoing champions Celtic had become almost an irrelevance within a mere 12 months, such was the ferocity of the Sounessian whirlwind. Second place was nowhere, not when Rangers were storming to their first title in aeons, anyway. And they weren't having it. The manager Davie Hay was sacked and replaced with the returning legend Billy McNeill, a three-time title winner during his first stint as Celtic boss, but coming off the back of a spectacular season south of the border which had seen him relegate both Manchester City and Aston Villa. The very early signs during the second reign of Caesar suggested more of the latter than the former. Celtic followed several embarrassing pre-season performances against lower-league Swedish opposition by going down 5-1 at home to Arsenal in a showpiece friendly, their heaviest loss on their own turf for 27 years.

No wonder, as star turns Johnston, Alan McInally and Brian McClair had departed during the summer. But Celtic were going into their centenary season and McNeill was in no frame of mind to succumb without a fight. His determined mindset was perfectly illustrated by his combative response to the loss of his entire strike force. McInally's departure was met with a shrug as he "wasn't familiar with him". Johnston's goals would be missed, but McNeill insisted he "isn't necessarily a severe loss" as "his off-the-field behaviour isn't something I would want to have to cope with. Don't forget he only came to Celtic in the first place because Watford thought he was too hot to handle." Only the departure of McClair to Manchester United raised hackles. "It was straightforward larceny! We were done, no doubt about that. How could any tribunal possibly expect us even to try to replace somebody like him with £850,000? The other upsetting thing about McClair and Johnston was that they both claimed to be Celtic supporters who would do anything for the club as long as the money was right. The directors made the money right – they were going to break the bank to hold them – yet they still went."

McNeill responded to the misery by signing the up-and-coming striker Andy Walker from Motherwell for £350,000 and the supposedly past-it attacking midfielder Billy Stark on the cheap from Aberdeen. The effect was immediate. Walker scored twice and Stark once on debut in a 4-0 league win at Morton and a pattern was set. The pair linked up marvellously with a rejuvenated Mark McGhee. In their first three league games, all wins, Celtic scored nine times, Stark with two, McGhee with three and Walker with the other four. A loss at Dunfermline gave McNeill a little pause for thought, but as Rangers had lost two of their first four matches, Celtic would still be the happier side going into the first Old Firm match of the season, at Parkhead.

They were certainly the happier coming out of it. Stark scored what proved the winner early on, then on the hour was wiped out by Souness, who, having already been cautioned for dissent, walked for the third time since coming to Scotland. The Rangers boss became involved with referee David Syme and a linesman in the tunnel after the match, calling Syme "a big fucking poof". He capped off a marvellous meltdown by tendering his resignation to Holmes, though he later calmed down enough sheepishly to withdraw it.

But the pressure was clearly back on Rangers. McNeill and Celtic had realised a spectacular turnaround in fortunes and by the time the second Old Firm match of the campaign came around in October they were already four points clear of their city rivals, two shy of the early leaders Hearts. A win for Celtic would surely see Souness's side out of the title race before October was through. And so it was do or die for the champions. Jock Brown – knowing full well that, with English teams out of Europe in the wake of the Heysel ban, all the hottest action was occurring up north these days – trilled excitedly into his STV microphone as Celtic got the ball rolling at Ibrox, "It's undoubtedly Britain's match of the day!"

It was on.

This game has a reputation as quite the rammy nowadays. And with good reason. Then again, here's the immediate response of the esteemed *Sunday Times* journalist Bob Ferrier: "The puzzle was that the match, in spite of the tensions of this age-old fixture, was never particularly vicious or vindictive." As ever, the truth lies somewhere in the middle. This match might be a grotesque nonsense, but it's not quite the extreme outrage than its legend could lead one to believe.

Despite Celtic's goal-rich start to the season, McNeill hadn't taken anything for granted. Walker, McGhee and Stark might have been racking them up, but another striker wasn't going to hurt, so in came Frank McAvennie from West Ham United (who initially wanted £1.5m, but settled for £750,000). He arrived in Glasgow on the same day Richard Gough swapped White Hart Lane for Ibrox in a £1.5m deal. Both expensive new arrivals would make quite an impression on this game. McAvennie had made his debut against Hibs a fortnight earlier, 24 hours after joining the club. He was patently unfit for that one, but soon got up to speed, scoring his first goal for his childhood favourites against Morton and thus went into the game at Ibrox in determined spirit.

Perhaps too determined. Early on, Tommy Burns hoicked an agricultural garryowen into the Rangers box from distance out on the left, forcing Chris Woods to palm over the crossbar. As the keeper flew through the air to deal with the difficult ball, McAvennie bowled into view and Nat Lofthoused him into the net. A fevered tone had been established from the off, a state of affairs additionally illustrated back up the field: Burns had been extremely fortunate to evade a full-blooded sliding scythe by Durrant, who had been hysterically skittering across the turf with combative intent while the Celtic man had been mid-hoof.

McAvennie had, perhaps unwittingly, lit the famous Rangers short fuse. Trevor Francis tried to inject a bit of class into proceedings by gliding in from the right and sending a skidder towards the bottom corner which Allan McKnight did well to parry. But his measured interjection counted for naught. The next meaningful passage of play would occur at the other end, in the Rangers area. On 16 minutes, Chris Morris sent a low cross into the box from the right. Jimmy Phillips slid in to guide the ball back to Woods, who gathered. In came McAvennie, late, more cheeky agitation on his mind. Cue bedlam, as first the striker, then the keeper, raised hands, throwing them around in a freeform fashion.

Woods grabbed McAvennie by the throat with one big paw, pushing him backwards. Butcher stepped in, bouncer style, shoving McAvennie violently in the chest. Woods moved in to continue the debate, but before he could get involved again, Roberts silently ambled up and, stealing in from the side, calmly introduced his fist to McAvennie's coupon, executing a sharp, snide rabbit punch before slipping away. McAvennie, then Woods were sent packing, despite arguably being the least aggressive pair involved in this particular hoo-hah.

McAvennie departed the scene quickly, on the advice of his teammate Peter Grant, for now playing the peacemaker. But Woods stood rooted to the spot in disbelief, blond, statuesque, before eventually stripping to the waist and giving Roberts his shirt and gloves, a pleasing homo-erotic counterpoint to all the tedious macho posturing. Butcher escaped with a booking, while the crafty Roberts was free to go about his new net-minding task without any censure whatsoever. In the stand behind, one Celtic supporting gentleman turned to the home support and repeatedly performed a *bras d'honneur*, the no-nonsense up-yours gesture of fist and forearm, a perfect response to the old-fashioned dukes-up shenanigans being played out on the field.

Roberts was immediately in the thick of the action, coming to the edge of his area to parry a shot from Grant, who had been sent clear on goal. However, he failed to repeat the trick when Mick McCarthy, another new signing from Manchester City, launched a basic clearance upfield on 33 minutes. Rangers, on the attack seconds earlier, were left light at the back and Walker skittered down the inside-left channel before drawing Roberts off his line and threading a marvellous low shot under the keeper into the far corner.

Two minutes later, Stark, in the centre circle, chipped a pass out right for Walker, who immediately wedged one back down the middle for the onrushing Grant. Butcher, tracking back, got to the ball first with a telescopic leg, but only succeeded in arcing it over the stranded Roberts and into the empty net. Grant celebrated by crossing himself, in and of itself a banal and insignificant act, but one which would guarantee him plenty of wearisome post-match hassle.

Celtic's goals had been decent – a lovely finish from Walker, a crisp move to force the second – but Rangers had clearly lost both their shape and the head. (A writer's exercise: how would things have panned out had Souness been on the pitch?) On 63 minutes, John McGregor

launched a long ball into the Celtic box. Butcher contested it with McKnight, then, as the two tangled on the floor, lamped the keeper upside the head for no discernible reason. A straight red, to go with the yellow he'd received earlier. It was surely all over.

But if this match was to become a classic, it needed a footballing narrative of note; by itself, a fight wasn't enough to cut the mustard. And here it was. Within 60 seconds, Rangers – down to nine men, with a defender in goal – hauled themselves back in it with an exquisite piece of football. Derek Ferguson wriggled free of a Celtic pincer movement in the middle of the park and slid the ball forward for Gough, who in turn shuttled it on for McCoist, making good down the inside-left channel. The striker smashed a shot off the left-hand upright and into the net. A marvellous goal amid the mayhem.

Celtic should still have glided home, but their efforts to put Roberts under pressure with high balls were weak and half-arsed. McNeill had opted to stick rather than twist in the second half, sending his team out with a safety-first mindset, and he wasn't minded to change the plan. Celtic suffered some bad luck – a Stark header looped over a stranded Roberts and twanged off the crossbar – but in truth they hadn't done enough to earn any of the good stuff. And sure enough, Roberts having otherwise held firm, the grandstand finish came on 90 minutes. Durrant sped past Anton Rogan down the right. The resulting cross was headed back out to the wing by McCarthy, but Durrant picked up possession again and looped in a second. McKnight came for the cross, flapped, and missed. Gough, in the role of emergency striker and loitering in the middle, scuffed the ball home from six yards as he fell backwards. Bedlam, bedlam, bedlam.

All that was left during the short period of injury time remaining was for Roberts, inflammatory gestures second nature, gormlessly to conduct the Ibrox choir in a rendition of the Sash. Ah well, Jock Wallace will have been proud, at least.

Jan Kiesiel, assistant manager of the Polish side Górnik Zabrze, was in the stands to run the rule over Rangers ahead of an upcoming European Cup tie. "I have never witnessed such scenes in Poland," he observed, before dryly adding, "We do not have boxers in our country." It was certainly a squalid affair and one which rattled on for months. "This has to go to the top of the house," spluttered Jock Brown on *Scotsport*, which is exactly what happened. Butcher, Woods, Roberts and McAvennie were all hauled before the beak. Butcher and Woods were found guilty of conduct likely to provoke off-field bother and fined £250 and £500 respectively. The case against Roberts was not proven, while McAvennie was found not guilty.

A shameful business, but then the denizens of the Broomloan Road Stand got their money's worth that day: four goals, three red cards, two haymakers, one last-gasp comeback, all on a plate, right in front of them. It might not have pleased the pious, but it was thunderingly good entertainment. Despite it all, it had been a great match.

By dint of the comeback, secured while down to nine men and with a clown in goal, Rangers felt they had won this particular battle with Celtic. But Celtic would win the war. Rangers, severely depleted now by suspension, nevertheless lifted the League Cup the following weekend, prevailing in a roller-coaster final with Aberdeen. But they could never quite haul themselves back into the title race, losing both of the season's remaining Old Firm fixtures. Celtic romped to the championship and completed a double in their centenary season with a victory over Dundee United in a Scottish Cup final remembered more these days for the glorious pelters copped by a shocked Margaret Thatcher than for McAvennie's last-gasp winner.

The following season would see Rangers win the first title in what would become a record-equalling nine-in-a-row run. Souness would be long gone by the time that particular achievement was in the bag, but it didn't matter. He'd already made an indelible mark on the Scottish game, energising the league with a memorable team of cartoon baddies who surely earned their place in the rogues gallery – an essential sub-section of football's rich tradition – alongside the likes of Estudiantes, Revie's Leeds, the Wimbledon crazy gang, the Brazil and Argentina teams of the late 1940s, and Goikoetxea's Athletic of Bilbao. Knock them if you like, but the league in Scotland has never been quite as entertaining since.

180

Eight Bells

"...the one surviving embodiment
of an organic living folk tradition."

Chants

A selection of terrace songs that helped shape the history of chanting

By Andrew Lawn

 "On the Ball, City"

Football fans have a proud tradition of chanting at football matches. These chants can be supportive or critical of their team, critical of the opposition, hostile, crude, humorous and on occasion seemingly pointless.

But why do we chant at football? Where did it start and how did we reach a point where football is considered an arena in which almost anything can be shouted, resulting in various obscene chants hitting the headlines on a regular basis?

Academic studies on football chants have compared them to a modern version of storytelling and folk music, with the influential folk musician Martin Carthy going as far as to label them "the one surviving embodiment of an organic living folk tradition", noting the content of the songs and their communal singing. Carthy states the similarities between the two: "a network of songs which evolved out of existing songs, sung by the people, adapted to meet the specific needs of a geographical identity and seemingly created by spontaneous combustion, the unheralded originators remaining anonymous."

This aspect of being 'by the people and for the people', found a perfect match in football. Football chanting as we know it has remarkably classical origins with Norwich City's "On the Ball, City" composed in the 1890s and originally sung with full piano accompaniment, the oldest still sung today. Some claim that "He Banged the Leather for Goal", written in honour of the Wolves striker Billy Malpass by Edward Elgar predates "On the Ball, City" but it has, anyway, fallen into disuse. Often credited to Albert T Smith, who would go on to become a director of the club, "On the Ball, City" predates the football club with which it is now synonymous, which was formed in 1902.

"On the Ball, City" was originally written for a local works team, but in the same way modern fans take tunes and inspiration from popular culture, Norwich fans adopted the song as their own and 120 years later it still rings out around Carrow Road. Unsurprisingly, given its 19th century conception, "On the Ball, City" sounds like no other chant you're likely to hear on the terraces elsewhere. Initially featuring two verses and a chorus, the song features none of the tub-thumping one-upmanship which characterises many modern chants and instead focuses fully on the club:

Kick it off, throw it in, have a little scrimmage,
Keep it low, a splendid rush, bravo, win or die;
On the ball, City, never mind the danger,
Steady on, now's your chance,
Hurrah, we've scored a goal!
City, City, City.

Once Norwich joined the Football League in 1920, "On the Ball, City" was exposed to fans across England and led to other jovial, club or location specific chants springing up, notably, "Play up, Pompey, / Pompey play up," sung as the bells chime at Portsmouth's Fratton Park, "Blaydon Races" at Newcastle and "Glory, Glory, Tottenham Hotspur" at White Hart Lane.

Early football chants were harmless and cheerfully parochial. It would be Cilla Black and the Beatles who would spark a change 40 years later.

 "You'll Never Walk Alone"

The parochial joviality of the pre-war football chant began to shift towards the more antagonistic ditties of today at the same time as pop music began to dominate the UK Top 40.

Nowhere were these shifts more pronounced than in Liverpool and it is no coincidence that the rise of one gave birth to the other. With an estimated 350 bands in the city at the beginning of the 1960s, the banks of the Mersey were fertile grounds from which a phenomenon that would dominate English popular culture for the next 50 years would grow.

As local acts, Cilla Black, Gerry and the Pacemakers and the Beatles leapt to the top of the charts, Liverpool's Kop picked up their nationally known tunes as a transferable vehicle for expressing local pride.

As the sports historians Andrew Ward and John Williams noted, "the Kop was always a noisy place. People shouted and roared, and there was banter and bad language. In the early sixties however, the noise changed. The Kop began to sing, and singing made the fans feel good. The Anfield Kop covered a succession of Beatles songs soon after they appeared. They sang the whole of Cilla Black's "Anyone Who Had a Heart" and adopted a new local anthem "You'll Never Walk Alone", a song from the musical *Carousel*, covered by Gerry and the Pacemakers.

Originally written as a show tune for the 1945 musical *Carousel*, "You'll Never Walk Alone" was sung to comfort the widow of Billy Bigelow, who had killed himself to avoid capture after a failed robbery. "You'll Never Walk Alone" caught the imagination of the Kop, remaining associated with the club to this day.

Such is the affinity between the club and Liverpool, the title featured on the club's crest and atop the famed Shankly Gates at Anfield. Shankly, for his part, would later pick the song as his final selection for BBC Radio's *Desert Island Discs* broadcast on the eve of the 1965 FA Cup Final win over Leeds.

Like Norwich's "On the Ball, City" before it, the full version of "You'll Never Walk Alone" is much longer than the now famous chorus, although the full lyrics continue to be sung prior to Liverpool home matches.

With its message of solidarity, support and loyalty, the chant not only caught on with fans at Liverpool, but has also been adopted by Celtic in Scotland – there are those who claim Celtic sang it first – and has a large following on the continent with fans of Borussia Dortmund, Mainz, Hoffenheim, St Pauli and Kaiserslautern in Germany and Feyenoord, Twente and Cambuur in the Netherlands all routinely belting out their own renditions.

"You'll Never Walk Alone" also captured another moment in the evolution of football fandom in Britain. Through their pop renditions the Kop became the focal point of chanting at Liverpool and with it began the culture of 'home ends' that would go on to shape both future chants and the game itself.

 ## "Those were the days, my friend..."

As the Kop grew in volume, its reputation spread across British football, hastened by a new breed of younger fan who began to follow their clubs home and away, aided by the introduction of cheaper transport via British Rail's 'Football Special' trains.

The rise of the Kop coincided with two League Championships for Liverpool and, naturally enough, it was mimicked. Vocal fans of clubs across Britain began to congregate in one area with local versions of the Kop, also known as 'ends', appearing across the country.

Four years after Gerry and the Pacemakers released "You'll Never Walk Alone", the creation of dedicated ends had spawned a new wave of hooliganism as away fans saw the home end as a prize to take with violence. Within ends, hooligan firms began to take hold and new identities were forged.

As hooligan firms took over and the quest to take ends became as important as on-field success, the main inspiration for chants switched from pop music to aggression. As a result chants began to draw on memories of violent skirmishes in faraway places, such as this from Everton:

Those were the days my friend,
We took the Stretford End,
We took the Shed,
The North Bank Highbury,
We took the Geordies too,
We fight for Everton,
We are the Street of Everton FC.
La, la, la, la, lala, la la la, la, lala...

Where "You'll Never Walk Alone" referenced the positive success of a proud son of the city and spoke of loyalty through dark times, "Those Were the Days" fondly recalls away games, not for on-field success, but for violence. Outright abuse and needless cruelty had become staple ingredients, and the height of wit now was to rip off old chants with violent equivalents, highlighted in the conversion of "You'll Never Walk Alone" into the rather more ominous "You'll Never Walk Again".

This change took place during games as well, with fans of clubs from rural areas such as East Anglia or the West Country beginning a game by being mocked with "You're going home in a combine harvester", transformed into "You're going home in a fucking ambulance" as the mood darkened and violence flared.

"Those Were the Days" is also notable in that the key identity expressed is that not of wholly of Everton, as the earlier parochial chants of "On the Ball, City", "Glory, Glory Tottenham Hotspur" or "Play up, Pompey" had been about Norwich City, Tottenham Hotspur and Portsmouth respectively, but of Everton's hooligan firm The Street.

The shift was complete. Fans now saw themselves as a group in their own right and chanting was one weapon in their armoury with which to hurt opposition fans. Chants were therefore no longer just about celebrating the identity of a place, but a masculine quest for status and social recognition.

An arms race of abuse had begun.

4 "Who's that Lying on the Runway?"

As outright hate replaced *Top of the Pops* as the main motivation for chanting, chants became even darker, foregrounding violence, death and disaster, rather than on-field success. Just as the best of chanting began on Liverpool's Kop, the worst of it originated there too; born in a burgeoning rivalry with Manchester United.

The two most successful English clubs, domestically and in Europe, Liverpool and Manchester United share a rivalry which runs deeper than football and takes in two fiercely proud cities. It began in the

Industrial Revolution as the two cities competed for economic prosperity and grew as the red footballing halves of both cities competed for supremacy at the top of English football, leading to a rivalry Sir Alex Ferguson described as "unparalleled".

The journalist Brian Reade summed up how unfriendly things had become when the two sides met for an FA Cup semi-final in 1985 saying, "There were re-enactments of medieval pitched battles in the streets, a Stanley knife exhibition in Stanley Park and, on the terraces, the kind of tribal exchanges you see in Gaza on a bad day."

These exchanges included one of the most infamous chants in English football, which rather than celebrating their glorious on-field pasts and well-stocked trophy cabinets, concerns a human disaster which had taken place in 1958: the Munich Air Crash. "Who's that lying on the runway? Who's that dying in the snow?" it began, before referring to Busby and his side stricken on the airfield.

A fierce rivalry was becoming marked with hatred and the rise of the Munich chant nearly two decades after the disaster highlights just how hateful it had become. Just over a month after that FA Cup tie, Liverpool themselves were involved in a tragedy as 39 fans died at Heysel at the European Cup Final between Liverpool and Juventus. Liverpool fans were widely blamed for the deaths. United fans saw Heysel as a chance for revenge for the Munich chant and marked what happened with chants of their own including "39 Italians Can't be Wrong" and "Murderers".

After the deaths of 96 Liverpool fans at Hillsborough four years later, United fans again used references to the disaster to chant abuse at Liverpool, which in turn helped some Liverpool fans legitimise their own continued referencing of the Munich Air Crash. As late as 2011 a youth-team match between the two clubs was disrupted by chants about Munich and Hillsborough.

 ## "There ain't no black in the Union Jack"

As fans began to use the tragedies as tools to abuse rival fans, the hate for players, both rival and otherwise, was more personal. Racism and homophobia, fuelled by a surge of extreme right-wing supporter groups, became commonplace on the terraces. As early as 1968 author Arthur Hopcroft noted that chants such as "Ey-ay-addio the Goalie is a Queer" and "Where's Your Handbag?" occurred at every league game, at every ground in the UK.

Racist abuse peaked on the terraces in the 1980s. Fifteen years after the 1965 Race Relations Act, footballers were routinely subjected to monkey chants. When Paul Canoville became the first black player to play for Chelsea in 1980, his own fans used the N-word to tell him he was not welcome. As late as 1988, the black Liverpool player and England international John Barnes was photographed nonchalantly back-heeling away a banana that had been hurled at him.

One such chant which began life on the terraces, but whose reach extended outside of the football grounds in the early 1980s runs,

There ain't no black in the Union Jack,
*Send those n*****s back,*
If you're white you're alright,
If you're black, send 'em back.

Such was the chant's popularity and reach that the UK's national flag is now seen by some as an overtly racist symbol, with the majority of England fans shying away from it in favour of the cross of St George.

While overt racism has been on the decline in part thanks to new measures to make it illegal, less obvious examples of racism and xenophobia remain common. As recently as November 2014, England fans were being asked to refrain from singing "No Surrender to the IRA" 17 years after the Northern Ireland Good Friday Peace Agreement.

Homophobic chants also remain sadly commonplace, particularly in games involving Brighton and Hove Albion. In April 2013, The Brighton and Hove Supporters Club and the Gay Football Supporters' Network collated a dossier of abuse which they submitted to the FA and the Football League, noting they had already spent more than 15 years trying to get the authorities to take the abuse seriously.

The dossier recorded homophobic specific chants by 72% of opposition fans over the course of the 2012-13 season, including: "Town Full of Faggots", "We can see you Holding Hands", "We Always Shag Girls," "What's it Like to Suck a Cock?" and "You're Queer and you Know you are."

The dossier helped shine a spotlight on homophobia in football, helping to kick off a campaign for homophobic abuse to be given the same legal classification as racist abuse. But it would take a single chant, sung in December 2008, to bring the two themes of racism and homophobia together and break enough societal taboos to spark a noticeable sea-change in the attitude towards football chanting from fans and the majority alike.

 "Sol, Sol, wherever you may be"

If one chant sums up the depths of hatred fans were able to express through the medium of chants it was that aimed at Sol Campbell by Tottenham Hotspur fans during their meeting with Portsmouth at Fratton Park in December 2008. A firm favourite after coming through the ranks, Campbell incurred the wrath of the Spurs fans who used to adore him, by leaving on a free transfer for their arch-rivals Arsenal in 2006.

On his return to White Hart Lane with Arsenal, Campbell expected some stick but was surprised by the level of hatred he encountered, including 4,000 white balloons and countless cards and flags emblazoned with the word "Judas" in blue. Among the fans releasing the balloons and holding the cards, Campbell saw his brother.

If that was a surprise, the level of abuse which Campbell continued to receive even after leaving Arsenal for Portsmouth proved truly shocking. When Campbell next faced Spurs, he was met with a chant to the tune of "Lord of the Dance", for which four people were arrested and later banned from attending any football match for three years (seven others had bans overturned on appeal).

Sol, Sol, wherever you may be,
Not long now until lunacy,
We won't give a fuck if you're hanging
from a tree,
You're a Judas cunt with HIV.

The official reason for the arrests was that the chant was homophobic, but in truth it could have been for any number of offensive elements. Taking each in turn, the chant first abuses Campbell for perceived mental health issues referencing a match between Arsenal and West Ham in 2006 in which Campbell asked to be substituted at half-time and left the stadium. Teammates admitted he had "worries" in his private life, which were interpreted by some to mean he was gay.

The third line continues the mental health theme, but as well as suicide, also references both Campbell's race and alleged homosexuality, recalling the only professional footballer in England to have come out as gay, Justin Fashanu, who like Campbell was black, and who took his own life by hanging. The image simultaneously conjures a suggestion of lynchings. After a brief deviation to again label Campbell a 'Judas', the chant returns to homophobia with the reference to HIV, a disease Campbell doesn't have but which disproportionately afflicted homosexual men in the eighties.

The Campbell chant was widely seen as a watershed moment. Campbell himself called it a "human rights situation" while it sparked a crackdown on abusive chanting, from both fans themselves and the authorities.

The season after the chant, banning orders in English football shot up 15% from the previous season to 3,391.

"Your teeth are offside"

Widespread revulsion at the treatment Sol Campbell received has not eradicated abuse but at least led to it being toned down, without losing the competitive ridicule and subsequent humour. Humour, like identity and rivalry, is a key ingredient of football chanting, particularly in England. As the social commentator AA Gill wrote, "Jokes are the English social currency, English women regularly report that a sense of humour is their first requirement in a mate [and] making mates and strangers laugh has a higher status in England than it does in almost any other country. Having a laugh isn't just a national cultural affinity, it's a large part of the behaviour and motivation of young English blokes. Football terraces are really, really funny and really, really horrible, both at the same time. It's the volume and the power, the huge wattage of anger, sharpened with malevolent wit."

However the use of humour, by its very nature, can lead to its audience being offended. Gill himself defines humour as "the sound of the bullies". Lots of football chants are indeed deliberately offensive in order to further foster the 'us v them' mentality, meaning chants are often exaggerated insults.

Take a chant which began at Manchester United and spread across fans of Premier League clubs during the 2013-14 season, aimed at Liverpool striker Luis Suárez. Banned for racially abusing Patrice Evra, and for biting Branislav Ivanović, Suárez was instead picked on for his appearance and performance with,

Your teeth are offside,
Your teeth are offside,
Oh Luis Suárez,
Your teeth are offside.

The chant picks on someone with power and wealth, in an original and ridiculous but still potentially offensive way, although for offensiveness it's not in the same league as the chant which Spurs fans greeted Campbell, or those United and Liverpool previously indulged in about Munich, Heysel and Hillsborough.

The chant spread across Premier League grounds as the season went on. It was also well-received in Europe and cited as an example of chanting and English humour at its best, with *L'Équipe* quoting the song and noting, "You can say what you like about England, there is a real football culture. And in the stands, humour inspired by Monty Python, silly, wicked and so funny."

The French broadcaster RMC picked up on the key roles played by humour and offence in football chanting, with their piece on the game, declaring that the invention of the chant made Manchester United fans their winner in the battle of the terraces.

Whether the chant is offensive or not is open to debate and subject to a myriad of contextual factors. The linguistics expert Barry Blake sums up the difficulties of classifying something as being either funny or offensive when he says, "humour is universal, although what strikes some people as funny will not strike others in the same way."

Chants can be offensive, they can be funny and they can also be funny and offensive. Sometimes they can also be inexplicably meaningless and quite frankly brilliant.

 The Wheelbarrow Song

The evolution of football chanting from show-tune through hate-fuelled abuse and good-natured ridicule ignores one final aspect of chanting which has sustained chanting as a social phenomenon, helping to bind fans to their clubs and each other: chanting for the sake of chanting.

While the chants citing incidents with intrinsic shock value – death, abuse or taboo subjects – make the headlines and give football chanting a bad name, this doesn't tell the full story.

Chanting is a way of expressing pride or worshipping something you are proud to identify with, in the same way that the sociologist Émile Durkheim described aboriginal clans coming together to worship the totem. Within these ritualistic celebrations, the aborigines experienced the social existence of their clan viscerally. The aborigines' emotions were focussed on the totem of the clan and, since the totem represented the clan, the aborigines were worshipping their own society.

Notts County's "Wheelbarrow Song" is a perfect example of this and sums up all that is good about football chanting. To the tune of football chant regular "On Top of Old Smoky", it is simply:

I had a wheelbarrow,
The wheel fell off.
I had a wheelbarrow,

The wheel fell off.
County, County, County.

Why then is this the perfect football chant?

First, its origins are disputed, rooted in folklore and the memories of famous comebacks or misfortune depending who you believe.

Secondly, it's simple and inclusive. It uses no divisive language or themes, but it brings a community together, finishing with a rousing rendition of "County, County, County."

Thirdly, it is self-deprecating; the inference being that as a club they are so unfortunate that even their wheelbarrow is broken.

Finally, it is completely irrelevant. It has nothing to do with football, until the final reference to County, and is all the stronger for it.

The sole point of the song is the singing of the song itself. It expresses no particular support, derision, masculinity or geographical relevance and yet perfectly encapsulates what it is to be a football fan: you get a new wheelbarrow, bundled up in it are ideas of potential, excitement and achievement, then just as everything looks good, the wheel falls off, the promise remains unfilled, the excitement turns to abject disappointment. Yet, despite all that, we still love the wheelbarrow. We'll get a new wheel, it'll be as good as new. We believe again.

That is not to say that football chanting and those who engage in it should be given carte blanche to sing whatever they want, and the continued crackdown of abuse which draws on prejudice should be wholeheartedly supported.

It is by no means all bad, however, and any group of people who can sing publicly about their broken wheelbarrow or, as Norwich City did, having relegation confirmed with a 2-0 home defeat and responding to away fans' taunts with,

We lose every week,
We lose every week.
You're nothing special –
We lose every week

is worth saluting.

Contributors

The Blizzard, Issue Sixteen

Stuart Roy Clarke has spent the last 25 years photographing football in its many guises. He began his ongoing project, *The Homes of Football*, in 1989. Twitter: **@homesoffootball**

James Corbett is a sports correspondent and award-winning author who has reported for outlets including the BBC, the *Observer*, the *Guardian*, the *Sunday Times* and *FourFourTwo*. His books include the *Everton Encyclopedia* and his collaboration with Neville Southall, *The Binman Chronicles*. He is currently working on a book about football governance. Twitter: **@james_corbett**

John Davidson is an Australian freelance journalist who lives in the UK. He writes for *FourFourTwo Australia*, *Inside Sport*, TheRoar.com.au, *Thin White Line* and *Leopold Method*, among others. Twitter: **@johnnyddavidson**

John Harding lives and works in North London and writes on a variety of topics, ranging from literary and sporting biography to cultural history and criticism. Past subjects include the footballers Billy Meredith and Alex James, boxer Jack 'Kid' Berg and poet and cartoonist Ralph Hodgson. He is also the Professional Footballers' Association's official historian. He is working on a study of the playwright Shelagh Delaney.

Joanna Howarth relocated to Sierra Leone in June 2014 to support the Craig Bellamy Foundation with their Fundraising and Partnerships. She now lives and works in Addis Ababa, Ethiopia, as a Fundraising and Communications consultant. Twitter: **@jo_howarth**

Andrew Lawn is a freelance columnist and the author of *Who are ya? Who are ya? Who are we?* which looks at why we chant at football matches and what those chants say about us as individuals and as a society. He is about to start a project looking at the differences between football chanting in the men and woman's game. Twitter: **@Lawny1986**

Greg Lea is a freelance football writer with work published by the likes of *FourFourTwo*, the *Guardian*, *When Saturday Comes*, *Squawka* and *Goal*. Twitter: **@GregLeaFootball**

Felix Lill is a German freelance journalist who works as an author for *Die Zeit*, *Die Presse*, *Der Spiegel*, *Neue Zürcher Zeitung*, *Tagesspiegel*, *Zeit Online* and others. He was awarded the Austrian Sports Journalism Award in 2010, 2011 and 2012. He was awarded the Austrian OEZIV Media Prize 2012.

Ben Lyttleton covers European football for the *Sports Illustrated* website and Bloomberg TV, among others, and is a regular guest on the *European Football Show* podcast. He is editorial director of *The Global Player* and the author of *Twelve Yards: The Art and Psychology of the Perfect Penalty Kick*. Twitter: **@benlyt**

Firdose Moonda is a writer living in Johannesburg. She writes primarily for ESPNcricinfo on South Africa and Zimbabwean cricket and ESPNFC, where she runs the Football Africa blog. She also appears regularly in Forbes Africa's publications, on the *Atlantic Post* and runs her own website at www.the-street-seen.com.

Scott Murray writes for the *Guardian*. He is co-author of *And Gazza Misses The Final*, a history of the World Cup through the medium of minute-by-minute match reports. He also co-wrote *The Anatomy of Liverpool*, and *Phantom of the Open: Maurice Flitcroft, the World's Worst Golfer*.

Stephen O'Donnell is the author of two contemporary football-themed novels, *Paradise Road* (2012) and *Scotball* (2014). He lives in Glasgow with his partner and their baby daughter and is currently collaborating on a book about the history of Scottish football, as well as working on another novel.

Louise Phillips lives in London. Her work has most recently appeared in the *Independent*, *New World Writing*, *Litro*, *McSweeney's Internet Tendency* and *3AM Magazine*. Twitter: **@Louloulips**

Dileep Premachandran is editor-in-chief of *Wisden India*. His love of football dates back to Bob Paisley's final season in charge of Liverpool. He lives in Bangalore with his wife and daughter, and wishes

Fernando Redondo was still playing. Twitter:**@SpiceBoxofEarth**

Javier Sauras is a nomadic journalist and photographer who has been wandering from Asia to Latin America during the last four years. He has written about Japan, the Philippines, Spain, China, UK and Bolivia. He is still on the road. Twitter: **@jsauras**

Paul Simpson is the editor of *Champions* magazine.

Jon Spurling writes for *FourFourTwo* and *When Saturday Comes*, and has written several books on Arsenal. He is currently working on a Charlie Buchan biography. Twitter: **@jonspurling1**

Jonathan Wilson is the author of *Inverting the Pyramid*. He writes for the *Guardian*, the *National*, *World Soccer*, *Fox* and *Sports Illustrated*. He is writing a book on the history of Argentinian football. Twitter: **@jonawils**

James Young has lived in Brazil for 10 years and writes about the country and its football for *Sports Illustrated*, *Rolling Stone*, ESPN, the *Independent*, *Folha de São Paulo* and others. He is the author of a collection of short stories set in Recife, *A Beer Before Lunch*.

Blizzard Subscriptions

Subscribe to the print version of The Blizzard, *be the first to receive new issues, get exclusive Blizzard offers and access digital versions of all back-issues FREE*

Subscription Options

Set Price for Four Issues

Get a four-issue subscription to *The Blizzard* — for you or as a gift — for a flat fee including postage and packing (P&P):

UK:	£35
Europe:	£45
Non-Euorpe:	£55

Recurring Pay-What-You-Like

Set up a quarterly recurring payment for each edition of *The Blizzard*. The recommended retail price (RRP) is £12, but pay what you like, subject to a minimum fee of £6 plus P&P.

See www.theblizzard.co.uk for more

Digital Subscriptions

If the cost of postage is prohibitive, or you just want an excuse to use your new iPad or Kindle, you can set up a subscription to digital versions of The Blizzard for just £3 per issue.

See www.theblizzard.co.uk for more

Information for Existing Subscribers

Free Digital Downloads for *Blizzard* Subscribers

Whether you have taken advantage of our set price or pay-what-you-like offer, for the duration of your subscription to *The Blizzard* you are entitled to download every issue FREE.

See www.theblizzard.co.uk for more

We very much value the commitment of our print subscribers and have a policy to make available new issues, special offers and other limited access events and benefits to print subscribers first.

About *The Blizzard*

Distribution & Back Issues
Contact Information
About Issue Sixteen

Buy *The Blizzard*

We want as many readers as possible for *The Blizzard*. We therefore operate as far as we are able on a pay-what-you-like basis for digital and print versions.

Digital Version (Current & Back Issues)

All issues of *The Blizzard* are available to download for Kindle, Android, iOS and PC/Mac at: *www.theblizzard.co.uk*.

- *RRP: £3*
- *Pay-what-you-like minimum: £0.01*

Printed Version (Current & Back Issues)

Purchase a physical copy of *The Blizzard* in all its luxurious, tactile, sensual glory at: *www.theblizzard.co.uk*. If you haven't felt our rough textured cover-varnish and smelled the inner genius, you haven't properly experienced its awesome true form. Read it, or leave it on your coffee table to wow visitors.

- *RRP: £12 (+P&P)*
- *Pay-what-you-like min: £6 (+P&P)*

Contact *The Blizzard*

All advertising, sales, press and business communication should be addressed to the Central Publishing Office:

The Blizzard
Ashmore Villa,
1, Ashmore Terrace,
Stockton Road,
Sunderland,
SR2 7DE

Email: info@theblizzard.co.uk
Telephone: +44 (0) 191 543 8785
Website: www.theblizzard.co.uk
Facebook: www.facebook.com/blzzrd
Twitter: @blzzrd

About Issue Sixteen

Editor Jonathan Wilson
Publisher The Blizzard Media Ltd
www.theblizzard.co.uk
Design Daykin & Storey
www.daykinandstorey.co.uk

Copyright
All content is ©Copyright The Blizzard Media Ltd and may not be reproduced without explicit consent. Thanks to Jeanette G Sturis at the Kingsley Motel, Manjimup, for kind use of Warren Walker's original sketches of Dog.

Stroke is the third biggest killer and the leading cause of severe adult disability in the UK.

Behind much of the Stroke Association's unique work are people just like you – people who want to do something powerful and lasting through their Will.

To find out more about leaving a gift in your Will please call us on **020 7566 1505** or email **legacy@stroke.org.uk**

stroke.org.uk

Registered as a Charity in England and Wales (No 211015) and
in Scotland (SC037789). Also registered in Isle of Man (No 945)
Jersey (NPO 369) and serving Northern Ireland.